Praise for *The Mom & Pop Store*

"[Spector] takes a close look at su[...] America . . . And guess what? The [...] be the essence of localism, entrepr[...] 21st century ideas." —**Carol Tice,** *Entrepreneur* **magazine**

"The stories that Spector has gathered are cheering testimonials to the value of hard work and creative retailing, heartwarming in this day of conglomerates . . . Readers who enjoy Capra-esque stories about plucky general merchandising outfits run by colorful individualists will enjoy Spector's book."
—**Michael Lindgren,** *Cleveland Plain Dealer*

"There's a great deal of good journalism in Spector's book, and it affirms what I've long believed: that this kind of small, family business is integral to the American experience." —**Gay Talese**

"Spector offers a love letter to American small-business people . . . His book truly sings when [he] recounts his childhood spent in his family's butcher shop and the practical wisdom he gleaned at his father's knee. Cheerful and charming, this is a heartfelt look at life on 'the other side of the counter.'" —***Publishers Weekly***

"The most intriguing parts of the book chronicle the struggle of each business to survive in a retail environment in which small businesses must adapt or fail . . . Lively lessons about business ethics and practices that Fortune 500 companies, the author suggests, would be wise to follow." —***Kirkus Reviews***

"This excellent book is about real America since 90 percent of all U.S. businesses are family owned or controlled, and though some are large, mostly they are mom and pops." —***Booklist***

"A warm and personal look at the entry point of American emigrant entrepreneurship. *The Mom & Pop Store* is part Studs

Terkel, part Bill Bryson, as Spector mixes family history with his vast knowledge of retail." —Paco Underhill, author of
Why We Buy: The Science of Shopping

"Every business lesson my dad ever taught me was built around the idea of treasuring every single customer. The resourceful entrepreneurs you'll meet in this captivating book live by that simple, but powerful, idea."
—Bruce Nordstrom, chairman emeritus, Nordstrom, Inc.

"We need more mom and we need more pop. Do you want to know why? Because they care. Caring matters. If you need proof, Robert Spector has it." —Seth Godin, author of *Tribes*

"These personal accounts and reminiscences of tenacity, pluck, resourcefulness, and integrity, peppered with a few shakes of history, could forever change your interactions with local businesses."
—Jennifer Rockne, director,
American Independent Business Alliance (AMIBA)

THE
MOM & POP STORE

True Stories from the Heart of America

ROBERT SPECTOR

WALKER & COMPANY
New York

Grateful acknowledgment is made to reprint excerpts from: "Departure and Arrival" in *World of Our Fathers*, copyright © 1976 by Irving Howe, reprinted by permission of Houghton Mifflin Harcourt Publishing Company; *Wheels of Commerce: Civilizations & Capitalism 15th–18th Century*, vol. 2, copyright © 1992 by Fernand Braudel, reprinted by permission of Armand-Colin; *I Know Why the Caged Bird Sings*, by Maya Angelou, copyright © 1970, reprinted by permission of Random House.

Portions of author's interview with Daniel Carney came from an interview conducted for *The Pizza Hut Story*, by Robert Spector (New York: Melcher Media, 2008).

Published by Walker Publishing Company, Inc., New York

All papers used by Walker & Company are natural, recyclable products made from wood grown in well-managed forests. The manufacturing processes conform to the environmental regulations of the country of origin.

LIBRARY OF CONGRESS CATALOGING-IN-PUBLICATION DATA

Spector, Robert, 1947–
The mom & pop store : how the unsung heroes of the American economy are surviving and thriving / Robert Spector.—1st U.S. ed.
p. cm.
Includes bibliographical references.
ISBN 978-0-8027-1605-7 (hardcover)
1. Couple-owned business enterprises—United States—History.
2. Small business—Social aspects—United States—History.   I. Title.
HD62.27.S64 2009
381'.14—dc22

2009019198

Visit Walker & Company's Web site at www.walkerbooks.com

First published by Walker & Company in 2009
This paperback edition published in 2010

Paperback ISBN: 978-0-8027-7765-2

1 3 5 7 9 10 8 6 4 2

Book design by Simon M. Sullivan
Typeset by Westchester Book Group
Printed in the United States of America by
Worldcolor Fairfield

For my sisters,

SANDRA SPECTOR GOLDBERG *and* BARBARA SPECTOR EISNER,

who were there, on the other side of the counter.

There is no man who is not in some degree a merchant;
who has not something to buy or something to sell.

—SAMUEL JOHNSON (1709–1784)

CONTENTS

INTRODUCTION

THE MOM & POP STORE—the small, independent trader—embodies our most basic and enduring commercial bond. From the wool merchants in the markets of King Hammurabi's Babylon in 2000 B.C., to the stand-alone bakeries in eleventh-century France, to the espresso shops on modern-day Main Street, *trade*—the exchange of goods or currency between buyer and seller—is the foundation of civilized society.

Retail, as the writer Christopher Caldwell noted, "is the exciting place where the economic order and the social order meet."

Not that any of these thoughts ever crossed my mind as a teenager slicing liverwurst in my father's butcher shop in the farmers' market in Perth Amboy, New Jersey. All I could think about was getting as far away as I could from the boiled ham, chop meat, pigs' feet, calves' brains, ham hocks, and head cheese that surrounded me. Never once, as I stuffed scraps of raw meat and fat into the grinder to make chop meat, did I think about my contribution to the "economic order and the social order," nor did I appreciate the fact that I was sharing this experience with Bob Dylan, whose first job was sweeping the floor of his father's Zimmerman Electric & Furniture store in Hibbing, Minnesota; or Colin Powell, who worked throughout high school at Sickser's Furniture in the Bronx; or Margaret Thatcher, who made change in her father's grocery store in Grantham, Lincolnshire; or Paul Newman, who once ran his father's sporting goods store in Cleveland, Ohio; or Tony Bennett, Warren Buffett, or Maya Angelou. I didn't know that being the son of a butcher placed me in the company of William Shakespeare, Nat King Cole, Marcel Marceau, Antonín Dvořák, John Harvard, John

Jacob Astor, Julian Schnabel, and Paul "Big Pauly" Castellano, the late head of the Gambino crime family.

It wasn't until I was almost fifty years old that I finally comprehended how those hours spent behind the counter had shaped my life and granted me the practical wisdom that has guided me ever since. At the time, I didn't even think I was paying attention.

I eventually learned to fully appreciate the impact that the shop had on my extended family (over four decades, Spector's Meat Market directly or indirectly benefited seventeen relatives), and on the lives of our customers. The T-bone steak that my father trimmed, the salami that my uncle sliced, and the rye bread that my mother sold found their way to the dinner tables of homes all over our community. A little bit of the Spectors, as it were, right there on your plate. This was brought home to me during the research of this book, when a high school classmate of my sister Sandra wrote a poem called "Memories" for their class reunion. Included in the lines written by Ann Romeo Kulick, who lived across the street from the farmers' market, was "There was Spector's, with rye bread in hand."

A few years ago, I wrote a book called *Category Killers* about the impact of so-called big-box retailers, such as Wal-Mart, Staples, Best Buy, Petco, and so forth on our consumer culture. Back then, when people asked me what project I was working on, my answer, "category killers," produced a blank stare. What's a category killer? But when I told people I was working on a book about mom & pop stores, practically all of them reacted with a smile because everyone knows what a mom & pop store is. "Oh, my grandfather had an Italian bakery," one person said. "My uncle was a butcher," said another, or "My parents had a tailor shop."

Almost everyone had a personal story about his or her favorite mom & pop store. My doctor, Bill Mitchell, told me about the time when he was eight years old and his mother sent him to the nearby corner grocery store in his Chicago neighborhood to get a quart of milk. This was in the 1950s, when milk came in glass bottles. Bill bought the milk, walked out of the grocery store, slipped on a wet spot, and dropped the bottle onto the sidewalk—shattering glass at his feet. As he began to cry (literally over spilled milk), the owner heard him and rushed out of the store to see what was the matter.

He gave young Bill another bottle of milk, free of charge. Fifty years after that experience, Bill recalled it as if it were yesterday.

Howard Schultz, the chairman of Starbucks Coffee, told me that when he was a young boy in Brooklyn, "I would go to the butcher store with my mom, and the butcher would show her chickens. My mother would say, 'No, I don't want that one; yes, I want that one.' The butcher placed a lot of importance on doing things right for her. After we were done, he'd always say, 'I'll see you next week, Mrs. Schultz.' You want to go into a place where you're appreciated, known, and respected."

Growing up, my favorite store was Penn's Confectionary, the little shop owned by the parents of my childhood friend Sharon Penn. Penn's was located a couple of blocks from my house, in the middle of a modest, tree-lined residential neighborhood. The shop carried a little bit of everything—candy, comic books, magazines, greeting cards, and Spalding High-Bounce rubber balls, which were ideal for stickball or stoopball games. Penn's centerpiece was a classic soda fountain counter where customers devoured ice cream sodas, fudge sundaes, banana splits, milkshakes, and egg creams. By the time Sharon, the oldest child, was fourteen, her father thought nothing of leaving her to run the store by herself for three or four hours at a time. On many a summer day, I'd dribble my basketball down our street, then over to the corner of Lewis Street and Brighton Avenue, to Penn's, where I'd park myself on a stool at the counter and keep Sharon company as we talked about girls (me) and boys (her). In between the times she was waiting on customers, she'd fix me a chocolate malted milk shake (with a raw egg, always), and let me read, for free, the latest Superman and Batman comic books.

It turns out I was having more fun than Sharon was.

"When I was fourteen, I never thought about what an awesome responsibility it was to be left to run the store by myself," Sharon Penn Sigmund told me. "My father was so interested in getting out of there, if I was nine years old he would have left me there."

And yet, her time working in the shop taught her valuable lessons.

"I knew that, even at fourteen, I was capable of running the store for three or four hours on my own. My mother taught me to always be organized and neat. Always recheck everything. Later in life I did surgical scheduling, where you had to be precise, because having the right equipment in the operating room was a matter of life or death."

"Mom & pop store" is such a familiar expression that it seems to have been around forever, but it's a modern term. The *Oxford English Dictionary* attributes the first usage to the December 20, 1962, issue of a publication called the *Listener*, which was distributed by the BBC in Great Britain: "These mom & pop stores certainly do not love the supermarkets."

(By the way, they still don't.)

Over the years, the term has gotten a bad rap. Businesses are belittled as being just "mom & pop operations"—small, insignificant, outdated. It's easy to understand why many people who run mom & pop stores don't want their businesses described that way because they feel it diminishes what they do.

Some owners of small, independent retail businesses reject the term because their stores are not owned by a mom and a pop. So when I use the term "mom & pop," I also mean mom & mom, mom & daughter, brother & brother, business partner & business partner, and life partner & life partner. To me, it's all mom & pop.

Mom & pop stores are not about something small; they are about something big. Ninety percent of all U.S. businesses are family owned or controlled. They are important not only for the food, drink, clothing, and tools they sell us, but also for providing us with intellectual stimulation, social interaction, and connection to our communities. We must have mom & pop stores because we are social animals. We crave to be a part of the marketplace. Before the bursting of the Internet-stock bubble of the 1990s, the so-called experts were telling us that we no longer needed brick-and-mortar shops because we were all going to be buying everything online, in our pajamas, at two in the morning. (Were these the same people who predicted the "paperless office" and the "thirty-hour workweek"?) They didn't realize that human beings are drawn to the market, the agora, the heart of town. We will always have mom & pop stores because we will always need them. Mom & pop stores have endured every new retail concept that's been thrown at them: department stores, chain stores, discount stores, mail-order catalogs, and the Internet. They are masters at adapting to their changing environment. That's why, after the apocalypse, the only survivors will be cockroaches and mom & pop stores.

With this book, I intend to reappropriate the term "mom & pop" to its rightful, honorable place.

The men and women who run these enterprises are heroes and heroines; they are authentic entrepreneurs who create, organize, operate, and assume the risk for their business ventures. That's why in order to run a mom & pop business you have to be a jack-of-all-trades (or a jill)—financier, buyer, merchandiser, bookkeeper, bill collector, adviser, referee, good neighbor, and community pillar.

The owner of a successful mom & pop store has to have more talents than the CEO of a Fortune 500 company—plus more integrity. Lora Lewis, who owns and operates Hotwire Online Coffeehouse in Seattle, told me that all her new hires are given a sheet of paper that lists pertinent contact information about the business. Under "human resources" is Lora's name and cell phone number. Under "payroll" is her name and cell phone number. The same thing goes for "schedule changes" and every other relevant topic. "They all laugh, thank goodness," said Lora, but the point is still made. After all is said and done, it's all her responsibility.

This book is no elegy for the shops that have relocated to the big Main Street in the sky. Their passing is a part of life, just like the death of a person or a pet. About a third of family-owned businesses survive to the second generation, and 16 percent reach the third generation. Only 3 percent make it to the fourth generation or further. Small independent retailers go out of business for many reasons: aging owners, family squabbles, absence of a successor, burnout, competition from large chain stores, new highways that bypass downtowns, ups and downs of local economies, evolving tastes and needs of their neighborhoods, changing demographics, urban renewal, loss of lease, hikes in rent, poor planning. Some indie traders are like shooting stars, meant to exist for a brief time; others persevere and become Pizza Hut or Nordstrom or the Geek Squad.

Newspapers often run retail obituaries about longtime stores or restaurants that are closing their doors. Here's a sampling of headlines that I've collected over the years:

IT'S LAST CALL FOR GUINAN'S PUB AND STORE

A COFFEE SHOP CLOSES, AND THERE'LL BE SAD SONGS DOWN AT MORY'S

CLOSING TIME FOR DINER THAT FED THE BODY AND SOUL

A DELI DESTINATION, NOW A PASTRAMI-SCENTED MEMORY

TOUGH TIMES FOR LOCAL INDIE BOOKSTORES

We bemoan the fact that the place is closing, but we can't remember the last time we gave the place our business. For three decades, a dear friend of mine was a very successful retailer in a major city, but because of changes in the local demand for his specialized product category, he was forced to close his store, which was a well-known, longtime landmark in his city. The local newspaper wrote the obligatory article about the store's demise, and customers came by to lament what had happened, and to buy a few items as mementos. My friend was gratified by the outpouring, but, he asked me, "Where were those people when I needed them?"

If we want independent retailers to stay in business, we have to patronize them. It's that simple. It's always been that simple. That thought was reinforced in me in 2006 at the New Jersey Information Center in the Newark Public Library, where I was staring at microfiche copies of the classified city directories, looking for businesses my grandfather had been involved in, before he and my father and uncle opened their butcher shop in Perth Amboy in the 1930s. On the introductory page of the 1930 directory, the publisher listed several reasons for buying a copy, but the payoff was the final reason: "If your neighbor has it to sell, give him your business. Like consideration from your neighbor adds prosperity to both."

In other words, if you've got something I need, I'll buy from you, and vice versa. That's what makes the world go 'round. Mom & pop stores are about neighborhood, about community, about my taking care of you and your taking care of me.

Today in communities, big and small, mom & pop stores are

more relevant than ever. They're not disappearing. Look around you. They are everywhere: the neighborhood grocer, butcher, dry cleaner, and barber. Today's mom & pop store is a trendy women's boutique that reflects the fashion vision of a former department store sportswear buyer. Today's mom & pop store is a hip bakery started by an erstwhile hedge fund trader, who wanted to capitalize on grandma's recipe for cupcakes.

A surprising marketing strategy shows just how relevant mom & pop stores are today. They were a key component in a 2008 advertising campaign by the *Atlantic* magazine that was aimed at grabbing the attention of young New York media buyers—the people who decide where to spend the advertising budget of their clients. Part of the strategy of the *Atlantic* was to advertise in unconventional venues, such as neighborhood restaurants, bakeries, and bodegas where the media buyers ate and shopped. For example, in a bakery showcase, between the corn muffins and the currant biscuits, there was a scone with a little sign that posed the provocative question, "Is war a sport?" along with the magazine's Web site and slogan. A spokesman for the ad agency was quoted as saying that the restaurants and shops were ideal locations to get the media buyers' attention because they are "places where people's brains are most at rest."

Mom & pop stores define the neighborhood. Jane Jacobs, who wrote about my old Greenwich Village neighborhood in *The Death and Life of Great American Cities*, pointed out that it's not the big retail chains that provide the characters on the streets of a neighborhood; it's the small businesses that do that. The neighborhood characters are people like Rob Kaufelt, the owner of Murray's Cheese Shop on Bleecker Street in Greenwich Village; John Nese, who runs Galco's Old World Grocery in Los Angeles; Willie Earl Bates, who revived the legendary Four Way Restaurant in Memphis, Tennessee, and all the other men and women you will meet in these pages. Each of them has invested blood, sweat, tears, time, passion, and dollars, and each has, in the process, created a unique neighborhood place.

Mom & pop stores continue to be a part of the immigrant entrepreneurial experience in ways that combine the old with the new.

I fondly recall riding a bus down Hillside Avenue in Queens with my book editor and marveling at the veritable "United Nations" of mom & pop stores on that bustling street in the most diverse community on the planet. It didn't matter whether the shop owners were from Ghana, Vietnam, or Ukraine or whether they were running restaurants, dry cleaners, or bakeries. Once they reached the shores of America, they instinctively understood the part they could play in their neighborhood.

Small independent traders are the most direct line to the people. In an article in the *New York Times* headlined HIP-HOP BETWEEN THE COLD CUTS, resourceful Latino hip-hop, dance, and rock bands talked about bypassing the big music stores and Internet music sites by selling their CDs at the corner bodega and the local barbershop. And one of the biggest recent hit shows on Broadway was the rap-and-salsa-inspired musical *In the Heights*, which centered its action on a bodega in the Washington Heights neighborhood of Manhattan.

MY AMERICAN ODYSSEY

FOR TWO YEARS, I traveled all over the United States and other parts of the world to interview men and women who are running successful mom & pop stores. My selection of stores was random, based on my travel schedule, recommendations, and gut feelings. At first, I was going to concentrate on traditional family retailers that had been in business for several generations, but that was too limiting. My sole criterion eventually evolved into finding the mom & pops that told a compelling story. Looking back on the topics we discussed, I found we covered all of the important ones: life, death, love, hate, family, friendship, neighborliness, hard work, entrepreneurship, creativity, adaptation, racism, sexism, anti-Semitism, civil rights, AIDS, immigration, capitalism, socialism, communism, war, freedom, urban renewal, sweet soul music, and corned beef on rye.

My odyssey took me to Los Angeles, Orange County, Portland, Chicago, Milwaukee, Cincinnati, Dayton, New York, Washington, D.C., Baltimore, Philadelphia, Pittsburgh, Miami, Savannah, New

Orleans—and Newark, New Jersey, where I was born, Perth Amboy, New Jersey, where I grew up, and back to my own community in Seattle, where I live. I also visited mom & pop retailers in Tokyo and London. I've had the honor and pleasure to interview people who own hardware stores, florists, butcher shops, fruit stands, barber shops, bakeries, coffee shops, home-decor stores, furniture stores, restaurants, groceries, delis, pharmacies, lumberyards, jewelry stores, and bookstores.

What all the entrepreneurs I interviewed have in common is a desire to run their own independent business. Why else would they and millions of other men and women like them ignore the conventional wisdom and the naysayers? It's because they are living a dream that will not die. It's too powerful and too seductive, even when it's a pain in the rear. A few of them were discouraged from going into the family business by their fathers—who told them they were never going to get rich. But money wasn't their primary motivation. Contentment and making an honest living were what they were after.

These men and women prove that anything is possible if you work at it, and work at it, and work at it some more. They share seven qualities: (1) a desire for independence, (2) a distinctive entrepreneurial belief that what they are doing is special, (3) passion, (4) persistence, (5) a willingness to work hard and to do whatever it takes to get the job done, (6) a connection to their community, and, most important, (7) an ability to adapt to change. It's not that they've simply figured out a way to make it work. It's that they continue to figure out how to make it work as conditions change—how to survive and thrive. Several of them have embraced the Internet, which has given them new opportunities for growth and for expanding their shopping community. Like all shopkeepers, they are deep-down optimists. They have to be, because every morning they unlock the doors of their stores, turn on the lights, prepare for the day, and wait for people to walk in and hand them money. Can you think of a better definition of an optimist? What they do is not easy. It's never been easy. But if it were easy, then everybody would do it.

I am indebted to them for letting me, a stranger, walk briefly into their lives to talk about what they love. They taught me many things, particularly that despite geographical, regional, racial, ethnic, political, and sexual differences, we all share a desire for a uniqueness of place that says, "This is where I live, and this is why it's special."

My fondest wish would be to bring them all together at the same time, so they could meet each other and compare notes. That would make for one interesting evening, especially if all the food people brought something special. The Hernandez brothers might bring fresh mango from their fruit stand, Los Pinareños Fruteria, in Miami's Little Havana district. I'd ask the Brummer brothers to pack some pastrami sandwiches from their Hobby's Delicatessen in Newark. For dessert, Norm Dinkel could supply us with strudel from Dinkel's Bakery in Chicago; or Willie Earl Bates could tempt us with sweet potato pie from the Four Way Restaurant in Memphis. But I digress. Alas, they will never meet because they're all too busy running their businesses. So, the next best thing is to get to know them and their stories in these pages.

This book is divided into three sections. The first, "Stories from Home," looks at my own family's story of how we got to have a butcher shop in the farmers' market in Perth Amboy, New Jersey. It also includes a fun look at pop retail history and at how the systems of trade that we use today—weights and measures, currency, shops—came into being. The second section, "Stories from the Road," contains dispatches from my retail odyssey, from the people I met along the way, and the wisdom they imparted. The third section, "Stories from the Community," bring us back home, and looks at the importance of the community, and how it sustains us through good times and bad.

Most people know mom & pop stores from only the customer's point of view. Here's what life looks like from the other side of the counter.

PART I

STORIES FROM HOME

Working-Class Hero

If you want to leave your footprints on the sands of
time, be sure you're wearing work shoes.

—ITALIAN PROVERB

FRED SPECTOR WAS A FINE MAN, a pious man," I heard the
rabbi drone at my father's funeral service at Temple Beth Mordecai in Perth Amboy, New Jersey, on May 11, 1990.

A fine man, yeah. Pious? I don't think so. When it came to pre-
serving Jewish traditions, the Spectors, my father's side of the
family, did the bare minimum.

"I'm going to make a real Jew out of you," my mother, Florence,
told my father in 1970 after he sold our butcher shop and retired.
What she meant was that she and Fred were going to be regulars at
Sabbath services every Friday night and Saturday morning at Beth
Mordecai. They could never do that while they had the shop because Saturday was our busiest day. Saturday's business determined
how you fared for the week. Oh sure, Dad was a regular every fall
on the important days—the High Holy Days—even though Yom Kippur services, which ran from nine A.M. to sundown, got pretty te-
dious by the middle of the afternoon. While my mother prayed all
day and fasted—no water or food passed through her lips—my father would invariably disappear. He would wander off to get something to eat at a restaurant and to smoke a cigarette or two. When
he returned to Beth Mordecai and took his seat next to my mother,
she would smell his breath—ham sandwich, coffee, and a Pall
Mall—and shoot him a disapproving look. Who was he fooling?
Certainly not my religious mother, who, before she married my

father, once seriously dated a man who eventually became a rabbi. "I could have been a *rebbitzen* [a rabbi's wife]," she used to joke.

(One of the ironies of the Spector family was that our home was kosher—at the insistence of my observant mother—but we did not sell kosher meat.)

At my dad's funeral, this rabbi knew Fred Spector, who died at age eighty-three, only as an old man who shuffled into Beth Mordecai Friday evenings and Saturday mornings. (Dad enjoyed the social aspects of being with men his own age. He was a schmoozer par excellence.) But the rabbi didn't know one of the most important parts of the story—that my father had been the owner of Spector's Meat Market, which had been started by my grandfather, my father, and my uncle in the 1930s, and was in our family until my dad retired. He was a businessman, a hustler, a go-getter, an improviser, a survivor, a mensch. As I sat in the pews at Beth Mordecai with my family and listened to this rabbi recite his clichés from Funeral Services 101, I got more and more irritated. I felt a knot in the pit of my stomach. I wanted to scream, "Enough!"

Earlier that day before the service, I had told the rabbi (whom I had just met), that I was going to speak about Dad for the rest of my family—my sisters and their husbands and children, and my wife and daughter. I had decided to entitle my eulogy "Working-Class Hero," from a song that John Lennon wrote after his days with the Beatles. The title was apt, because my father *was* a working-class hero, an immigrant with an eighth-grade education, with an advanced degree from the proverbial school of hard knocks. I had intended to quote a line or two from Lennon, but when I reread the lyrics I was reminded that they are among the most depressing ever written. But I did keep "Working-Class Hero" as my theme.

As I sat in the synagogue, I thought back to when I was nine years old, and my third-grade teacher, Mrs. Kreisher, gave us an assignment that, in retrospect, was odd: "Ask your father if he enjoys what he does for a living." At that age, I was old enough to grasp the fact that my father was a butcher, but I had rarely watched him work. I just knew that I didn't see that much of him. He was out of the house long before I got up for school. And when he came home at the end of the long workday, he could usually be found on his recliner chair—in the sun parlor of the upstairs apartment in the two-family house we owned on State Street—sound asleep and snoring like a buzz saw in front of our twelve-inch black-and-white DuMont TV set.

So, one day, home from Number 7 School, I raced up the stairs and ran to the sun parlor, where Dad had just awakened from a nap. I stood at his side and asked, "Do you enjoy what you do for a living?"

He didn't hesitate. "No."

That was it. It was not an essay question. I was so surprised that I couldn't think of a follow-up question, other than "Really?"

He nodded. End of discussion.

Looking back, I realized that I had asked him the wrong question. The *right* question should have been: "Are you proud of the way you've taken care of your family?" For that, I know he would have answered, "Yes."

My father may not have enjoyed what he did. I can't imagine that getting up at three or four o'clock in the morning almost every day of your life, dealing with the subfreezing New Jersey winters, trying not to get too angry at his older brother, Sidney (my dad's employee), and all the other stuff he had to deal with would fall under the heading of "enjoyment." Nevertheless, Fred Spector—like any hardworking proprietor of a mom & pop store—did what needed to be done.

When I was a few years older, I got to watch him do it. There are few businesses other than a family-run store where the children of the owners can fully appreciate what their parents do for a living. We are there to see it firsthand, to make our own contribution to the family enterprise, to learn what's good and what's not so good about the business, and to consider whether we want to do this for a living. If I hadn't worked alongside my father, I would have missed a significant part of who he was.

"Robert will now say a few words about his father," announced the rabbi.

I kissed my wife, Marybeth, stood up, and paused to collect myself. Then something startling happened: I felt the spirit of my father wash over me. It was warm and chilling, reassuring and bracing. As young man and boy, I had spent many, many hours in Beth Mordecai—on Rosh Hashanah, on Yom Kippur, on the Sabbath—but I had never ever experienced a single spiritual moment. But I did on this day, at this time.

The last major speech I had given—in this very synagogue, thirty years earlier—was my bar mitzvah speech. Like most people, I avoided public speaking. It wasn't merely the usual fears that everyone has. For my entire life, I have been a stutterer. It was not debilitating, but it was frustrating. Sometimes I'd trip over a word or two; sometimes I'd be unable to blurt out a word, particularly if the word started with *M*. (Ironically, I married a woman whose name begins with *M*.) But at this moment, thanks to the spirit of my father, I was no longer afraid. I confidently walked up to the podium and looked out on his children, grandchildren, nephews, nieces, friends, and customers who had come to pay their respects to this working-class hero. I smiled, took a deep breath, and then told the story of Fred Spector as I, his only son, saw him.

For six days a week for forty years, he rose before the sun to tend to his business. Because of his workload and responsibilities as the owner of a small retail business, we never took a family vacation all together. There were a few summers when my mother and my older sisters, Sandra and Barbara, and I would spend a couple of weeks in a rented bungalow "down the shore" at Bradley Beach, right next to Asbury Park. Dad would arrive on Saturday night, and go back early Monday morning. That was the extent of his time off.

I liked the fact that he was his own boss. Sure, the business was modest, but at least it was all his. As a kid, I occasionally accompanied him to the slaughterhouses—the abattoirs (and doesn't saying it in French make it sound so much nicer?)—where I would find myself standing in a large walk-in meat freezer, where the only colors were the white of the fat and the blood red of the skinned and quartered carcasses that dangled from tenterhooks in front of my face. The room smelled of sawdust, frozen flesh, and the aftershave lotion worn by burly butchers talking business. Even though I couldn't have verbalized it at the time, I could sense that these men respected my father. Of course, it helped that he paid his bills on time—and that he was good for a joke.

At work Fred possessed an abundance of nervous energy. I never saw him sit down. There was always something to do: make chop meat, open a can of boiled ham, slice pork chops. He'd light an un-filtered Pall Mall and take a drag or two. Then a customer would appear and he'd set the cigarette on the edge of his pockmarked chopping block, and immediately forget about it, while it burned away to ashes that dropped to the sawdust-covered floor.

His shop was his realm, where he loved to joke with the customers. He had a wonderful sense of humor. I once saw him joyfully greet a favorite female customer with the words: "I had a dream about you last night!"

"You did?" she said, flattered but embarrassed, glancing at my mother, who was standing right there.

"Yes. Yes," he insisted, with a big smile. "I dreamt I sold you this gorgeous leg of lamb," which magically materialized in his hands for her admiring inspection. She laughed. My mother laughed. More important, the customer bought the leg of lamb.

I once asked him how they make salami. His answer: "You don't want to know."

When I learned to slice cold cuts, my father hammered home to me the importance of slicing the *whole* salami, the *whole* bologna, the *whole* head cheese, particularly the ends because, he explained, "The profit is in the ends."

It works this way: Once a salami, for example, has been sliced down to the last three inches or so, you put a nice new salami in the front of the showcase for the customer to see, placing the smaller piece behind the new one. When a customer asks for a pound of salami, you simultaneously take out both salamis, walk over to the slicer, and put the small piece in first and then the new salami behind it. You slice the rest of the original salami and then the new one to complete the pound.

Some of our customers were not fond of this practice. One time a guy yelled at my father: "Spector, don't sell me the ends! I don't want the ends!" Without skipping a beat, Fred pointed to my then-teenage sister Sandra, and said, "You see my daughter? You see how pretty she is? She *only* eats the ends."

During my college graduation ceremonies, Franklin & Marshall College president Keith Spalding asked all of us in the class of 1969—dressed in our caps and gowns—to stand up. "It's an academic tradition, as a sign of respect, to doff one's cap," he said, "so I doff my cap to you. And while you're standing, please give your parents a round of applause," which we dutifully did. As I later learned from my sister Barbara, my father responded, "Well, that was worth twenty thousand dollars."

As I told these stories at the funeral, people laughed, cried, and laughed again. I felt that I had paid back the old man. I was never closer to him than I was at that moment.

My dad and I had nothing in common. He was an immigrant; I was an American. He was forty years old when I was born, much older than my friends' fathers. We never had a bonding experience. We never had a "moment." His lesson to me about the birds and the bees was reduced to: "Be careful." He knew nothing about sports; I was obsessed with sports. Whenever I'd be watching a Yankees game on TV, he would come into the room and the only question he'd ask was, "Where are they playing?" I never knew if he was actually curious about where the game was being played (he had never been to any major cities other than New York and Philadelphia) or if he was just trying to make conversation. "Detroit," I would grunt, or "Chicago," without looking up, as I concentrated on watching Mickey Mantle swing for the fences.

One of my best friends was Billy Dubin, whose father coached basketball, baseball, and tennis, and who taught Billy how to switch-hit in baseball, and how to hit a sweet backhand in tennis. Was I jealous! I once grumbled loudly, within earshot of my father, "I wish I had a dad like Billy's, who would play ball with me."

My father had never played sports in his life. He had emigrated to the United States at age fourteen, and almost immediately went to work for his father. At five foot eight inches tall and two hundred plus pounds, he was not in great shape. So imagine my surprise when he came to me one day and said, "Let's go out to the backyard and play catch." Play catch? Really? I got my Spaldeen rubber ball (which I had purchased at Penn's Confectionary), and we walked down the back stairs of our two-family house, down to the paved backyard we shared with two other houses and three garages. I had spent many hours in the backyard playing wiffle ball with friends, but I had never been there with my dad.

This, I assure you, was not the final scene from *Field of Dreams*.

I handed him the ball and backed up a few feet for a short throw. He tossed it to me, weakly, ineptly, embarrassingly. It might have been the first time he had thrown a ball. I softly tossed it back to him. He didn't have the slightest idea of how to catch it. It bounced off his hands. He awkwardly ran after it. I had never seen him run before. My heart sank. I was ashamed—and a bit queasy. I had to bring this to an end. "That's enough . . . Thank you," I said, but I didn't mean it.

My relationship with my father was formed working at the butcher shop in the farmers' market on the corner of Smith and Elm streets in Perth Amboy. Filling almost a city block on the edge of the downtown retail core, the 1.31-acre market property was almost completely dry dirt except for a twelve-foot-wide paved strip covered by a sloped roof that started at Smith Street, Perth Amboy's main shopping drag, and ran two hundred feet along Elm. At the very end of the paved strip was our shop, which was situated in a thirty-foot-wide storefront that anchored the farmers' market. (Picture the cross end of a T square.) Garage-style doors were kept open during business hours, leaving us exposed to the elements year-round, particularly those subfreezing New Jersey winters.

I don't have a picture of Spector's Meat Market, except for the one I carry around in my head. No one ever stopped to take a snapshot for posterity. There was work to be done, customers to be waited on, pork chops to be sliced, floors to be swept. Take time to pose for pictures? Are you kidding? Get your hands out of your pockets, kid, and get to work! So, there is no shot of my old man at his band saw, poised to cut a side of beef into a neat row of steaks. There is no tangible evidence that any of us were ever there. But the memories—good and bad—are still with every member of my family who ever wrapped a white apron around his or her body and waited on customers.

When I close my eyes and think about those days, I am transported to the 1960s. It's early in the morning. I see farmers dressed in newsboy caps, flannel shirts, work pants, and heavy woolen coats. They're igniting fires in large barrels to keep warm in the dawn darkness of winter. They're setting up from the backs of their trucks their displays of apples, pears, melons, and tomatoes, eggs and (live) chickens. I hear them barking out—in Italian, Russian, Portuguese, Greek, Hungarian—opinions and gossip about everything from the price of local peaches to the price of local politicians.

Every Saturday morning, at six o'clock, a young Perth Amboy resident named Stan Baranowski and his brother would dash out of their unit in one of the city's public housing projects and race over to Smith Street, where they would flag down farmers who were driving their trucks to the market. Stan and his brother helped farmers unload their trucks for "a quarter or half a buck," he told me as he recalled life back then. "After you were done, you'd run back over to Smith Street and find another farmer driving in, and help him set up. If you were lucky, you'd make a couple of bucks for the morning."

By six thirty in the morning, women customers—their hair covered in kerchiefs—would materialize out of the fog. "Fresh Jersey tomatoes," the Swallick brothers would call out to them. "Finest plums in the market," the Sosas yelled to get the shoppers' attention.

To this day, in markets and bazaars all over the world, this scene is repeated. It's an exhilarating feeling to be a part of a farmers' market that is being set up to meet the day. The energy of all these independent mom & pop operations makes everyone move a little faster and want to make their display a little more inviting. Fernand Braudel, the business historian, captured that liveliness in his description of the famed Les Halles market in Paris, in the sixteenth century, where six thousand peasants "came in the middle of every night half-asleep on their carts bringing vegetables, fruit, flowers; and the hawkers would draw people to their stalls, shouting, 'Live mackerel! Fresh herrings! Baked apples! Oysters!' . . . 'Here's a good country coat! Here's a fine jerkin!'" In medieval London, the shopkeeper or his apprentice would be out in front of the shop calling out to passersby: "What lack ye? What lack ye?"

I've seen variations of this theme in the Grand Bazaar in Istanbul, the Kensington Market in London, at a roadside fruit stand in Port of Spain, Trinidad, and a nighttime street market in Bangkok. No matter where you are, in any mom & pop enterprise, the first order of business remains the same: Grab the customer's attention.

THE RELUCTANT BUTCHER

SEPTEMBER 24, 1960, the first Saturday after my bar mitzvah, at age thirteen, I began working in the shop. Prior to that, my Saturdays were spent attending bar mitzvah lessons and Sabbath services at Temple Beth Mordecai with all my friends. But once I had become a "man" in the Jewish religion, Saturday for me was market day, until I left home for college in the fall of 1965.

One of my first jobs was to roll down the green canvas awning—emblazoned in white lettering with the words "Spector's Meat Market"—to signal that we were open for business. I felt an unexpected pride and pleasure in this small task, this morning ritual. Perhaps because this awning—other than the side of our red truck—was the only printed evidence to the outside world that there was something called "Spector's Meat Market."

But let's not get too nostalgic here. By the time I began working in my father's store, the farmers' market was a tattered eyesore. Let me amend that: It looked like crap. The V-shaped roof that was intended to protect people from the rain had lost so many shingles and boards, and was so full of holes, that it resembled the Swiss cheese we sold at twenty-nine cents a pound. The part of the block that was covered with dirt had enormous ruts that no one bothered to fill up. The three old wooden structures could have been knocked down by a colicky toddler. In 1962, the assessed valuation of those structures was twenty-four hundred dollars.

Winos and other vagrants used the unlocked, abandoned storage areas to sleep off the night before. In the morning, some of them would stagger over to our store and ask my dad if they could help load or unload things from our truck, or do some other odd job. He usually found a task for them. After they finished their work, Fred would slip them a couple of bucks, and then watch them totter their way across the street to the Pulaski Tavern to drink up their earnings. I remember one, whom my father called "Yussel," which is Yiddish for "Joseph." Yussel was tall, thin, gaunt, and beaten down, with an enormous, disfiguring growth on his chin, the kind of guy who sucked hard on every cigarette as if each puff was his last. During the infrequent times that Yussel was sober, he was a good worker, and Fred liked him enough to joke around with him. Alas, on one hot summer Friday night, Yussel was so drunk he fell asleep on the nearby railroad tracks and was run over by a train filled with weekend vacationers heading down to the Jersey Shore.

One of my jobs was to retrieve water to clean our showcases. On the market property there was a locked bathroom (basically a sink and toilet encased in old slabs of wood) a couple of hundred feet away on the other side of the dirt-covered block that Yussel and his compatriots called home. In the early dawn darkness, I would hike over with my bucket and prepare myself for the stench that would greet me. The place reeked of urine and cheap wine. Before I opened the door, I took a long, deep breath and held it in, my cheeks expanding like Dizzy Gillespie's. Once inside, I filled up my bucket as fast as that water would squirt from the tap, then slammed the door shut and exhaled. Phew! As I walked back to our shop, my water bucket by my side, I pretended I was a farmhand out on the plains, tendin' to the mornin' chores. As the sun began to come up over the central Jersey prairie, I'd break into "Oh, What a Beautiful Morning" from Oklahoma!

During summers and holidays, I worked at my father's other store on Whitehead Avenue in South River, New Jersey, about a thirty-minute ride from Perth Amboy. This was a real store. It was self-contained with a front door and a bathroom. Like the shop in Perth Amboy, the floor was covered in sawdust. Outside was a tiny farmers' market, which took place only on Wednesdays and Fridays, and comprised a small handful of vendors who sold eggs, poultry, fruit, and vegetables.

Friday was the big market day in South River, whose biggest claim to fame is being the hometown of former Washington Redskins quarterback Joe Theismann. On every Friday that I wasn't in school, I had to get up at three thirty in the morning with my father and ride over to the shop in Perth Amboy. (When you're used to rising at seven thirty, getting up at three thirty is brutal.) There was a lot to do: load up the refrigerated unit in our truck with all our stuff—Genoa salami, liverwurst, Canadian bacon, fatback, tripe, steaks, pork chops, and dozens of other items, including carving knives and cleavers—and then head to South River, where we unloaded everything and set up for business. Twelve hours later, we would pack up everything we had brought with us, head back to Perth Amboy, and unload it all, in order to be ready for Saturday's market. That made for one . . . long . . . day.

In the South River store, we sold herring, which we kept in a brine-filled barrel. When the customer placed her order, I would extract the herring from the barrel with a pair of tongs, wrap it in wax paper and old newspaper, and then put it into a paper bag. We sold a lot of herring and we went through a lot of old newspaper. As a future journalist, I learned a vital lesson about the ephemeral life of newspaper stories: Today they're important; tomorrow they're for wrapping dead fish.

(This was not a new concept. In the seventeenth and eighteenth centuries, book publishers often sold pages from failed books to grocers, butchers, and apothecaries for use as wrapping paper, or to cookshops to make pie cases.)

When I was old enough to drive, my father dispatched me to his wholesalers to pick up boxes of canned hams, pork butts, and the like. I looked forward to those assignments because they got me away from waiting on customers. I couldn't have cared less about the business, I'm ashamed to say. Have you ever shopped in a family-owned store and been waited on by a pimply teenager behind the counter, who's there because he has to be there? You just know that he wants to be somewhere, *anywhere* else. He's completely indifferent to you and to what you need. He's just going through the motions, watching the clock. That was me. When I walked over to a customer and asked to help her, I saw the reluctance in her eyes. I could almost hear her think, "I don't want this kid waiting on me. I remember how he sliced the salami too thick last week." The customer would usually smile and say, "I'll wait for your father." It might have been twenty degrees and snowing, but she was going to wait for my father. Or my uncle. Or my cousin. Anybody but me.

My transparent apathy sent my normally placid father into fits of rage. "Get him out of here, Florence," he'd sputter to my mother. She was always there to intercede on my behalf, to make sure I could skip off early to cover our high school football game for the school paper, or during basketball season, to go participate in varsity basketball practice (where, alas, I was the last man on the team).

It took some doing to get my father mad at me. He was remarkably easygoing and slow to anger, which made him the polar opposite of his father and his brother, who both had volatile tempers. (My grandfather, I am told, once threw a three-pound rye bread across the dinner table, which he aimed at Uncle Sidney's head.) Sidney's son, Harvey, told me about the time when Harvey was a teenager, and he got into a fender bender when backing up our truck. "My dad got so excited about it," Harvey recalled, some six decades after the incident. "But Uncle Fred took it in stride. He just said, 'Don't worry about it. Just be careful next time.' "

GRINDING WORDS, NOT CHOP MEAT

For me, Saturday high school football games were work. I was paid to cover them by the *Newark Star-Ledger*, *Newark Evening News*, and WCTC-AM radio in New Brunswick. Down on the field, I kept track of statistics (rushing yards, passing yards, etc.), and after the game I interviewed the coach, got a good quote, and then phoned in the results.

My college summers were spent working the night desk as a sportswriter for our local daily paper, the *Perth Amboy Evening*

News. Volunteers from around Middlesex County would call in the results of Little League, Babe Ruth League, and American Legion baseball games, and I would take down the details and compose quick recaps, such as "Joe Jones hit a two-run home run and Tom Smith pitched a four-hit shutout as First Bank & Trust beat Perry Brothers Furniture 4–0 in Perth Amboy Little League Action."

After graduating college, I wrote newspaper advertising copy for the Bamberger's department store chain, at its flagship store on Market Street in Newark. Although I didn't particularly like the job, I loved walking into the store before opening hours, taking the escalator (never the elevator) up to the advertising department offices on the eighth floor, and soaking in eight floors that were chock-full of stuff—suits, dresses, cosmetics, mattresses, couches, lamps, stereos, books, toys, and candy.

Eventually, I moved to an apartment in Greenwich Village with a couple of friends, hoping to launch my writing career. It was a checkered career at best. For four years, I was a staff journalist for a menswear newspaper called *Daily News Record*. I later hammered out press releases for a boutique public relations firm on the Upper East Side. In between, I wrote jokes for third-rate Borscht Belt comedians, radio personality Don Imus, and the comedy team of Jerry Stiller & Anne Meara. I ghostwrote magazine articles for a TV personality and came up with questions for contestants on game shows.

Rarely did I ever think again about Spector's Meat Market, except, perhaps, for the times when I was in a mom & pop butcher shop or grocery store, staring at the owner's apathetic teenage son working behind the counter, and thinking, "Boy, am I glad that's not me."

In the fall of 1977, I left New York for Seattle. Not long after I arrived in the Northwest, I discovered Pike Place Market, with its high stalls of fruit and vegetables, vendors of fish, meat, and flowers, ethnic food stands, craftspeople, and street buskers. The market, I soon discovered, was the heart and soul of the city, and it was there that I rediscovered a part of my own heart and soul. Every time I visited Pike Place Market, I felt at home. I found myself lingering in front of the butcher shops, staring longingly at the pork chops and cold cuts that reminded me of those days in Perth Amboy—the days I had chosen to forget.

Eventually, I became the stringer for Fairchild Publications, which publishes *Women's Wear Daily* and a wide assortment of trade newspapers. A stringer is a nonsalaried regular contributor to a publication—in other words, you get paid by the story, in this case, by the column inch. As it turned out, being a stringer was an ideal job for me. I had discovered early on that I was a terrible employee because I could never buy in to any agenda other than my own. But as an independent stringer, I could generate as many articles as I could sell.

Fortunately, at the time, Seattle was an up-and-coming city, with interesting businesses such as Nordstrom, Starbucks, and Eddie Bauer, and apparel manufacturers such as Union Bay, Generra, and Tommy Bahama. I wrote about retail, apparel, home furnishings, footwear, supermarkets, travel, and cable television and I was able to generate a decent income. I was becoming an enterprising businessman—just like my father and grandfather. To this day, I work just about every day of the year with an immigrant's drive and hunger. Like my father and grandfather, I am constantly looking for the next opening, the next opportunity.

What did I learn about taking care of editors, who were my customers? As a self-employed person, I have always made sure that I give great customer service. I keep editors apprised of my progress on projects, so they don't have to call me. I send thank-you notes. I make it clear that I appreciate their business. Gay Talese, whose parents, Joseph (a master tailor) and Catherine, ran a dress shop in Ocean City, New Jersey, once expounded on the lessons he absorbed helping out in the business: "I don't do hatchet jobs . . . I never try to take advantage of people. I certainly win their confidence, but I don't betray it. Why? I think I learned that in the store . . . You can't betray your customer."

LESSONS FROM THE SHOP

My mother died of cancer of the liver in 1982. She had been well enough the previous year to fly to Seattle, for my wedding to Marybeth Armitstead. My father was my best man.

My mother was a home hospice patient, and during her final days I stayed with her and Dad in their two-bedroom apartment at an apartment complex called Harbor Terrace, where most of the retired Jews of Perth Amboy moved when they sold their homes. For the last forty-eight hours of her life, I gave her injections of morphine every four hours. Finally, at three in the morning on October 27, with my sister Barbara and me at her side, she died. The moment she passed away, I felt a burst of energy, a *swooooosh*, leave the room. It was startling. At that moment, I saw death not in terms of finality, but as a transfer of energy from one dimension to another. Witnessing her death was my mother's final gift to me.

During all of this, my father was sound asleep in the next room. The next order of business was to break the news to him that his wife of forty-seven years was gone. But before I woke him up, I went into the bathroom and slowly washed my hands and face. Then I opened the door of his bedroom, sat down at the side of the bed, and looked at him while he slept. I put my hand on his shoulder and gently roused him. As his eyes slowly opened and he saw me, I said, "Dad, she's gone." When the reality hit him, he blurted out a pained cry. As I held my father in my arms to console him, he began to sob.

Dad and I didn't get close until after my mother died. Before that, whenever I called home and he answered the telephone, he always said hello and then, "Here's your mother." After she died and there was no go-between, I'd fly from Seattle back to Perth Amboy to visit him, and we would sit at the dining room table, sometimes looking out the window to Raritan Bay and Staten Island, and talk—man-to-man, father-to-son. He told me he was proud of me. That was all I needed to hear. I didn't need to hear that from my mother, because I knew she had loved me unconditionally.

• • •

Five years after my father passed away, I wrote a book called *The Nordstrom Way: The Inside Story of America's Number One Customer Service Company*, about the famed Seattle-based retailer. I had become an expert in customer service, of all things. I began to get requests to speak to corporate groups. Public speaking? Me? The kid who stuttered?

Why not? I took presentation-skills training and learned some technique. Trainers can't teach you to be fearless when addressing an audience, but I already had that, thanks to my experience giving my father's eulogy five years earlier. To this day, I carry that feeling with me wherever in the world I give speeches. It is my rock, my source of strength and courage. It was the final gift from my father.

When I first began putting together my PowerPoint presentation about Nordstrom's culture of customer service, I was surprised to find myself reflecting back on Spector's Meat Market. I was amazed at how much I remembered about how my father and mother ran their business, and (most surprising) how their principles could apply to Fortune 500 companies.

I began to appreciate all the lessons I had learned—when I didn't think I was paying attention.

"Before I learned about customer service from Nordstrom," I would tell my audiences, "I learned about it from my parents." I'd put up a slide with a photo of my mother, father, sisters, and me, at about a year old. Is there a more shameless way to get the audience on your side than to show them your baby pictures? I'd talk about how my parents operated their business, how my father could multilingually sell salami and spare ribs and pork chops in Russian, Ukrainian, and various Slavic languages. And then I'd ask, "Do you have people on your staff who can conduct business in four or five languages? That's pretty good customer service."

I'd tell them about the customer I remember best and most fondly: Mrs. Trasky, a tiny, white-haired lady who used to take the bus every Saturday for the three-mile trip from her modest house in the little town of Keasbey, on the outskirts of Perth Amboy, to the farmers' market, where she sold doilies and handkerchiefs edged with lace that she crocheted herself. Winter or summer, there was Mrs. Trasky dressed in a simple cotton print dress, long, black cloth coat, and a babushka (head scarf). In the winter, she wore mittens that were cut off at the finger tips. She had four children, but never spoke of a husband. Toward the end of the day, Mrs. Trasky would put away her needles, bundle up her doilies and handkerchiefs, and then shop the market for fruit and vegetables. Her last stop would be Spector's Meat Market, where she would buy her cold cuts and other provisions. By this time, Mrs. Trasky's bags were heavy and full. Fred never wanted Mrs. Trasky to have to lug her bags to the bus stop, ride back to Keasbey, get off the bus, and walk the three long blocks to her house.

"Robert," my dad would call to me, "drive Mrs. Trasky home," as he tossed me the keys to the '62 Buick Skylark. Oh boy, a chance to get away from the market! I grabbed Mrs. Trasky's bags, put them in the backseat, opened the passenger door for her, and off we went. When we got to her house, I placed the bags on her kitchen table. Now *that* was customer service.

(I once asked my sister Barbara why she thought Mrs. Trasky received this special treatment. She replied, "Mrs. Trasky was a single woman raising four children. Dad's mother raised four children in Russia, while our grandfather was here in America. Dad understood what Mrs. Trasky was going through, and wanted to help her whenever he could.")

"Back when I was working in the butcher shop," I would tell my corporate audiences, "the thought never crossed my mind that my father was an expert on customer service. He never read a book about customer service. He never heard an expert like me talk about customer service. How did this guy get to be so smart? The answer is that he knew instinctively what it took to take care of the customer. Customer service is the same thing, whether it's Spector's Meat Market or it's Nordstrom."

The stories I tell these corporate audiences are about one neighbor serving another neighbor, about the importance of community, about the simple power of the mom & pop store. They are about what I learned from my mother and father, and what I learned in the town where I grew up. People would invariably come up to me after my speeches and tell me, "I loved the stories about your father. My parents had a shop and they always talked about the importance of taking care of the customer."

I had spent a good portion of my life searching for a mentor, someone who could point the way for me, and give me the benefit of his experience. I never ever considered that that person could possibly be my father, or that I would ever write about him. But, after he died, I realized that my father taught me the value of hard work, the importance of a timely quip, and the joy of schmoozing. Long after his death, I finally realized that all along he had been my mentor.

2

Perth Amboy

The map of America is a map of endlessness, of
opening out, of forever and ever. No man's face would
make you think of it but his hope might, his
courage might.

—ARCHIBALD MACLEISH (1892–1982)

SMITH STREET BEGINS TO UNFOLD at the cross section of Front
Street, by the dock where Perth Amboy passengers once caught
the ferry for the two-mile ride across Raritan Bay to Staten Island.
At the beginning of the twentieth century, Smith Street was the primary route from New York to the Jersey Shore, via the Staten Island ferry, a service that ran from 1709 to 1963. In the 1920s, John
D. Rockefeller, returning from his estate in Lakewood, could be
seen handing out shiny dimes to Perth Amboy's young people as his
car waited for the ferry back to the New York side.

Smith Street was and is the city's "main street," the pathway to
the mom & pop stores that have always dotted the neighborhoods
of my home town. A haven for immigrant shopkeepers for more than
three centuries, Perth Amboy is as good a place as any to talk about
mom & pop stores.

Nestled at the intersection of the Raritan River and the Arthur
Kill (a derivation of the Dutch word *kull*, or creek), in the eastern
part of Middlesex County, Perth Amboy is a blue-collar, working-
class, big-shouldered town in the dense midsection of New Jersey—
Exit 127 on the Garden State Parkway, Exit 11 on the Jersey
Turnpike—twenty-nine miles from Manhattan, seventy-six miles
from Philadelphia.

Originally founded in 1664, the town was settled officially in 1683 by a group of twelve British men known as the East Jersey Board of Proprietors, a group that included William Penn, who upon viewing the land declared, "I have never seen such before in my life." Owing to its location and natural resources, it was variously described as "a convenient town for merchandise, trade, and fishery," as well as "a sweet, wholesome, and delightful place proper for trade," thanks to its safe harbor, navigable river, and fresh water, "and hath, by many persons of the greatest experience and best judgment, been approved for the goodness of the air, soil, and situation." With those credentials, the town was made the capital of East Jersey.

Perth Amboy came by its odd moniker over the course of many decades. In the beginning, it was called, variously, "Ompoge" or "Ompo" or "Ompoye," which translated to "elbow" or "point" (describing the shape of the land) in the language of the Lenni Lenape Indians of the Algonquian nation. The name gradually evolved from Emboyle to Amboyle to Ambo Point to Amboy.

In the 1680s, one of the area's first investors (most of whom lived in Scotland) was a Scotsman named James Drummond, who was the Earl of Perth. Thanks to Drummond, the Amboy area soon became a destination for men and women who were leaving Europe for religious and political freedom. Among the new refugees were Quakers, Dutch, Scottish Presbyterians, French Huguenots (Calvinists), and English Roundheads (Puritan supporters of Parliament during the English Civil War). In 1685, two hundred freedom-seeking Scottish Presbyterians left the port of Leith, Scotland, aboard the ship *Henry and Francis* for the fifteen-week journey to the New World. Those who couldn't afford the fare of five pounds sterling were expected to spend four years as servants to the proprietors of East Jersey. Once they fulfilled that obligation, they would be declared freemen and awarded a bounty of twenty-five acres of land and a new suit of clothes.

But something happens to immigrants when they reach the soil of the New World: They grasp the concept of freedom. By the time the *Henry and Francis* rounded Sandy Hook and dropped anchor at Amboy Point, many of its passengers considered themselves to be *already* free, thank you very much. They had endured nearly four months at sea—and an outbreak of fever that killed more than half of them. Many of the survivors settled in East Jersey and were granted refuge by James Drummond, the Earl of Perth. These new settlers paid their tribute to Drummond by referring to the town as, variously, New Perth, Perth Town, or Amboy Perth. It was initially referred to as Perth Amboy in 1692, and eventually became the first incorporated city in New Jersey, with a royal charter from King George I.

The old joke of how Perth Amboy got its name goes like this: The Lenni Lenape Indians spotted the Earl of Perth dressed in a kilt and asked him, "Perth am girl?" "No," he replied, "Perth am boy." I didn't say it was a good joke, just an old one.

The East Jersey Proprietors platted the land, divided fifteen hundred acres into 150 ten-acre lots, and vowed to erect "by the help of Almighty God with all convenient speed, a convenient town." Appropriately, one of the first businesses in town was the Long Ferry Tavern, established in 1684. Two years later, it was declared that every Wednesday was Farmers' Market Day, and that two seasonal fairs would be brought to "Perth-town" every year. The town was not without a farmers' market for almost the next three hundred years. By the early eighteenth century, the market days were every Tuesday and Saturday except for Christmas. In Perth Amboy and towns all over colonial America, public markets and fairs were essential to progress and development.

THE MOM & POPPING OF AMERICA

AMERICA WAS, AND has always been, a country of opportunities for those with enterprise, guts, and determination. By the time the Pilgrims landed at Plymouth Rock, and permanent English settlements were developed, the New World had become a brand new market for English products sold by English traders, who had helped to bankroll many of the expeditions. Francis Bacon wrote in *Of Plantations* that the most successful colonists would come from the ranks of the practical vocations: "gardeners, ploughmen, labourers, smiths, carpenters, joiners, fishermen, fowlers, with some few apothecaries, cooks and bakers."

Mom & pop stores popped up very early in New England. In 1651, a pioneering entrepreneur named George Corwin established a general store in Salem, Massachusetts, that sold fabrics, hardware, toys, needles and thread, and most everything needed for the frontier. As the population increased, the number of general stores increased accordingly. These stores sold mainly *dry goods*—merchandise that was not weighed or poured. They didn't sell much in the way of perishable goods because they didn't have the necessary facilities to preserve them. The enterprising frontier housewife had to grow most of her own food, but for her other needs she periodically visited a town market, or waited for an itinerant peddler to show up. In that respect, retail in the American colonies in the seventeenth century bore little difference to retail in the eleventh century.

Coins were not generally circulated on the frontier in the New World, so there was much bartering with the natives for beads, knives, hatchets, powder, shotguns, corn, and cattle. By the eighteenth century, retail as we know it today was established with small shopkeepers, who were also known as "petty tradesmen." These shops were where consumers spent their money to buy the things they needed (as well as things they probably didn't need). As Karl Marx wrote in *Das Kapital*, "A society cannot leave off producing any more than it can leave off consuming."

By the latter part of the eighteenth century, many colonists were concerned as much about economic repression as they were about political rights. The Stamp Act of 1765 imposed a tariff on all legal documents in the colonies, revenue intended to pay for the British Army's presence in the colonies. In response, the merchants and traders of Philadelphia boycotted the importation of goods from the mother country. This act of defiance upset affluent settlers, who counted on receiving the latest fashions from London. The Stamp Act was repealed a year after its imposition.

As the United States became more populated, shops abounded. Morris Birkbeck, writing about the settling of the Midwest in *Notes on a Journey in America* (1818), pointed out that "on any spot

where a few settlers cluster together . . . some enterprising proprietor finds in his section what he deems a good site for a town, he
has it surveyed and laid out in lots which he sells or offers for sale
by auction." This nascent town takes the name of its founding father. Next, wrote Birkbeck, "a storekeeper builds a little framed
store, and sends for a few cases of goods; and then a tavern starts
up, which becomes the residence of a doctor and a lawyer, and the
boarding-house of the storekeeper as well as the resort of the weary
traveller." That's a perfectly apt description of the origins of Perth
Amboy.

TAKE PERTH AMBOY, PLEASE

IN THE EARLY eighteenth century, publicity-minded local merchants and civic boosters dubbed Perth Amboy *portus optimus*—
the greatest port. Alas, it never made it as the greatest port. It never
made it as the greatest anything. Nevertheless, it was a great place
to grow up. Perth Amboy doesn't lack for history. In 1791, when
New Jersey became the first state to ratify the Bill of Rights, it was
done at Perth Amboy's city hall, a building that is still in use today.
On March 31, 1870, a month after ratification of the Fifteenth
Amendment to the Constitution ("The right of citizens of the United
States to vote shall not be denied or abridged by the United States
or by any State on account of race, color, or previous condition of
servitude"), Thomas Mundy Peterson, custodian of School Number 1, became the first black voter in the United States. He later
was the city's first African American to hold elected office, and the
first to serve on a jury. Today, the building where he swept the
floors and took out the garbage bears his name, Thomas Mundy Peterson School.

If New Jersey is the butt of New York jokes, then Perth Amboy
is the butt of Jersey jokes. I take a perverse pride in that.

For example, the novelist Fletcher Knebel (*Seven Days in May*),
writing a tongue-in-cheek "New Jersey Dictionary" for the op-ed
page of the *New York Times*, defined "utopia" as "what people seldom have in mind when they retire to Perth Amboy."

Russell Baker, the *Times* humor columnist, once wrote, "I now have enough letters from incensed readers to fill this space for a week, which enables me to extend my Perth Amboy vacation long enough to get a fresh coat of mosquito bites."

The *New Yorker*'s Brendan Gill, writing a scathing review of a 1985 Broadway play, rhetorically asked why the production was even mounted. Answering his own question, Gill presumed that all the people associated with this flop "were not thinking, they were simply glad to be at work." That explanation, Gill concluded, "may suffice in any of the numerous widget-manufacturing plants in Perth Amboy, but it doesn't suffice on Broadway."

In the 1951 film *An American in Paris*, Gene Kelly portrayed a starving painter named Jerry Mulligan, who tries to sell his works on the Left Bank. In one scene, a strolling American exchange student stops in front of Mulligan's oils and, assuming that the artist is a Parisian, begins to tell Mulligan, in French, what he thinks of the paintings. Mulligan shuts him up with the line: "I'm from Perth Amboy, New Jersey."

James Thurber (an Ohioan) had a quirky fascination with Perth Amboy, which is where the title character grew up in *The Secret Life of Walter Mitty*. In his semi-autobiographical *My Life and Hard Times*, Thurber wrote, "I had been trying all afternoon, in vain, to think of the name Perth Amboy. It seems now like a very simple name to recall and yet on the day in question I thought of every other town in the country, as well as such words and names and phrases as terra cotta, Walla Walla, bill of lading, vice versa, hoity-toity . . . without even coming close to Perth Amboy."

CRUISING SMITH STREET

ALTHOUGH SMITH STREET, the seven-block-long main shopping drag in Perth Amboy, had the occasional national chain—F. W. Woolworth, Kresge, Thom McAn shoes—what I remember best is the vast array of small shops. Before the then-new Menlo Park shopping mall, a few miles away, would begin to siphon away shoppers, every Friday night, when the stores stayed open until nine o'clock, Smith Street was the place to see and be seen. If there wasn't a high school dance, a football pep rally, or a basketball game, Perth Amboy's teenage drivers spent a good portion of the night cruising (crawling, really) up and down Smith Street, looking for friends—our own version of *American Graffiti*. There were two popular diners, both owned by Greeks: the Crystal Lunch and the Coney Island, within seventy-five feet of each other. After a dance or a game, if you were a student at Perth Amboy High School (Amboy High, as we call it), you congregated at the Crystal; if you went to our city rival, St. Mary's High School, you hung out at the Coney Island.

On Saturdays, when the Amboy High Panthers won a home football game, the marching band, cheerleaders, and student body would lead an eight-block victory procession from Albert G. Waters Stadium, eventually marching past the mom & pop stores on Smith Street (where the owners would stand outside their stores and wave at the students in the parade), and then turn the corner to our ivy-covered high school (built in 1898) on State Street, where we would gather to sing the alma mater ("To thee, the school we love so well, a swelling song we raise"). Picture Bedford Falls from *It's a Wonderful Life*, but with a Jersey accent.

Seaman's Pharmacy (which opened in 1863) at 82 Smith, was Perth Amboy's answer to Bedford Falls's Gower's Drugstore, with its old-fashioned soda fountain and sixteen-seat-long marble counter, where one could spot Perth Amboy native Charles "Bud" White, the veteran character actor best known for playing the school principal, Mr. Brewster, on *The Patty Duke Show* on television. Later that night, Bud might be at the Barge seafood restaurant by the waterfront, nibbling on fried shrimp and tossing back libations with some of the locals, or maybe with a prominent actor like Robert Ryan, who was Bud's fellow cast member in *The Front Page* on Broadway.

Roth's Furniture, Littman's Jewelers, Schlesinger's School Supplies, Plaid 'n' Tweed clothes, Roy's Young Men's Shop, Allyn's Shoes, the Kotton Shop, and others were not just stores or centers of consumption. These small-business men and women were the parents of friends and classmates; representatives of our community; members of our churches, synagogues, Kiwanis, and parent-teacher associations; and sponsors of our bowling and Little League and Babe Ruth League teams.

If you decided to turn down Madison Avenue, one of the busiest side streets, you'd walk past Jack Rubin Jewelers, where we bought our high school class rings, and Fishkin Brothers, which was founded in 1912 by Russian immigrants and remained in business until 2004. Although the store initially sold just cigars and cigarettes, over the years the Fishkin family traded in bathing suits, underwear, horseback-riding equipment, and bicycles, but it was its matchless selection of photographic supplies—from refrigerated professional film to the latest cameras and lenses—that drew professional photographers from all over the New York metropolitan area, and as far away as Philadelphia.

(Small stores that sell a little bit of everything have been in existence for centuries. For example, William Davison, who had a shop in Alnwick, Northumberland, England, in the 1800s, was a bookseller, stationer, and printer, as well as an apothecary. He also sold hair and nail brushes, scales, compasses, mathematical instruments, and musical instruments and their accessories, such as violin strings, bridges, pegs, and hair for the violin bows.)

Across the street from Fishkin's was Pollino's Barber Shop, patronized by David T. Wilentz, who in 1935 as the state attorney general successfully prosecuted Bruno Hauptmann in the "trial of the century"—for the kidnapping of the Lindbergh baby. He eventually headed the biggest law firm in the state and was a longtime Democratic Party heavyweight. In Perth Amboy and Middlesex County, if someone wanted to get something done or get their kid hired for a particular government job, standard advice was: "See Dave." Wilentz's son, Robert, became chief justice of the New Jersey Supreme Court. His daughter, Norma, married Leon Hess, who once owned a single oil truck, eventually became an oil magnate (Hess Oil), and later yet became the owner of the New York Jets football team.

Continuing down Madison, past Capri Pizza and Leslauer's Jewish deli, you'd saunter into Mizerak's Billiards. The owner's young son, Steve, grew up to become arguably the greatest pool player in the world, and the star of Miller Lite beer television commercials.

Jewish shopkeepers once dominated the stores on Smith Street and in the neighborhoods. Today, the last surviving store on Smith Street owned by a Jewish family is Fink's Department Store, which sells bedding, bath, draperies, curtains, and other home-decorating items. Howard Fink, a third-generation owner of the business, runs it with his two sons—Robert, who is now managing the store, and Daniel. Howard's grandfather, Benjamin, an émigré from Russia, opened the shop in 1923, selling women's ready-to-wear apparel and other soft goods. Back then and through the 1970s, the shop was at another location on Smith Street and Madison Avenue around the corner from Shaarey Tefiloh, the orthodox Jewish synagogue, and the YMHA. Today, the space where the original store once stood is Elliot Fink Memorial Park, named after Howard's father.

Fink's is a throwback to the time when every town had independent stores that sold ready-made home fashion products. "Stores like this don't exist in the New York/New Jersey area anymore," Howard Fink told me. "We're doing things that the big department stores can't do. You go to Bed Bath & Beyond, and you find a lot of 'beyond' but not much bed and bath. After getting hundreds and hundreds of calls from around the country looking for window curtains to match shower curtains that they bought at Penney's or Bed Bath & Beyond, we started our Web site, shopfinkshome.com which has become a very good tool. Seventy percent of our volume— twenty percent of our traffic—is from out of town. We get business from word-of-mouth advertising, as well as from people who used to live in Perth Amboy. We have a good mix of the inexpensive and expensive. We work on a keystone markup [doubling the wholesale cost price to arrive at the retail price]—far less than our major competitors. If we get an extra ten percent on top of that, we're very happy; we feel like we're ganefs ["thieves," in Yiddish]."

Howard Fink loves his business, but he's a realist. At the age of fifty-six, he thinks about the future. "If you told me that I could get a half-million dollars for this building, which my father and grandfather paid twenty-two thousand dollars for thirty-five years ago, it makes you think. If my kids didn't want the business, I could rent the building and retire. Several years ago, I went down with what I thought was bronchitis, but turned out to be congestive heart failure. You start reevaluating your life and begin looking at your options."

West of the center of town, the quality of shops steadily declined. The imaginary line of demarcation was a little concrete sidewalk bridge over the railroad tracks for the Jersey Coast trains that connect Perth Amboy to Newark and New York to the north, and the Jersey Shore to the south. At the end of that block, you'd find the farmers' market, which was a center of commerce on Tuesdays, Thursdays, and Saturdays from the 1930s through the 1960s. Evelyn "Evie" Mariolis recalled that on Saturdays "you couldn't even walk on the street, the market was so busy. People were lined up from one end of the street to the other end. You had to fight your way through." She speaks with a Tony Sopranoesque Jersey accent (pronouncing our home town "Per-TAM-boy").

Evie and her family ran Texas Lunch, a small twenty-four-hour-a-day diner at 252 Smith, around the corner from the market. If Perth Amboy was an ethnic melting pot, Texas Lunch was the stove. Greeks, Italians, blacks, Poles, and Hispanics—among others—sorted out politics, sports, and gossip over a plate of breaded pork chops or liver and onions.

"We used to get all the meat from your father—stew meat, chop meat, pork chops," Evie reminded me. "I remember a time in the late forties when somebody owed my father money. They didn't have any money, so they gave him a cow and a goat. All of a sudden, when meat was scarce, my father thought about that cow. He said to your father, 'What do you think, Fred? Do you think we can slaughter 'im?' Your dad says, 'Why not? We cut 'im. We go fifty-fifty.' "

On many a Saturday morning, I'd be eating breakfast at Texas Lunch at five thirty with dad and Uncle Sidney, a man with curly hair and a bristly disposition. Even at that hour, in the winter's darkness, Texas Lunch was filled with caffeine, commotion, and conversation. I loved the thin slices of French toast with powdered sugar. For Fred and Sidney, breakfast was a huge hard roll that was covered with poppy seeds and slathered with butter like icing on a cake, which they washed down with "regular coffee"—i.e., lots of cream and sugar. With eating habits like that how did Sid live to ninety-four and Fred to eighty-three?

There were times when Fred and Sid used the Texas Lunch for more than eating. Back in the days when my family still lived in Newark, one winter night, when it snowed fifteen inches and they were stranded in Perth Amboy, they slept in a booth at Texas Lunch. Soon after that episode, my family and my uncle's family moved to Perth Amboy, so they no longer had to make the long commute.

A WORKING-CLASS TOWN

MY PERTH AMBOY was an industrial city. When I was growing up in the 1950s, a smokestack economy attracted immigrants from many lands, including Russia, Poland, Hungary, Czechoslovakia, Ireland, Italy, Puerto Rico, and the West Indies. White Anglo Saxon Protestants were in the minority, and just about everybody could be described as "working class."

In the early 1900s, 25 percent of the entire world's silver supply and 22 percent of the world's copper supply came from Perth Amboy. From the city's large coal dock, coal was transported to New York City and beyond on the Lehigh Valley Railroad, thanks to industrialist Asa Packer, who also built Perth Amboy's biggest hotel, the Packer House.

Every morning, workers toted their lunch pails into the local factories: Raritan Copper Works, Anaconda Copper Mining, American Smelting & Refining, Hatco Chemical, Witco Chemical, Hess Oil, and Chevron Oil. Barber Asphalt Paving once refined much of the asphalt east of the Mississippi. The Atlantic Terra Cotta Company transformed the city's rich clay deposits into the terra cotta detailing for the United States Supreme Court building, the Philadelphia Museum of Art, and New York's Plaza Hotel and Flatiron Building.

Back then, half the population of forty thousand worked right in town, which boasted 85 churches and 165 saloons.

"You would smell the smoke from the factories, and you'd say, 'That's not smoke, that's money,'" recalled Austin Gumbs, my former high school English teacher (and later the superintendent of schools), whose father emigrated from Anguila in the British West Indies. "Because every Friday, everybody got a paycheck out of that smoke."

But in the 1970s, the factories and industrial firms, the backbone of Perth Amboy, began to close. Part of the reason was that the state of New Jersey enacted some of the nation's strictest environmental enforcement laws, which essentially redlined old industrial properties in urban areas. The law effectively said that a new buyer would be liable for all the past harm done to the environment by that property. It would have been possible for some incubator or small-scale manufacturing to have filled those old buildings and generate economic activity, but the law essentially prohibited that. As a result, businesses that had long thrived in the city were fleeing or just closing down, which resulted in a shift of the burden of taxes from industry to residential property owners. In Perth Amboy's heyday, two thirds of the taxes were paid by the industrial base. By 1989, three quarters of the tax base was residential.

By the end of the seventies, the waterfront and the marina—the jewels of the city—were falling apart. Close to 40 percent of the downtown stores were boarded up. Crime was rampant. People were leaving. At the same time, Perth Amboy continued to be what it had always been—a port of entry for immigrants, but this time the newcomers were Hispanic. First they came from Puerto Rico, and later from Mexico, Ecuador, Peru, and the Dominican Republic. In 1988, Perth Amboy, which was notable for its assimilation of various minorities, was rocked by the shooting of two Mexican brothers by an off-duty policeman, causing a rampage in the downtown commercial district. Today about 75 percent of the population of forty-eight thousand is Hispanic, representing virtually every Spanish-speaking country. With almost no manufacturing base, Perth Amboy is a poor town, with a median annual household income of about forty-three thousand dollars—not much in high-tax New Jersey.

Today, on the corner of Smith and Elm where the farmers' market used to be, there is an eldercare nursing home—a homely three-story building that began to show its age right after it was built in the early 1970s. It is a dull, ugly edifice, with all the curb appeal of the Berlin Wall.

Evie Mariolis closed Texas Lunch in 2002. One of the reasons, she told me, was the increased paperwork that local and state bureaucracies demand of small businesses. "Years ago, you didn't have to fill out all these forms. When you're off work, you eat up your day fillin' out forms. I finally said, 'I've had it.'" Evie is still there, but the one-story building is no longer Texas Lunch. Rather it is the office of Family Foot Care, which is owned and operated by Evie's daughter, Elaine Mariolis, a doctor of podiatric medicine. Elaine's advertisement in the weekly newspaper, *Amboy Beacon*, lists all the foot ailments she treats: bunions, warts, corns, and calluses. And it prominently features the words "Se habla Español."

COPA DE ORO

MANY OF THE names of the stores on Smith Street and in the neighborhoods reflect Perth Amboy's financial state: 99 Cent Dreams, 99 Cent Power Store, Warehouse Outlet, and Family Discount Furniture. The largest downtown store is a discounter called Kids City. But, as always, there are also independent mom & pop stores, such as Fashions by La Femme, Flowers 'N Things, and Pretty Girl of Perth Amboy.

Perth Amboy is an Urban Enterprise Zone, which is part of a federal-government-sponsored program intended to persuade entrepreneurs and investors to develop projects in blighted neighborhoods by offering tax incentives and regulatory relief. Under this program, consumers pay a sales tax of 3.5 percent, which is half that of the New Jersey statewide rate of 7 percent. The city has used government funds to spruce up Smith Street by planting trees, installing Victorian-era streetlights, benches, garbage cans, and red brick sidewalks. But at 306 Smith—the poorest retail section of a poor city—these amenities were nowhere to be found. When I was growing up, this area, which is a couple of blocks from the site of the old farmers' market, was where the poor or lower-income Greeks, Poles, Hungarians, and Italians lived and did their business. Today, the area is still run down; only the ethnicities have changed.

Copa de Oro, a bar/nightclub, is a modest little operation in a one-story building with red brick on one side of the entrance (a windowless, gray door) and painted white brick on the other side. The only window is above the door, so there is no view of what's going on from the street. Inside, it's dark—like most bars—day or night. On a cold December Saturday afternoon, I visited Copa de Oro to speak with the owner, Reyes Ortega. I learned about Rey when my sister Sandra sent me an article in the local newspaper, the *Home News Tribune*, headlined I AM AN AMERICAN: FROM UNDOCUMENTED ALIEN TO VOTING PROPERTY OWNER, ORTEGA IS LIVING THE AMERICAN DREAM.

When I walked into Copa de Oro, I was greeted warmly by Rey, a stocky man with jet black hair, moustache, and goatee that matched his hip-length black leather jacket. He looks much younger than someone born in 1955. The front of the room is dominated by a large pool table, but no one is playing pool. Several of the customers are sitting on bar stools, chatting in Spanish and listening to high-energy Latin music.

The thirteenth of seventeen children, Rey was born in the west-central Mexican state of Michoacán, which is dominated by the Sierra Madre mountains. Pointing to a large map of Mexico, which is on the wall near the front door of the bar (near a photograph of the Mexican national soccer team), Rey proudly showed me the location of Michoacán. He was seven years old when his father passed away, leaving Rey and his four younger brothers to be cared for by his mother. His other siblings had either left home or died young.

"Since I was a small boy, I have tried to be independent," he told me. "I've tried to do good for myself and my family. I worked very hard to help my mother feed my four younger brothers."

In 1972, at the age of sixteen, Rey departed his hometown of Tiquicheo, one of the oldest cities in Mexico, and headed north to the United States. "When I left my family and my girlfriend in Mexico, my intention was to stay for two years in the U.S., and then come back." He made his way to Chicago, but was unable to find steady work. A cousin, who was living in New Jersey, told Rey that there were opportunities in the Perth Amboy area. He took his cousin's advice and was soon hired on to do landscaping at a toy factory outside of town. Eventually, he landed a job inside the factory, driving a tractor. He later got a job with a meat distributor, A. N. Weissman & Sons, where he worked the night shift, driving a forklift in the shipping department.

"Back then, I wasn't speaking any English. My supervisor asked me if I was going to go to school to learn English. I said, 'Yeah.' He said, 'Tomorrow, you get up early, and go to school.' I found the dates for the next classes, and the next day, I showed them to my supervisor. Soon after, I started school, and learned English." A. N. Weissman & Sons, where Rey worked for fifteen years, "treated me good. They allowed me to go to school and work. That was very nice of them."

To make enough money to buy a house, he took a second job at a chemical plant. In 1986, Rey, by then the father of three young children, bought his first house on Madison Avenue between Patterson and Lewis streets, which is just two blocks from the house where I grew up at 119 State Street. His four children attended the same schools I did.

Ortega had not envisioned himself as the owner of a small business; it just worked out that way. In the summer of 1985, he gave a party for his son Joel at a club that was then known as "Bamboo." After the party, the owner—a Puerto Rican man who had lived in Perth Amboy for many years—told him, "Rey, in one or two years, I'm going to retire. I'm going to put this place up for sale. Maybe you'd like to buy it."

"I didn't have any money," Rey recalled. "How am I going to buy it? I just bought my house, and I was already working two jobs." But the owner of Bamboo was insistent. "I tried to avoid him. When I was walking down Smith Street, I'd walk on the other side of the street from the bar, so that I wouldn't run into him. He really wanted to sell it to me. One day, he saw me on the street and he said, 'Rey, I don't know why, but I want you to buy my business. Something tells me that you are the right person to take care of it.'"

The owner's asking price was $299,000, which was way out of Rey's neighborhood. The owner asked Rey for a counteroffer.

"Right from the top of my mouth, I said $225,000. I don't know where that came from. That was a big difference in price. I was hoping he'd say no."

The owner walked around the bar and thought for a few minutes about it before finally agreeing to the deal.

"I thought, 'Jesus Christ, what did I do?' I was scared."

The owner wanted a down payment of a hundred thousand dollars, but Rey could only manage a loan of seventy-five thousand dollars from his bank. With twenty thousand dollars borrowed from one of his brothers and an additional five thousand dollars from other relatives, he scraped together enough money to swing the deal. In 1989, Reyes Ortega became an American entrepreneur, the proud (and anxious) owner of a mom & pop operation in Perth Amboy. The problem was that he had no idea how to run a business.

"That was my main concern. In those days, I didn't even drink. As part of the deal, the guy who sold it to me stayed on for a month to teach me the names of the liquors, how to order, how to buy the kind of liquor the customers like."

Once he took over, Rey renamed the club Copa de Oro or Golden Cup. He became the owner, the bartender, and chief cook and bottle washer for the twelve-hundred-square-foot space that today employs four family members, including his son, Joel.

Rey told me his story across the street from Copa de Oro at a Dominican restaurant called El Monumento, where the waitress greeted him warmly, and then brought us some coffee—its bitter taste cut by milk—in Styrofoam cups. Rey cautioned me that the coffee was very hot. He was right. While we talked, a steady stream of locals filed in and out of the shop, and everyone stopped by our table to say hello to Rey, shake his hand, and exchange a few pleasantries in Spanish.

"Does everybody know you?" I asked. He chuckled, but clearly he is a man who is respected in the neighborhood.

"I was working in the community even before I had the business. When my kids [who are now in their twenties] were in school, I was a member of the PTA. Little by little, as I got more involved in my business, different issues would come up. People would need help. You hear about them in the bar. I'd speak to attorneys and doctors," who could help people in the community with their problems.

In 1988, after sixteen years in the United States, Rey, an undocumented alien, applied for his green card at the immigration office in Newark. In 2002, he became a U.S. citizen. "I wasn't afraid to do it, but I was so busy working, and my kids were small. I started learning about the U.S. I like history. I liked the Constitution of the United States, even though the Mexican Constitution is very nice. I liked learning about the U.S. It was a nice experience. It's something special you feel inside of you. I believe that everyone should commit to the country."

The same year he became a citizen, Rey and some of his business friends formed the Perth Amboy Merchants Association (PAMA), of which he is president. With the slogan "Working for your business" ("Trabajando para su negocio"), PAMA's mission statement emphasizes "the inclusion of all businesses in the growth and redevelopment of the community."

"We get involved in a lot of things. We have town meetings. We have seminars to teach people how to get a loan, how to run a business, how they can protect themselves. We explain the local laws and how they can be affected by them."

Rey described himself as a community activist, with particular concerns about labor and immigrations laws—which is not surprising considering his personal history. To make his stand, he made a run for the New Jersey General Assembly—as a Republican, a political species as rare in Middlesex County as it is in Berkeley, California. Rey ran against the deeply entrenched Democratic machine and lost by several thousand votes. All things considered, it was a respectable showing.

The long-term future of the town is positive. The downtown mom & pop businesses are thriving, with few vacancies in the retail core. The city is going through profound changes as the town leaders try to move it toward gentrification—or perhaps the term is regentrification. The longtime mayor (voted out of office in 2008 after two decades) brought in many millions of federal and state dollars to spur development of homes and condominiums. Perth

Amboy has always had a lot going for it, particularly its location. It's a stop on the Jersey Central train line, less than sixty minutes away from Penn Station in New York. Many wealthy people who live in Manhattan and other upscale communities dock their boats at the Raritan Yacht Club, which is the second-oldest yacht club in America, established in 1865.

Rey expressed concern over gentrification. "If we continue going the way we're going, it's not good for us. People like me, we need the poor people to survive for our business. Perth Amboy in the near future is going to be a city of rich and poor. People like us are going to have to move out. You think the well-off people from New York are going to stop in my place to have a drink?"

Rey intends to stay and fight for himself and his community. Reflecting on the value and importance of following his American dream Rey said, "As long as a person has the disposition to do it, it can be done."

My immigrant grandfather would have heartily agreed.

3

Zeyde (Grandfather): Founder of Our Family Business

The whole of the American Dream has been based
on the chance to get ahead for one's self or one's
children. Would this country ever have reached the
point it has if the individual had always been refused
the rewards of his labors and dangers?

—JAMES TRUSLOW ADAMS, HISTORIAN (1878–1949)

IN THE LATE WINTER OF 1909, my grandfather Israel Spektor left behind in his home village of Kapeigorad, Ukraine, his wife, Mindel, and their four children: nine-year-old Sidney, seven-year-old Yetta, five-year-old Bella, and three-year-old Fred. Kapeigorad was a small commercial town in the province of Podolia in the Pale of the Settlement (the source of the phrase "beyond the pale"), the place chosen by Nicholas II for the Jewish people to live in the Russian Empire. Like the other villages, Kapeigorad had a marketplace where peasants like my family sold their wares for survival.

On March 10, 1910, five days short of his thirty-second birthday, my grandfather arrived at Ellis Island on the ship *Campania*, out of Rotterdam. The 622-foot-long vessel carried two thousand passengers—six hundred in first class, four hundred in second class, and a thousand in third class, including Israel Spektor, my *zeyde* (*zey'·deh*)—the Yiddish word for grandfather.

"Your father is in America" was a verse in a popular lullaby—"Shlof, Mayn Kind" ("Sleep, My Baby")—that was written by

Sholem Aleichem and sung by mothers whose husbands followed the same path as my grandfather:

> Sleep, my baby sleep. Your father is in America.
> In that wonderful country, he eats white bread every day.
> When there is a sound at the door, he does not flinch.
> It is not the officers of the Czar but only the wind.
> Sleep, baby, soon you will join him.

In my grandfather's family's case, his wife and children would not be able to join him for eleven years. *Eleven* years.

As Henry Roth wrote in the classic novel *Call It Sleep*, the motley collection of immigrants on ships like the *Campania* painted a colorful picture, "a matrix of the vivid costumes of other lands, the speckled green-and-yellow aprons, the flowered kerchief . . . yellow boots, fur caps, caftans, dull gabardines." My grandfather, who later changed his name to Isadore Spector, was one of the more than two million Jews who fled Russia between 1899 and 1914, when it was ruled by the last czar—the brutal Nicholas II—who sanctioned pogroms and other atrocities against the Jews.

Writing in the *Forward*, the Yiddish-language newspaper, in 1909, Russian-based correspondent A. Litwin suggested, "If they could afford it, half the Jewish workers in the big cities and all in the small towns would emigrate. They save up the hundred rubles for the ticket for years, adding a groschen [coin] to a groschen, going half-naked, borrowing and pawning."

Researching my grandfather's journey brought me to a U.S. government records office on Varick Street in Lower Manhattan, where I found on microfiche the *Campania*'s passenger manifest when my grandfather was on board. Under the column headed "occupation," virtually every immigrant on that ship was listed as a "laborer." Laborer, laborer, laborer—all the way down the manifest of some twelve hundred names. The only one who was not designated as a "laborer" was my grandfather, who listed himself as "carpenter." Hah! There is no carpenter gene in the Spector family! My father could barely hammer a nail into a wall and I'm not much better. Clearly, my grandfather's claim is the first recorded example of Spector bullshit in the New World. It would not be the last.

My grandfather's resume inflation was hardly unique, as Irving Howe observed in *World of Our Fathers*: "If one does speak 'broadly,' it ought to be suggested that some of those 'tailors' and 'building workers' were also *luftmenshen* [*sic*, men who could not hold on to a job] who assigned themselves occupations in order to get past Ellis Island. And the category of 'skilled laborer' employed by U.S. immigration authorities had only the haziest relevance to the Jewish workers who came over, since many of them were small craftsmen and artisans without industrial experience."

FREEDOM

I WAS ONCE invited to New York to be a keynote speaker at a conference of grocery-store executives from the United Kingdom. The group asked me to join them on several of their outings in and around Manhattan, including a visit to Ellis Island for a banquet in the Great Hall. I had never been to Ellis Island, which had fallen into disrepair by the time I was growing up. I was looking forward to seeing the renovation of the facility and the exhibits that went with it.

We boarded the ferry that departed from the Lower West Side of Manhattan and soon began our short trip out of the harbor. As we began to reach the deeper waters of the Hudson, I saw the Statue of Liberty in the distance. Whenever I see Miss Liberty, whether in a picture or in person, I am transfixed because she symbolizes the promise of America. The sight of her never fails to bring a tear to my eyes. What did my grandfather think as he caught a glimpse of her for the first time? What did my father think? What did my mother think? Why hadn't I ever asked them?

We departed from the ferry at Ellis Island and strolled through the entrance and entered the Great Hall, where all the millions and millions of immigrants had been processed after their arrival. Pictures of that time show thousands of them seated close together in what looked like church pews, penned in by chain-link fencing or scaffolding, enduring hours of queuing and questioning about their medical conditions and legal status before being released from the bureaucracy, or worse, being turned away and sent back.

"They put us into lines, all kinds of lines. If you had visibly something wrong with you, like if they saw your eyes red, or something, they'd put color chalk on you," recalled Katherine Beychok, who was a Russian Jewish immigrant in 1910, and whose quote is part of the permanent exhibition on Ellis Island. "If it was something else, if you were with a cane or something, it's another chalk and you go into a certain other line. If nothing visible there, they put you in lines, regular lines . . . And the doctors and everybody that was supposed to interrogate us were dressed in uniforms . . . [that] had a terrible effect on me . . . we were scared of uniforms. It took us back to the Russian uniforms that we were running away from."

In another part of the exhibit, a letter dated November 21, 1906, from the Office of the Commissioner of Immigration, Department of Commerce and Labor, Immigration Service, described the previous day's bill of fare in the immigrants' dining room: "Dinner: beef stew, boiled potatoes and bread. Smoked or pickled herring for Hebrews. Crackers and milk for women and children." When my grandfather arrived three-and-a-half years later, could the food have improved that much?

By contrast, the night I was at Ellis Island for the corporate event, the Great Hall was a sea of decorated tables covered with floral-design plates, silver flatware, and crystal wineglasses. We dined on ravioli stuffed with mushrooms and Asiago cheese, Atlantic salmon, braised brisket of beef, oven-roasted potatoes, and grilled asparagus, fennel, eggplant, and yellow squash. Grabbing a glass of a fine California cabernet sauvignon, I left the din of the diners and walked outside behind the main building to search for my grandfather's name, which I knew had been inscribed on the Wall of Honor, along with the names of a half-million other immigrants whose families had made donations. I kept walking along the steel wall, which forms a circle around the part of the island that faces Manhattan and New Jersey, until I found my grandfather's name. I stood there and ran my fingers over the letters. Then I raised my glass and saluted Isadore Spector—this pretend carpenter, this patriarch—and thanked him for taking his journey and making his sacrifices, so that his grandchildren and great-grandchildren could be born free in America.

After being processed at Ellis Island, Isadore headed to Newark, where his sponsor, Bernard Weitzer (my grandmother's brother), owned a tobacco shop. Weitzer was typical of the waves of immigrants who used the mom & pop store as a way up—as a way to connect in the New World.

My grandfather was one of the 250,000 immigrants who settled in Newark between 1880 and World War I, when the population ballooned to 350,000. By the 1920s, Newark boasted sixty-three live theaters, forty-six movie theaters, and an active nightlife. Market and Broad streets—the "Four Corners," as it is known—was one of the busiest intersections in the United States, with four major department stores, including L. Bamberger and Company (later acquired by Macy's). "Mecca of visitors as it has been through all its long history," Newark merchants boasted, "they come in hundreds of thousands now when once they came in hundreds."

Like New York City, six miles to the east, Newark was "undergoing a powerful and dynamic transformation," wrote the Newark-born novelist Philip Roth. Immigrants like my grandfather helped to make it boom, settling in Clinton Hills, which was the southwestern section of the city adjacent to the Weequahic neighborhood—the Jewish ghetto that would become the geographic and emotional center of many of Roth's novels. At one time Newark boasted about fifty synagogues and seventy thousand Jewish residents. Weequahic High School was the Harvard of New Jersey high schools. Theodore Liebman, a prominent architect in New York, told me that when he went to Pratt Institute to study architecture, he was number one in his class, but at Weequahic High School, he was only number thirty-five.

As Roth once told the *New York Times*, "In my childhood imagination, Newark was always the East Coast of the American mainland. Beyond that was the Hudson River, which was not that easy to cross in the old days. New York was to us as Europe was to

New York. So when people say to me, 'You came from New York,' and I say, 'No, Newark,' and they reply, 'Well, it's the same,' I say, 'No, it wasn't.' "

Proof that Newark attracted enterprising independent retailers could be found in this original idea for publicizing the opening of Lewitt's drugstore, at Market and Washington streets: "Our store was opened on July 2, 1921, at which time the Louis Carpentier–Jack Dempsey fight took place. The excitement and enthusiasm displayed by all at that time are now a matter of history. We figured—why not capitalize on this interest by announcing the returns of the fight from our store?" the owner wrote to the *Newark Evening News*. Murray's, a famous café that "had been announcing all important events to the sporting public for the past fifty years," had recently gone out of business, so Lewitt's decided to fill the void. The store was able to get a direct open wire to the New York offices of the *Evening Journal* and the *New York American*, which would transmit the blow-by-blow description.

Although the preparation was time consuming and expensive, "the results obtained was worth it all. Our corner became famous over night and we were the talk of the town for many months thereafter." The owner boasted that a crowd "estimated at over thirty thousand people lined the curbs and walks of both Market and Washington Streets" to follow the results. The police captain in charge "remarked that never in the history of Newark did he remember such a news hungry crowd."

The promotion brought "all the sporting men of the city to our store, and inasmuch as our stock of smokers' articles is the largest of any drug store in the state, we get them coming to us for their needs." Lewitt said that were it not for his publicity stunt, most of those customers would have passed the store by, assuming a drugstore wouldn't carry such a complete line of tobacco products.

THAT MAN IS YOUR FATHER

IN AN EFFORT to curtail immigration, Congress passed the Quota Act of 1921, a temporary measure that set monthly immigration allocations for each nationality. By this time, my grandmother and three of her four children (Yetta, Bella, and Fred) had made their way to Romania; the elder son, twenty-year-old Sidney, had joined his father a couple of years earlier. World War I had impeded the flow of refugees out of Europe, with about 136,000 still trying to emigrate to America.

Romania was one of the primary stopping-off points for Russian Jewish refugees on their way to the piers of Rotterdam, Antwerp, Bremen, or Hamburg, from where they would sail to America. In 1921, that country was populated with about forty-five thousand Russian Jewish refugees who were attempting to emigrate. Authorities tried to get a handle on these huge numbers of people by removing them from the border communities to the interior of the country. By the end of that year, of the twenty-two thousand Jewish refugees still in Romania, a mere four thousand were permitted to stay.

Fortunately, that year my grandmother and her three teenage children were able to book passage on the *Nieuw Amsterdam* out of Rotterdam. The *Nieuw Amsterdam*, which had been built in 1906, carried 2,886 passengers, including 440 in first class, 246 in second class, and 2,200 in third class, which is where my family was, crowded together with fellow impoverished immigrants from all over Europe.

They arrived at Ellis Island on April 23, 1921. According to the passenger records, my father was listed as "Franke Spektor." His original name was Ephraim, so I guess "Franke" was close enough. Whatever his name was, my father, who had turned fourteen during the voyage from Rotterdam, hadn't seen his father since the age of three. After my family went through the seemingly endless queues as they were processed through Ellis Island, they exited the doors of the great building and looked out into the throng of people waiting for their family members. My grandmother pointed to a face in the crowd and informed her children in Yiddish: "You see that man over there? That man is your father."

As difficult as it was for my grandmother and her children, they were among the lucky ones. Every Spector family member got through. A small percentage of families who went through Ellis Island had to be split up if a parent or a child was denied entry for a medical or legal reason. I can only imagine my grandmother's anxiety as she watched over her three teenagers as they proceeded from line to line to line, stepping closer and closer to freedom.

Unlike my grandfather, many immigrant men abandoned their wives and children back in the old country and started a new life and a new family in America. When he was a teenager in Newark, my father ran into a boy he had known from his village in Ukraine. The boy's father had deserted him and the rest of his family.

"I saw your father yesterday," Fred told him.

"My father is dead," answered the boy.

"No, I just saw him. He's alive."

"He's dead to me."

Many years later, when I was a child, I'd walk with my parents along the boardwalk at Bradley Beach, which was a great promenade for people watching, especially Jewish people watching. Many times my father would run into men and women who had traveled on the same boat with him to America, when they were all young. He'd describe them in Yiddish, as his "*shif shvester*" (ship sister) or "*shif bruder*" (ship brother), with a big smile on his face. It was obvious that Fred shared a lifetime bond with them. I could see how happy he was to see them (and vice versa) and how they talked about how their lives had turned out in this new country.

REACHING OUT AND UP

BEFORE GETTING INTO the meat business, my grandfather had tried his hand at a few other enterprises. The first one we knew of was Guarantee Fur Dresser Inc., which made fur pieces that were used as trim on ladies' garments. His next enterprise was Sunrise Honey Company. "Headquartered" on Jellif Avenue, behind the family house on Peshine Avenue, the warehouse was equipped with a machine that blended sugar, water, and caramel to produce some sort of ersatz honey. The bottles were filled on a conveyor belt, and the caps and labels were put on by hand. My family would sell the "honey" at farmers' markets in Perth Amboy and Englishtown, New Jersey.

In the 1940 Newark city directory, Isadore listed himself as a baker. My father, Fred, then thirty-three, was described as a butcher in Perth Amboy. None of them had any formal training. My father used to say that he was a "self-taught" butcher. It was as if the Spectors woke up one day and decided they were butchers, so let's open a business. Theirs was the typical immigrant's aspiration for advancement. The author Anzia Yezierska, who wrote about Jewish newcomers to the Lower East Side in the 1920s, considered this "eternal desire to reach out and up" to be "the predominant racial trait of the Russian immigrant."

To be successful in a mom & pop business, you must be strong, resilient, and demanding. Those words describe my zeyde. But there was an even better word to sum up his personality. I interviewed two of my older cousins, Seymour Handler and Harvey Spector, who worked closely with Zeyde and my father and uncle in the market. I asked them the same question separately: "What word immediately comes to mind when you think about Zeyde?" They both said the same thing: "Tough."

"Zeyde was a tough guy," said Seymour. "He was no-nonsense. He was big in size and character. At the market, he was a tyrant."

My grandmother, Mindel, would sell the bread and rolls. At lunchtime, she served potted chuck meat and made sandwiches for all the workers and "was so full of life," recalled Harvey Spector. "She, too, was a tough old bird. It was nothing for her to come home after a full day's work and make supper that evening and breakfast the next morning for everybody. She was the boss. She even bossed Zeyde around." My grandmother died when I was a year old. My grandfather died when I was four-and-a-half. I have only a few hazy memories of him. The most vivid is when I was about two, playing in front of our house on Treacy Avenue in Newark, and he knelt down to give me a piece of candy.

Saturday was the big market day, the day you made your money for the entire week. Before the New Jersey Turnpike was built in 1951, my relatives would leave Newark at three o'clock in the morning in order to get to Perth Amboy (seventeen miles away) by five o'clock, to get ready for the day. Every Saturday morning, Zeyde would walk across Treacy Avenue from our house to the house of my father's sister, Yetta, and awaken her teenaged sons, Paul and Seymour. "Zeyde would walk up the three flights of stairs to my bedroom and shake me. No words," Seymour recalled. "Then he would go down the stairs to the car and wait. You knew what you had to do. You got up, got yourself together, and headed out the door."

For Zeyde, it was all about keeping busy and moving the merchandise.

When he was twelve years old Robert Bialecki, now in his mid-seventies, worked for my grandfather. "In the wintertime, when it was cold, I would put my hands in my pockets to keep warm. Your grandfather would say to me, 'Get your hands out of your pockets and find something to do.' When the bread got hard from the cold, he would tell me to put the bread in a big bag and jump on it, to soften it up."

On the other hand, he was a generous man. Ernest Horvath, who worked for Zeyde in 1938 as an eleven-year-old, told me: "Your grandfather was very nice to me. He gave me a job, helping to unload his truck. He trusted me, and treated me as if I was a grown-up person. My family was very poor, and he always gave me leftovers like bread and rolls and hotdogs."

My cousin Seymour said that "the bread that we didn't sell at the end of the day, Zeyde would distribute to the other houses on our street. He never rang the bell or left a note. He would just put the bread in the vestibule of the houses and leave."

Harvey Spector described our grandfather as "always a hustler, always looking to sell more products to more customers. He could not stand a lazy person. He pushed people. He pushed himself to do more, to do better. There was nothing that he wouldn't take a chance on. Nothing could stand in his way. He would find a way, whether it was money or favors. Zeyde had balls."

He had the heart and guile of an entrepreneur. If there's an obstacle in your way, you simply go around it. Rules were made for other people. When asked how he managed to secure a driver's license when his English was lacking, he would smile, and recite the Yiddish expression *Az men shmirt, fort men*, which literally translates to "If one smears, one rides," but in my grandfather's street-peasant vernacular it meant: "Grease the way, and you shall go forward."

TENDING TO THE FAMILY BUSINESS

SPECTOR'S MEAT MARKET'S showcases were crowded with chop meat, steaks, pork chops, bacon, etc., and a wide variety of lunch meats. That area was patrolled by my grandfather, father, uncle, cousins, and a few nonfamily employees, who dodged and elbowed and shoved each other in the tight space between the showcase and a work shelf that was loaded with cleavers, slicers, grinders, and knives.

"When I think of the market, the first thing that comes to my mind is pain," recalled Harvey Spector. "I had to mix frozen clods—red meat, no fat at all, right from the bull—with scraps and fat to make chop meat. We would cut the frozen meat on the band saw. The clods were frozen; the weather was frozen; I was frozen. It was so painful that I would be crying. It was warmer in the freezer than it was outside."

Before I was born, on Saturdays, my father, grandfather, uncle, and cousins would work in the Perth Amboy market until about two o'clock in the afternoon. Then they would pack up their truck with platters of precut pork chops, steaks, and roasts, and other provisions and drive about an hour to the market in Englishtown, where they had a large group of regular customers. The Spectors had a standing arrangement with a local man to pack their showcases with ice right before they arrived in Englishtown, where they unloaded the platters off the truck and placed them in the showcases to take care of the customers who were awaiting their arrival. The Spectors would continue to work at that market until eight or nine o'clock.

In Perth Amboy, around the corner from the farmers' market were two big, new supermarkets—A&P and Acme—which carried pretty much the same basic meat offerings as we did. When I was a small boy, I would often accompany my parents to the A&P to buy groceries. I generally stayed with my mother to make sure that she bought Kellogg's Sugar Frosted Flakes, because they advertised on the *Superman* program, starring George Reeves.

Glancing to the rear of the A&P, I would see my father, his back to me, hunched over the meat showcase, lifting up packages of frozen pork shoulders or hams or chop meat, and checking out A&P's prices. Our prices were competitive. We had a loyal clientele who would stand outside in the freezing cold, teeth chattering, waiting patiently, because they knew they could get specialty ethnic foods— fatback, salt pork, Genoa salami, black headcheese—and that my father and uncle knew enough Russian, Ukrainian, Polish, and Hungarian to converse (and joke) with them in their native tongues.

"You never waited on somebody else's regular customer," recalled Bill Kodilla, a nonfamily employee. "I would never work on your father's customer or Sid's customer." Bill had one amusing line that he used over and over again. When a customer requested his corned beef to be sliced *lean*, Bill invariably asked, "Which way do you want it to lean?"

MY MOTHER'S JOURNEY

SPECTOR'S MEAT MARKET was a *mom* & pop business. For decades, my mother, Florence, worked a couple of days a week in the market, right alongside my dad.

Women have found ways to carve out their niche in the marketplace ever since the early days of commercial civilization. In the glory days of Rome, women with an artistic bent could engrave gems, set pearls, and create gold leaf jewelry.

In sixteenth-century London, in the section of Cheapside ("cheap" roughly translates to "market" in medieval English), husbands encouraged their wives and daughters to sit outside their shops or in the doorways, where they would converse with—and attract— potential customers. To quote a seventeenth-century ballad: "if thy wife be fair and thou be poor, let her stand like a picture at the door." Shakespeare's *As You Like It* has the character of Jacques saying of the women of Cheapside, "You are full of pretty answers.

Have you not been acquainted with goldsmiths' wives and conned them out of rings?"

Back then, the only way a woman could participate in a "man's trade" was if she were a widow of a freeman, which entitled her to assume her husband's membership in his guild in order to take over the business. Consider Mrs. Arabella Brown, who, upon her husband's demise in 1760, took over his Trunk, Chest, Box Maker & Undertaker business in the Southwark section. Her advertising message to the public read, in part, that "Arabella Brown (widow of John Brown) Begs Leave respectfully to acquaint her late Husband's Friends, and Customers and the public in general, that she continues carrying on the Business for the support of herself and Family; humbly requesting their Favours and assuring them of the utmost Exertion to fulfill their Orders with Punctuality and Dispatch."

During the eighteenth century, mom & pop stores—where the wife had (almost) equal billing with the husband—were becoming more widespread. There were "David Jacobs and his Wife, Necklace Makers," and "Susanh. & Jonatn. Coleman, Breeches Makers." In Sandwich, England, Jacob and Anne Silver ran two separate shops across the street from each other. Jacob was a bookseller, Anne a grocer and haberdasher.

In a popular ballad of the time entitled "Chandler's Shop" a courting couple dream of opening their own general merchandise store—a chandler's shop:

> HE: Oh, Sally Sime, when we get wed,
> SHE: Why, Sammy Sly, we'll do as we said,
>   Extravagance we both will drop,
> HE: And open up a chandler's shop
> SHE: Yes, so we will, and Sammy, dear,
>   You shall draw the table beer;
> HE: And to the customers you shall chat,
>   For Sally dear, you're fond of that.

My mother was a pretty woman, about five foot three, a nice figure in her day, and dark auburn hair, which was one of her few vanities. She regularly visited the beauty parlor for her hair to be colored and her fingernails to be manicured and polished. She was unflaggingly polite—sincere, but not cloying. She always had a smile and a kind word. And like everyone else in our shop, she was a hard worker. She was used to that. Before marriage, she had worked several years at the H. L. Green five-and-ten store in Newark, so she knew how to close the sale.

Florence's domain was a forty-five-square-foot space to the left of the meat showcase, where she sold bagels, hard rolls, onion rolls, crullers, and jelly doughnuts (my favorites), all for a nickel apiece (the price in 1960), as well as chocolate cakes, cheesecakes, and various breads, including four-pound rye and pumpernickel (eighty-five cents) from Pechter's Bakery, which is still operating today in Kearny, New Jersey.

My mother had taken her own circuitous route to the farmers' market. She was born Feiga Okner in the Ukrainian village of Bershad in 1912, the youngest of eight children of Sarah and Rueben Okner, a Jewish couple that managed the estate of a wealthy landowner. Like slaves in the antebellum American South, my forebears were given the name of the landowner, Okner. Forty-seven-year-old Rueben died in 1915 when Feiga was three; Sarah died a year later. Feiga was left to be raised by her brother Zalman, who was almost twenty years her senior.

My uncle Zalman was a mild-mannered man, who had a quiet internal grit—and a zeal for survival. In 1912, when he had just turned eighteen, he faced conscription into the army of Nicholas II. A Jew in the army of the Czar? Not a good long-term future. To render himself unsuitable for military service, he chose to blind himself in one eye. According to his daughter, Beatrice, he probably used lye. One drop onto his cornea would do it. The lye's calcium hydroxide splashed onto his cornea—the front surface window of the eye through which light passes. Trickling into the surrounding tissue, the lye set off an inflammatory reaction, immediately scarring everything it touched, causing the tissue to become opaque. Within a week, the lye had so damaged the tissue that the nerves stopped sending pain signals to his brain. After a couple of months, the pain subsided completely. But for the rest of his life, Zalman had the use of only his left eye. He never drove a car.

During the first two decades of the twentieth century, thousands of Jews were being slaughtered, among them Zalman and Feiga's grandfather, who was executed in an infamous 1920 pogrom in his home province of Podolia. His corpse was discarded in a massive common grave with those of six hundred other Jewish men. By this time, Zalman had married Bessie Teplitzky, a strong, oval-faced girl from another village, whom my mother welcomed to the family with open arms and the ingenuous words of a little orphan: "I am your dowry."

Zalman schemed to raise the necessary money to pay the price of freedom for himself, his new bride, and his little sister. He sold grain on the black market. They forged documents to make it appear that Feiga was the child of Zalman and Bessie. Bessie, at age twenty, was too young to have been ten-year-old Feiga's mother, so they doctored their birth certificates to make Bessie six years older than she actually was, and made my mother two years younger—a little white lie that my mother enjoyed perpetuating for the rest of her life.

(Today when I hear discussions about "illegal immigrants" I am reminded that without deception my mother—and probably my paternal grandfather—would not have made it to the United States.)

Just after sundown, on a cold night in December 1921, Zalman, Bessie, and Feiga stole away in the direction of the Romanian border. (A year later, the Union of Soviet Socialist Republics was officially established.) They were fired upon by Russian soldiers and bribed border guards with the dwindling possessions in Bessie's dowry. The trio trekked in the night through woods and over mountains, slept on wooden synagogue benches, and hid in the cellars of righteous gentiles, but they could not make a sound lest they be discovered. Remaining in Bucharest, Romania, for almost two years (during that time Bessie gave birth to Beatrice, the first of what would be three daughters), the family arrived at Cherbourg on the coast of Northern France, finally booking passage to America— and to freedom. Sailing on the Cunard White Star Liner SS *Berengaria*, a 919-foot-long ship that carried almost five thousand passengers, Mr. and Mrs. Zalman Okner and their children arrived at Ellis Island on September 12, 1922.

After a year spent with relatives in Philadelphia, they moved to

Newark, where there was a job waiting for Zalman in a cousin's store. Their first apartment in 1923 was on Prince Street, the bustling commercial center of the city's Jewish community (comparable to Orchard Street in Lower Manhattan), where peddlers' wagons lined the streets in front of the assorted mom & pop shops. It was on Prince Street that Abner "Longy" Zwillman, the "Al Capone of New Jersey," once peddled fruit and vegetables from a rented horse and wagon.

Zalman went to work for his cousin, Morris Forster, who owned a retail shop, Star Electrical Supply Company. The company was founded in 1905 by Morris's father, Samuel, a Russian immigrant who started out as a peddler of light bulbs on the streets of Newark. Zalman worked for Star Electrical for the next forty years. Today, the store is still in business in Newark, although they've changed locations a couple of times. Joe Forster, the current owner, is the grandson of the founder. As a child and young man, Joe worked with Zalman, who "ran our electrical supplies department," said Joe. "He was the only one who knew where everything was. He was old-school. Meticulous. He was on the go from the time he got to work until the time he left." Although Zalman passed away in 1970, "there are still boxes in the store with his handwriting on it—part Yiddish, part English, and part Russian."

I never saw Uncle Zalman at work at Star Electrical; I never saw him as a "clerk" in the store. My most vivid memories of him are from Passover Seders, where Zalman, the patriarch of his family, sat at the head of the table among some twenty or so relatives, and presided over the prayers (completely in Hebrew) with enormous dignity and piety. Although my sisters and I were not their grandchildren, Uncle Zalman and Aunt Bessie never differentiated between the three of us and their seven grandchildren. We Okners were and remain a tight-knit extended family. I can't say the same for the Spectors.

PART II

STORIES FROM THE ROAD

4

The Rise of the Merchant

If you are unskilled in the arts of buying and selling,
the market will teach you.

—PROVERB

A PICTURE OF THE Perth Amboy Farmers' Market in the late
nineteenth century shows a dirt-covered city block, with two
parallel rows of horse-drawn wagons, from which the farmers sold
their wares. The backs of the wagons faced inside; the horses faced
outside. The space in between the two rows of wagons was crammed
with hundreds of shoppers, with barely enough room to elbow past
each other. No wonder, when my grandfather first set eyes on the
market in the 1930s, he exclaimed to his sons: "It's just like the old
country!"

Actually, it was a lot like the old, old, old country. Markets have
been around ever since one person had what another person needed.
The earliest known instance of buying and selling dates back to the
city of Çatalhöyük, in Anatolia, Turkey, in 7500 B.C., when tools
made of obsidian glass were traded for flint from neighboring Syria.
Three millennia later, farmers brought their wares from the country to the public markets of the early Mesopotamian civilizations
(between the Tigris and Euphrates rivers), where they would haggle
and cajole and contribute to the growth of the local economy.
Whether in ancient Greece or China or Africa or Mexico, wherever
there were motivated buyers and sellers, there was a market.

From before the common era to the Middle Ages, most people
lived off the land and were responsible for providing their own food,
clothing, and shelter. As agriculture was developed and animals were

domesticated, humans transformed themselves from hunters and gatherers to buyers and sellers. Once farmers began producing more fruits, vegetables, etc. than they needed for their families they made their way to the nearest markets where they could exchange their surpluses for products they didn't have the time or the aptitude to make or cultivate: bread, tools, meat, cloth, leather, and candles, which were produced by local craftsmen. Ever since, history has shown us that an individual motivated by profit is able to achieve more for himself—and for the local citizenry—than any market-controlling government. The market, as messy as it often is, remains the place where humans need and depend upon each other. Adam Smith, the eighteenth-century moral philosopher and political economist, once aptly observed that "it is not from the benevolence of the butcher, the brewer, or the baker that we expect our dinner, but from their regard to their own interest." Smith was not criticizing the shopkeepers, but merely stating a universal truth.

In order to eke out a living among a small population, the operator of a small general merchandise, all-purpose country store in eighteenth- and nineteenth-century America had to be clever, versatile, and resourceful. To survive, he might also operate a tavern, cut hair, and serve as the local postmaster, which made his place of business the economic and social center of the community. But by the end of the nineteenth century, this independent operator was being squeezed out by new forms of retail distribution, such as five-and-ten stores, led by F. W. Woolworth's, which debuted in Lancaster, Pennsylvania, in 1879, and the S. S. Kresge Corporation a few years later. Writing in the *New York Times* in August of 1902, a journalist bemoaned, "The old-fashioned grocer who was required to know many things about the art and mystery of his trade [is being converted into] a vendor of packet goods so that a large proportion of the grocer's work of the present day could be accomplished almost equally well by an automatic machine delivering a packet of goods in exchange for a coin."

A few years after the introduction in 1909 of Henry Ford's first T model automobile, newly mobile Americans became less dependent on (and less loyal to) the local general stores and specialty mom & pop stores, and more interested in newer, bigger, more sophisticated, and more complete retail chain store options, such as Sears Roebuck & Co. and Montgomery Ward & Co., which eventually expanded to thousands of stores and became ubiquitous in small- and medium-size towns and cities, thanks to the rise of mass production. Even before they had begun to build brick-and-mortar stores across the country, both of those giant retailers offered consumers the option of shopping from their massive mail-order catalogs.

(Less than a century later, Wards and Sears and Woolworth's were buffeted by the harsh competitive realities of retail. Woolworth's closed its last doors in 1997. After several attempts at reinvention, Wards went out of business in 2001. Today Sears is a weak giant trying desperately to find a way to survive.)

Discounting provided another option for consumers on a budget. In Kemmerer, Wyoming, in 1902, James Cash Penney opened the Golden Rule general store, a mom & pop operation that became the foundation of the giant JCPenney discount retail chain. Eventually, the United States was flooded with scores of national and regional discount shops, which sold products below list price and could operate on lower margins. And why not? "One of the accepted axioms of selling is that when demand is created for a type of marketing institution, one will arise to satisfy that demand," wrote Penrose Scull in *From Peddlers to Merchant Princes: A History of Selling in America.* "The discount store was just such a response." The catalyst for the rise of discount stores was as basic as trade itself: Who can resist a good deal?

Some populist politicians tried to find ways to help independent retailers who lacked the purchasing clout to get the same kinds of deals and terms that manufacturers offered to the chains. In the 1920s, the antichain forces included nearly three hundred local or national organizations, which boasted more than eight million members, or almost 7 percent of the population of the United States at the same time. A few pols based their reelection campaigns on their antipathy to chains. Governor Huey P. Long, the notorious "Kingfish" of Louisiana, was quoted as saying that he would rather his state be occupied by thieves and gangsters than operators of chain stores.

A typical example of this sentiment is found in the following excerpt from the 1922 book *Meeting Chain Store Competition*: "Every retailer who has to meet chain store competition thinks he needs no one to tell him what a chain store is. To him it is a cut-rate competitor managed from the outside by a soul-less corporation." Throughout the 1930s, individual states enacted special taxes targeted at the big chain stores, which accounted for more than 60 percent of the more than four thousand department stores in the country. By the 1950s, the five-and-ten concept had become tired and tattered around the edges, so enterprising retailers turned to a new generation of discount stores, such as E. J. Korvette, Wal-Mart, Kmart (which grew out of Kresge's), Target, and Woolco (an offshoot of Woolworth's).

In 1956, the U.S. Congress passed the Interstate Highway Act, which earmarked twenty-five billion dollars to construct the forty-one-thousand-mile interstate system. When the New Jersey Turnpike was completed in 1951, the *Newark News* gushed that the highway "opens vistas never before seen by even those who live in the regions through which it passes, for its wide right-of-way opens to view hundreds of miles of expanse that always before has been kept from view by the trees or underbrush." Whatever the lofty goals of the Interstate Highway system, the new superroads damaged Perth Amboy and other small towns, because they diverted people from downtown to the suburbs and, eventually, to suburban malls, which were anchored by traditional department stores.

Throughout the history of retail, some new format always has been "killing" the mom & pop store, but somehow it always survives.

MERCHANTS AND MIDDLEMEN

THE SPECTORS WERE middlemen. We were the guys between the producers and consumers. We didn't raise the cattle or pigs or lamb, and neither did we bake the onion rolls, bagels, rye breads, or cheesecake. As middlemen, we were following in the tradition of buyers and sellers throughout recorded history. Today, one thinks of mom & pop merchants as kindly and neighborly, but it was not always thus. In medieval social circles, the shopkeepers who didn't make the goods they sold were despised, distrusted, and disrespected. They were considered parasites and exploiters of labor. A nineteenth-century English social critic branded shopkeepers as "locusts . . . who create nothing, who add to the value of nothing, who improve nothing . . . and who live well, too, out of the labour of the producer and the consumer." Friedrich Wilhelm Nietzsche, the nineteenth-century philosopher, once wrote, "Merchant and pirate were for a long period one and the same person. Even today mercantile morality is really nothing but a refinement of piratical morality."

Merchants as a class were considered decadent and immoral. In *The Odyssey*, Homer describes what happened when Princess Nausicaä, the comely daughter of King Alcinous and Queen Arete of the Phaeacians, came upon the shipwrecked Odysseus on the beach at Scheria, and then brought him to the palace court to meet her parents. A court nobleman at first glance found Odysseus to be weak and pensive and possibly a *merchant* "of greedily gotten gains." Insulted, Odysseus responded by looking "fiercely on him" and demonstrated that he was nobody's pushover by lifting up "a monstrous stone," heaving it a far distance, and revealing that he was Odysseus, damn it, not some effete trader.

The more the merchant accumulated wealth and influence, the less popular he became. Writing in *The Republic*, Plato, who railed against commercialism, thought it would be a good idea if the merchants of Athens were separated from the aristocracy—and forced to live with cobblers and masons. A citizen, Plato believed, should be punished for transacting business deals or becoming an *emporus*, a traveling salesman.

In medieval England, merchants, unlike craftspeople, were part of the establishment, and worked with the crown to ensure their hold on commerce in their towns. Merchants and merchant guilds controlled all aspects of business practices, including prices, quality, weights, and measures. Craft guilds were confined to regulating the quality, working hours, and working conditions of their members, and overseeing the various levels of skills: masters, journeymen, and apprentices. Not surprising, merchant guilds and crafts guilds were in a constant battle for commercial power.

As commerce became more sophisticated, middlemen known as "private traders" found their way around the closely monitored public markets by buying wheat, barley, sheep, wool, poultry, rabbit skins, sheepskins, and so on directly from farmers and other vendors. (Today's television commercials that tout "factory-direct buying" are a reminder that there are no new strategies in retail, just new riffs on the old ones.)

Being part of the establishment did not mean that merchants were beloved. Many of them were accused of taking advantage of the naïveté of the illiterate producers of goods on one end, and the unsuspecting buyers of goods (the customers) on the other end. No wonder they were often held in ridicule.

Charles Miner, an early nineteenth-century United States congressman from Pennsylvania, once noted, "When I see a merchant over-polite to his customers, begging them to taste a little brandy and throwing half his goods on the counter,—thinks I, that man has an axe to grind."

THE PRICE IS RIGHT

EVER SINCE ONE person sold something to another person, pricing has been an issue. Thousands of years ago, merchandise was not standardized, so neither were prices. Haggling was the order of the day. It was said that shopkeepers possessed "tricks enough to delude [customers], and rarely shall they stir out (like sheep engaged in briars) but they shall leave some fleece behind them." Aristophanes and other playwrights of comedies often wrote humorously about the give-and-take between buyer and seller in the marketplace, which is where we find a yeoman farmer character named Dikaiopolis in Aristophanes' play *Archarnians*, written ca. 425 B.C. Forced to live in Athens during the Peloponnesian War (to be safe from marauding Spartans), a homesick Dikaiopolis bemoaned:

> *I think about my farm, I long for peace.*
> *City life: I hate it. I want my village.*
> *No salesman there, no "Buy! Buy! Buy!" —*
> *It's share and share alike, it's bye-bye "Buy!"*

Savvy shoppers were constantly trying to outwit shopkeepers. Some would dress down, so they looked poorer than they actually were in hopes of negotiating a lower price based on their ability to pay. Some opted to deal with the master of the shop rather than his apprentices, because they were convinced that they would be able to get a better price from the owner himself. Most of the time, the opposite was true. For that reason, most canny masters minimized the time they left the apprentices to run the shop on their own. (In the Middle Ages, only the owner of the shop or studio was officially considered a merchant.)

What do we buyers and sellers get out of this competitive exercise of give-and-take? Adam Smith, the political economist, speculated that man's "propensity to truck, barter and exchange one thing for another" was probably "the necessary consequence of the faculty of reason and speech. Nobody ever saw a dog make a fair and deliberate exchange of one bone for another with another dog."

For most of recorded retail history, there was no such thing as a "fixed price" on merchandise. In France in the fourteenth century, producers and retailers were known to conspire among themselves by whispering in each other's ear, uttering coded words, or exchanging predetermined signals. It wasn't until the middle of the eighteenth century that fixed prices, marked clearly on tags, were popularized by haberdashers, who were an organized group of general merchandise shopkeepers (middlemen), who sold everything from spurs to girdles. Flint and Palmer's, a haberdashery and drapery on London Bridge, is considered by some retail historians as the first fixed-price-no-haggling-thank-you-very-much cash shop.

In 1780, James Lackington tried to bring fixed prices to bookselling, in his legendary shop the Temple of the Muses, in London's

Finsbury Square. Bookselling had been Lackington's path from poverty to wealth, taking him from traveling purveyor of meat pies at the age of ten to shoemaker's apprentice at fourteen. Lackington (who also wrote ballads on the side) created an inexpensive circulating library in 1775 before moving in 1789 to the Temple of the Muses, an architecturally stunning building, with floor-to-ceiling shelves of books, an atrium extending over the central information desk, and swaths of natural sunlight for reading. In Lackington's time, prices of new books were not set because buyers and sellers made no differentiation between new and secondhand books. Some copies were classified as in "neat" condition, some as "damaged"— not unlike what online shoppers find today on the Amazon.com Web site.

A CASH BUSINESS

JAMES LACKINGTON, WHO was in his day the equivalent of Leonard Riggio, chairman of Barnes & Noble, was renowned for making his fortune as a cash-only bookseller at the Temple of the Muses. In that regard, he offered these observations in his book, *Memoirs of the First Forty-five Years of the Life of James Lackington*:

> It was some time in the year seventeen hundred and eighty that I resolved from that period to give no person whatever any credit. I was determined to make this resolution from various motives. I had observed that when credit was given, most bills were not paid within six months, some not within a twelve-month and some not within two years . . . The losses sustained in interest of money in long credits and by those bills that were not paid at all; the inconveniences attending not having the ready money to lay out in trade to the best advantage, together with the great loss of time in keeping accounts and collecting debts, convinced me that if I could but establish a ready-money business without exceptions I should be enabled to sell every article very cheaply . . . When I communicated my ideas on this subject to some of my acquaintances I was much laughed at and ridiculed. It was thought I might as well attempt to re-build the Tower of Babel as to establish a large business without giving credit.

I determined to make the experiment, and began by plainly marking in every book, facing the title, the lowest price that I would take for it . . . I was obliged to deny credit to my very acquaintance . . . [and] . . . to the most respectable characters . . . not even to the nobility.

Spector's Meat Market was also strictly a cash business. There was no cash register and no receipts. All the money was kept securely in the three pockets of my father's and mother's white aprons—singles in the right pocket, big bills in the center pocket, coins in the left pocket.

Our system wasn't primitive, perhaps a couple of steps up from primitive. When man first started trading things, he kept track of the number of fishes or pots of grain that were owed to him by scratching some symbols on the wall of his mud house with a splinter of wood or a stone chip. His more sophisticated descendants counted with stones or grains of corn; later, more advanced civilizations calculated with a square board, made of wood, stone, or metal, upon which was a layer of fine sand for recording figures with lines, points, or other symbols. By about 300 A.D., the Greeks and Romans were calculating with an abacus, as were the Chinese and Japanese. Bookkeeping remained archaic until the 1880s and the introduction of cash registers, which saved time and effort—and made it more challenging for clerks to be dishonest.

Once people started exchanging commodities, they needed a simple form of currency. They used various materials: cotton cloth, copper bracelets, gold dust, chickens, horses, seashells, dried fish, or cubes of salt (which had a downside: they dissolved in water). The first coins, as we know them, were used around 2000 B.C., in the form of metal tokens, which served as receipts for quantities of grain placed in granaries. Paper money was invented in China, in about 800 A.D.

When currency began to replace bartering in the market place in the Middle Ages, there needed to be a way of deciding the worth of equivalent goods in order to keep trading above board, and to minimize confusion, which was widespread. Weights and measures differed between districts and towns, and even within the same town.

Some purchases were neither weighed nor measured. Shoppers would buy "a salmon as thick as a man's arm" or a piece of cloth that was "two ells wide between the fists." (The ell, the equivalent of the modern yard, was the length of the arm of King Henry I.) Local officials periodically met to determine the prices and weights of bread, ale, and other staples, and to set up a ruling court to enforce accuracy and fairness. Not surprising, cheating was common. Bakers might plant weights in loaves of bread. Sellers of dry goods were known to stretch a bolt of cloth or fold it in order to camouflage defects.

Punishment for dishonesty was swift, painful, and embarrassing. Cheaters were either fined or, worse, sentenced to the pillory or stock, which were prominently set up in marketplaces. Offenders were locked into the wooden devices with their arms, legs, and heads placed through holes, in a humiliating position. Next to them, there might be a written notice that detailed their offense. In Sicily, if a vendor charged his customer even a single *grano* over the established tariff, he could be sent straight to jail. In early fifteenth-century France, where aldermen were granted the right to inspect the bakeries, bakers who were third-time offenders were brutally tossed onto tumbrels (carts used for transporting prisoners) and bound up like sausages. This form of torture lasted almost two hundred years.

As the son of a butcher, I've always been sensitive to the bad public relations that the profession has had to deal with. Typical is this comment from the nineteenth-century economist William S. Jevons: "A good butcher makes high wages because his business is a greasy one, besides being thought to be cruel." In the Middle Ages, butchers were thought of as deceitful and tricky. They might pin some fat onto a piece of meat to enhance its appearance, or leave all the blood in their meat in order to increase the weight.

Bill Kodilla, an affable crew-cut ex-Marine who worked for my dad on Saturdays (the rest of the week, he was a grinder in the Singer Sewing Machine factory), told me that Fred's only instructions were: Be honest. Treat the customers right. Before being hired on by my father, Bill had worked for another butcher who ran a small shop on the other side of the Perth Amboy Farmers' Market. "I lasted two weeks with that guy," he recalled. "I quit because you had to cheat. He used to put a piece of meat on some paper, put it on the scale, and pull the paper down, which would increase the weight another couple of ounces. I just figured that it wasn't worth it. That butcher didn't last too long, once word got out."

As the proverb says, "Since no man is an island in the market, think of yourself but think of the market too."

Bill recalled the time that the Middlesex County inspector of weights and measurements paid a surprise call on Spector's Meat Market to make sure we were on the up-and-up.

"I was waiting on a regular customer, a Polish woman from Carteret," said Bill. "I put the items that she had already purchased on the counter. Then the inspector started grabbing the packages to see if they were weighed correctly. The customer said to the inspector, 'What are you doing?' He said, 'I'm going to reweigh them.' 'No you're not.' 'I have to.' She said, 'I don't give a goddamn what you have to do. It's my meat. I'm going to buy it. You leave it alone.' He said, 'I've got to see if you got a right count.' She said, 'I *know* I got a right count.' "

If you run a mom & pop store in an unethical way, you can't last, particularly in a small community. Today, there is no stock or pillory in the marketplace, just word of mouth. Mom & pop stores live—and die—by word of mouth, because after all is said and done all they have is their reputation and their good name. There is no corporate name to hide behind. Looking at the rampant dishonesty and avarice that helped to bring about the recession of 2008 and 2009, one might feel nostalgic for the days of stocks and pillories, where the crooks could be embarrassed and punished for the entire community to see.

"If somebody didn't believe that the meat weighed four pounds, six ounces, my dad or your dad would have the customer come around and look at the scale," recalled my cousin Harvey Spector. "We gave the customers a lot of freedom, which they didn't have at other meat markets. If a customer wasn't happy, Zeyde would make things good. He would take a salami or a loaf of bread, throw it in a bag, give it the customer and say, 'This will make up for it.' "

When you don't have a cash register, and you're dealing only in cash and coin, you can easily make a mistake. It still pains me to think about the time when my mother made change for a customer and mistakenly gave him a hundred-dollar bill instead of a ten-dollar bill. At the end of the day, when she realized what she had done, she was heartsick because that money represented much of the week's profit. (To this day, if a shopkeeper gives me back too much change for my purchase, I will immediately point out the mistake, no matter how small. Whenever I do, I hear my mother saying, "That's a good boy, Robert.")

CREDIT AND CREDITORS

EVER SINCE WHOLESALERS began offering credit to shopkeepers, and shopkeepers began offering credit to customers, there has been a pressing need to be able to size up people's ability to pay. After all, the base word *creder* means "to believe." Do I believe you're going to pay me? Credit has always been a dodgy proposition. Retailers historically were often quasi bankers, who lent money and charged interest. No wonder that it was said that the shopkeeper lived between those who owed him money and those to whom he owed money. As a poetic French retailer complained in 1632:

> *You break your back, and to be paid.*
> *You must be patient if delayed.*

Consider this collection of letters to a creditor that was written by a frustrated merchant in Lyon, France, during the spring and summer of 1669:

- "We write you these lines to enquire once more when you will be pleased to pay us."
- "Monsieur, I am much astonished that my often repeated letters have so little effect; one should at least have the goodness to reply to an honest man."
- "We should never have believed that after having assured us that you would come to the shop to settle your account, you would have gone away without saying a word."

- "I do not know how one should write to you, as I see you pay no attention to the letters I write you."

Beatrix Potter, the children's book author, wrote a wonderful little story about the downside of credit in *The Tale of Ginger & Pickles* (1904). Ginger, a yellow tomcat, and Pickles, a terrier, opened their own little general merchandise shop, where they sold items such as red spotty pocket handkerchiefs, sugar, snuff, and galoshes, and were more than happy to liberally give unlimited credit to their customers. Their only other competitor in the village was Tabitha Twitchit, who did not give credit.

Although their sales were ten times that of Tabitha Twitchit, Ginger and Pickles had no money because no one ever paid them. Alas, they eventually had to close the shop. Soon thereafter, the shop reopened—under the new ownership of Sally Henny Penny, who, wrote Potter, "insists on being paid cash; but she is quite harmless."

Sometimes, even famous customers don't pay up. For a lecture tour of the United States, Oscar Wilde, the playwright, once purchased a wide-brimmed soft felt hat at Lock & Co. Hatters on St. James's Street in London. (There are some famous photographs of Wilde wearing that hat, which were taken by Napoleon Sarony when Wilde toured New York.) Wilde had been a regular at Lock & Co. and had made several purchases over the years, including a folding opera hat that was bought on credit on February 14, 1895, for the launch of his play *The Importance of Being Earnest* at St James's Theatre, which was around the corner from the shop.

Soon after, Wilde was arrested and convicted of gross indecency and sentenced to two years of hard labor. After his release, he was never able to get his life back together, and he eventually died at age forty-six, in 1900. The bookkeeper at Lock & Co. prudently put a line through his overdue account, which was never settled—until November 30, 2000. On the centenary of Wilde's death, a Mr. Royston du Maurier sent a check for five pounds to Lock & Co. to pay for the hat and to remove Wilde from the shop's ledger of bad debts. In an accompanying letter, Mr. du Maurier described himself as an artist who, like his hero Wilde, had known "feast and famine."

In the old days, credit was local. That was one way to keep

people honest. You knew the person you owed money to. But that's the ideal, not necessarily the reality. Bob Wassler, who with his family owns Wassler's Meat Market in Cincinnati, told me that his grandfather's theory "was that if you gave people credit, the next time you see them, if they are walking near the store, they will cross the street, so they won't have to walk past the store. In theory, he's right. But we did give credit."

Colin Powell, the former secretary of state, recalled growing up in the forties in the South Bronx, where most people didn't have checkbooks, much less credit cards. Powell remembered that the owner of the kosher chicken market gave his customers credit, which he kept track of in a lined school notebook with a black marble cover. "A customer didn't have any money on hand, but needed a can of something or a loaf of bread," Powell told me. "The owner added it up on the brown paper bag. And then he would take that sum and write in by hand into this notebook. There was page after page of people who owed him money. But he knew that he could trust them because they were all neighbors. And if you couldn't pay this month, you must really be having trouble, so I'll take you for another month. That was the credit system."

Howard Fink of Fink's Department Store in Perth Amboy is one of the few small retailers in the United States who allows customers to buy items on layaway, a practice that was popular during the Great Depression, but pretty much disappeared with the popularity of credit cards.

"People want the three-hundred-fifty-dollar bathroom set, but they don't have the money in their pocket. They don't want to put it on a credit card. They may be near their limit or they don't want to incur the interest charges. So, they put it on layaway. People ask, 'How much do I have to put down and how long do I have to pick it up?' As long as you pay on it, it's OK. Not a problem."

(Layaway made a comeback among retailers big and small in 2008 as a result of the recession. Layaway provided an alternative to consumers who had maxed out on their credit cards. During the holiday buying season, Kmart made layaway a focus of its national advertising campaign. There's even a Web site called Elayaway.com.)

In South River, where my father had a second store, there was a nearby busy dress factory, which employed mostly Eastern European immigrant women who dressed in long dark wool coats. Their hair was covered with head scarves, their mouths were filled with gold and silver teeth, and their names were spelled in a long series of consonants with a vowel (usually a *y*) placed here or there for variety. They were our customer base. These women didn't have checking accounts, but they did have my father, who was their banker. On Friday, which was payday, they bought their provisions from Fred, and then endorsed their paychecks over to him. He subtracted the amount of their purchase and gave them back the difference. I can still see Fred sitting at our dining room table in the evening, counting out the day's take, sorting the bills, and stacking up the green-colored checks from that shirt factory.

RULES AND REGULATIONS

ONCE TRADE AND markets were established, trade laws became a necessity. In terms of the relationship between buyer and seller, very little has changed over the past four thousand years.

The oldest recorded codes of trade law were established around 2000 B.C. by the überefficient King Hammurabi, who ruled over Babylon, which was to become the political and intellectual center of Western Asia. Under the Code of Hammurabi, citizens were required to record and sign every significant purchase, and ensure that a third-party witness verified the transaction. To give an extreme example of the enforcement of proper marketplace behavior, one of the laws stipulated that "if outlaws hatch a conspiracy in the house of a wine seller and she does not arrest these outlaws and bring them to the palace, that wine seller shall be put to death."

Towns enacted their own laws to monitor and control trade. In the Middle Ages, a newly established market required a government permit that could be rejected if the proposed market was too close to one that was already in business. Traders were assigned a specific space within the market. Craft guilds regulated all aspects of their trade, including prices and work standards, in order to protect their reputations from dishonest practitioners. For example, in

1346, the Guild of Weavers of Bristol declared that "if the threads are thin in the cloth, or are too far apart, the cloth and the instrument on which it is worked ought to be burnt."

On a visit to London, I stopped by Guildhall, which was built between 1411 and 1430, and is a monument to the tradition of guilds and the ritual of taxation, and a center of government in the City of London. It was to the Guildhall where representatives of the Twelve Great Livery Companies (trade associations) came to pay their taxes. Looming above the Great Hall is the main cornice, with a frieze or band of decoration of the Arms of England, the City, and the Twelve Great Livery Companies (and their banners). These trade associations—whose names were preceded by the phrase "the Worshipful Company"—included (in order of precedence) the Worshipful Company of Mercers, Grocers, Drapers, Fishmongers, Goldsmiths, Skinners, Merchant Taylors, Haberdashers, Salters, Ironmongers, Vintners, and Clothworkers. There would eventually be 108 livery companies covering every imaginable trade and specialty.

Shopping hours were strictly regulated for a wide variety of reasons. One rationale was to ensure that all customers had the same opportunity to buy the same quality of goods. Another reason was to protect the buyer who might arrive at the marketplace near the end of the day, when the lighting (from candles) was poor, and he or she might not be able to notice shoddy work or poor quality. It was forbidden to sell meat by candlelight. As one shopper in Paris in the seventeenth century observed, "It is dangerous to buy unless one knows the trade well, for they have marvelous skill in restoring and patching up what is old so that it appears new. As the stalls are badly lit, you think you have bought a black coat, but when you take it into the daylight, it is green or purple or spotted like leopard skin."

Sometimes you couldn't even trust *booksellers*! In the eighteenth century, many booksellers were also publishers (as well as, occasionally, apothecaries). Authors such as Dryden, Defoe, Marvel, and Pope were commissioned by bookshop owners, who paid them by the hundred lines. Strewn about the bookshops were unbound sheets of manuscripts, for the customer to read on the premises, or to take home to be bound. Some unprincipled booksellers would clear out their slow-selling books by covering them with new title pages and new authors' names. Unsuspecting bibliophiles might find that they had bought the same book twice.

Profit was frowned upon in some circles. In fifteenth-century Great Britain, consumers were protected by the regulation of "scot and lot" (tribute and allotment), which was a municipal tax, subject to the individual's ability to pay. Medieval retailers could be criminally charged for "forestalling" (speculating), "engrossing" (hoarding), and "regrating" (profiteering). A middleman "forestalled" the market by buying goods in advance and "regrated" (resold) them for a profit or held them back to create an artificial shortage, which, of course, increased the price.

THE FIRST SHOPS

THE ORGANIZED BUYING and selling of merchandise began through traditional markets, which were held in specific places on specific days of the week. Because these markets sold only goods that were indigenous to their particular region, they needed to be augmented by itinerant fairs, which a couple of times a year brought food staples, supplies, news, and gossip from other parts of the known world. The fair (from the Latin "feria," or holiday) was a great treat for the people who lived far out in the countryside. Nowhere else could a citizen find in one place sights such as jugglers, tumblers and sword swallowers, fireworks and bonfires, two-headed calves and fortune-tellers, musicians and singers—and be able to partake in gambling, sex, and even the occasional legitimate business deal.

Eventually the role of fairs was reduced to entertainment and merriment. A new, steady way for people to buy things developed: permanent retail shops. The first retail shops were created around 650 B.C. by the Lydians (who lived in what is now the western Anatolia region of Turkey), but it took nearly two millennia for the idea of fixed-place shops to catch on. In Western Europe, these first "stores" (sometimes merely rented stalls) were operated by artisans such as bakers, butchers, tailors, and cobblers, who initially had sold their wares only at markets that were open only on officially designated days. (The ruling authorities mandated these controls in order to better supervise commerce and protect consumers from charlatans.)

In due course, these independent artisans sought a way to trade their goods whenever they desired, so they began selling from the front of their townhouses. The display space was the bottom half of the front door, while the upper half of the door served as an awning and as a barrier between the house and the street. These townhouses created a sense of predictability and consistency to the retail process. The largest spaces served as workshops, warehouses, and showrooms, and they enabled customers to check out the merchandise whenever they wanted to, and to have time to deliberate over a purchase.

The word "shop" in old Saxon or German means the porch, vestibule, or lean-to of a residence. Each workday morning shopkeepers or their apprentices would "unbutton" their shops by letting down their dressing board and setting out a display of their goods. Eventually, shopkeepers installed colorfully painted boards, which were hung on brackets, to identify their particular line of business.

Gradually, the idea of fixed retail districts grew more sophisticated, and shops became a part of the urban landscape. In the twelfth and thirteenth centuries, towns were created with a strategically located marketplace (generally near the church or the castle) where stalls were created for traders and craftspeople. More sophisticated town plans included side roads and back lanes so that deliveries could be made in the rear of the buildings. City planners provided for houses and shops that faced the streets, which enabled shopkeepers to deal directly with the customers, who stood in the street. Shopkeeper and customer transacted their business over a dressing board or counter, which was pulled up at the end of the day to become a shutter.

In Italy, where it was easy to add a commercial space to a home, some artisans lived above the shop, and others lived right in the shop, which helped to save money on expenses. According to Leon Battista Alberti's treatise on architecture in 1471, "Within the city, the shop, or *bottega*, that lies beneath the house and provides the owner with his livelihood should be better fitted out than his dining room, as it should appear more in keeping with his hopes and ambitions." Because the bottega was open to the public, it could be more easily monitored by the authorities.

The downside of public shops on fixed premises included potential theft and fires—and damages caused by overstimulated celebrants at festive events. In 1575, when the people of Florence heard the rumor of the birth of a male heir to Duke Francesco de' Medici, local shopkeepers immediately closed their shutters, wrote a diarist, "because of their worries that the plebeians would act according to their custom and put the goods in shops to the sack."

Each new century brought more sophisticated, artistic signage, sometimes to excess, as the signs kept getting bigger and bigger. Some signs reached out over the streets, occasionally falling and squashing potential customers.

Perhaps the most extreme example of signage goes back to 300 B.C. and the Colossus of Rhodes, the 110-foot-high statue that stood on a fifty-foot pedestal on the island of Rhodes, an important economic center. As merchant ships sailed into the harbor off the southwestern tip of Asia Minor, where the Aegean Sea meets the Mediterranean, the statue of the patron god Helios was the sign that Rhodes was open for business.

With economic development came even more specialization. Merchants such as grocers, who sold their products by weight, were distinguished from drapers and tailors, who sold their products by measure. Eventually there were differences between bakers of white and brown bread, and between workers in new leather (cordwainers) and those in old leather (cobblers).

Fixed-place shops offered an advantage that modern consumers can appreciate: People could buy what they wanted, when they wanted. They didn't have to plan their purchases in advance or have to deal only with a traveling peddler who carried a limited amount of goods. They didn't have to worry about when they might have another chance to buy a particular item.

The idea of grouping merchants by their specialty—fish, meat, cloth, etc.—goes back to the days of the Roman emperor Trajan who at the beginning of the second century A.D. had built the world's first multipurpose mall, with shops, places to eat and drink, as well as office space. There was the *holitorium* for vegetables, *boarium* for horned cattle, *suarium* for pigs, *vinarium* for wine merchants, and *piscarium* for fishmongers.

Other specialty retailers eventually found their own streets and districts to ply their wares. The great mosques of the Muslim world were surrounded by shopping streets (*souqs*) and inns to accommodate traders (*khans* or *caravansaries*) and specialized craftsmen, with their own unique form of segregation, as Fernand Braudel described in *Civilization & Capitalism*:

> A series of craftsmen [specializing in the same trade] ranged in concentric circles in a traditional order which always reflected notions concerning what was clean and what was unclean. Perfume and incense merchants, clean [because they were devoted to the sacred], were next to the Great Mosque. Near them were silk weavers, goldsmiths and so on. At the outer limits of the town were to be found the curriers, blacksmiths, shoeing smiths, potters, saddlers, dyers . . . grouped . . . as a convenience for customers and traders alike.

In thirteenth-century Europe, there were separate individual halls that featured sellers of wine, leather, shoes, and furs. In Paris, butchers were segregated in their "shambles"—open-air slaughterhouse and meat-market districts, because the sights and smells of dead meat and blood offended shoppers, fellow retailers, and churchgoers. In the middle of London's shambles, a street once called Stinking Lane eventually was rechristened to the slightly improved Butchers' Hall Lane. London's famed Cheapside market district (the home of John Milton and Geoffrey Chaucer) was surrounded by Honey Lane, Milk Street, Bread Street, and Poultry Street.

ROMANCING THE GOODS

As RETAIL BECAME more sophisticated, and the competition grew more intense, shopkeepers and apprentices developed new skills to attract customers. Shopkeepers publicized their places of business and their wares with promotional tools such as printed trade cards, newspaper advertising, and directories. Displays were used to try to get passersby to at least slow down for a little window-shopping. As a Frenchman visiting London wrote in 1663, "There is no city in the world that has so many and such fine shops. For they are large and their decorations are as valuable as those of the stage. The scene is new everywhere which exceedingly pleases and attracts the eye as we go along."

How merchants treat their customers is, of course, an essential element of staying in business. Daniel Defoe, best known as the author of *Robinson Crusoe* (and the son of a butcher), wrote about how shopkeepers should comport themselves in his book *The Compleat Tradesman* (published in 1727): "The Retail Tradesman must furnish himself with a competent stock of . . . patience which is needful to bear with all sorts of impertinence. A tradesman behind his counter must have no flesh and blood about him; no passions; no resentment. He must never be angry, no not so much as seem to be so, if a customer tumbles him 500 pounds worth of goods and scarce bids for anything."

A master of a high-end shop was advised by *The London Tradesman* in 1747 "to speak fluently, though not elegantly, to entertain the ladies; and to be master of a handsome bow and cringe; should be able to hand a lady to and from her coach politely, without being seized with a palpitation of the heart at the touch of a delicate hand, the sight of a well-turned and much exposed limb, or a handsome face."

A typical early eighteenth-century London retail establishment was Fribourg and Treyer's snuff shop in the fashionable Haymarket district. The following are a few of the management regulations for its staff:

- Let every order be dispatched as soon as possible if by Coach or by Waggon the first after receipt of your order.
- Clean the Counter of everything before you put up an order, for fear other articles be packed with it, and sent wrong; always restore all goods to their proper situations after serving a Customer.

- Never leave the Shop without a member of the Family in it.
- Never omit any Business till to Morrow if it can as well be done to day, for no one knows, what the Morrow may bring forth.

We followed those rules at Spector's Meat Market. Although there was nothing fancy about our operation, and not a whole lot of romancing the merchandise, my mother did her part to provide a pleasant shopping experience in her little space, where she sold baked goods.

We offered large, four-pound loaves of rye bread and pumpernickel. If some customers didn't want to buy the whole loaf, we were happy to sell them a half or quarter loaf. My mother would take out her big bread knife and neatly cut the bread to the preferred size. She would do the same thing with the cakes we sold. After cutting the cake in half, she would use another knife to cut into two pieces the top half of the cardboard box that the cake came in. Finally, she'd take some string and tie together the two pieces of cardboard to make one neat little improvised box, leaving enough string for a handle so that the customer could easily take the package home. And she would top it all off with a smile and a thank-you.

5

Working Alongside Mom & Pop

The father who does not teach his son his duties is
equally guilty with the son who neglects them.

—CONFUCIUS (551 B.C.–479 B.C.)

FOR MOST CHILDREN of owners of mom & pop stores, the first
time they see what their parents do for a living—and are old
enough to grasp the reality of the situation—their reaction is either
love at first sight or "get me outta here." I, of course, belong to the
latter group; I had no interest in becoming a butcher, and my father
expressed no desire for my carrying on the family business, except,
perhaps, as a joke. He didn't want me or my sisters to struggle like
he and my mother had.

Nevertheless, I am *fascinated* by the second-, third-, fourth- and
fifth-generation retailers I met who just *love* the business and enjoy
working (at least most of the time) with their father, mother, aunts,
uncles, siblings, and cousins. I saw those emotions reflected in the
eyes of John Nese, owner of Galco's Old World Grocery in the Los
Angeles suburb of Highland Park, who recalled with sweet fond-
ness "the first time my father took me to work at the downtown
store when I was four or five years old. I worked with him one
whole summer. I dusted the shelves and snacked on the Twinkies."

John is a stocky, solidly built man in his sixties with a ready
smile, who favors an outfit of a yellow polo shirt, shorts, white socks,
sneakers, and a fire-engine red apron. As we sat in the back stockroom of the store, listening to the hum of the refrigerator motors,
he told me that his family had been involved in the grocery business "for eons," although they were not the original owners of

Galco's, which opened in 1897 in downtown Los Angeles. The shop came by its moniker by combining the surnames of the founders, Galiota and Cortopassi, Italian immigrants who couldn't speak English. Because they were unable to find other employment, they opened a little store, which is a path that immigrants have taken (and always will take) to gain an economic foothold in America. John's grandfather made pepperoni for a sausage company and his uncle was a produce vendor. His parents, Louis and Rose, grew up next door to each other in the Chavez Ravine area, which since the late 1950s has been the site of Dodger Stadium, the home of the Los Angeles Dodgers baseball team. "Before the Dodgers built the stadium, my grandfather used to walk up Adobe Street every morning at six o'clock to get to the hills where he herded his goats." In the early 1940s, Louis Nese became a partner in Galco's. As Louis told an interviewer in 2000, "When I was a boy, my brother and I did all the dirty work. Our bedroom was in the stockroom—not on a mattress, but on top of melon crates."

In the mid-1950s, as the Little Italy of Los Angeles was morphing into Little Chinatown, the Neses moved the business to Highland Park, which at that time had lots of Italian patrons who bought Galco's Italian cold cuts, groceries, and their famous sandwich on a french roll, called the Blockbuster. The sandwich (which is still made in the store today) consists of cooked salami, ham, mortadella, mustard, mayonnaise, cheese, and pickles. The Blockbuster got its name in the 1950s, when the heavyweight boxing champion Rocky Marciano, visited the store, and asked for a sandwich to go. He took one bite and declared, "Hey, this is a real blockbuster!"

John graduated from the University of Southern California in 1967 with a major in food distribution and history. He could have gotten a job in the corporate world and by now would have been close to retirement. But that's not what he had in mind. He told his father that he wanted to work in the store. "My father said, 'You'll make a living but you won't make any money.' I told him how important it was for me to walk in here and to be able to hear the motors running. I had lots of ideas for different things I wanted to do around the store. I said, 'You know, Pop, if I work in the store, at least I won't be cubbyholed in some corner in some job and do the same thing for the next forty years, and be unhappy. He looked at me, shook his head, and said, 'You're a damn fool. Make the money.'" John laughed as he recounted his father's reaction, and then he smiled with quiet satisfaction when he told me that virtually every day for the next four decades, until they passed away, "I worked with both my parents."

Over that time period, in order to survive, John Nese was forced by market conditions to radically change the nature of his business (as we will see in a later chapter). But throughout the changes, he has never lost his love for his store and his passion for taking care of his customers.

Ever since brothers Marc and Michael Brummer were kids, there was always something special about visiting their father, Sam, at his restaurant, Hobby's Delicatessen in Newark, New Jersey. "When I was fourteen years old, I used to love to come here in the morning to watch the place open up," said Michael, an energetic, fast-talking deli guy. "It would be pitch black, then the lights would come on, and all the turkeys would be put up. And all of a sudden the smells of the food would come in. The bread man, a big tall man, would walk in the door, singing. You'd give him the order for the day. Other deliveries would come in. It was very exciting. A lot of it was just hearing the stories, the joking, the schmoozing. Today, we open between six and six thirty, as soon as there's coffee. If someone's knocking on the door, they get in. If we know you and you knock on the door and the coffee's not ready, you can come in and wait for the coffee."

Hobby's, which is located in the heart of downtown Newark, is a classic. When customers walk through its doors on the corner of Branford Place and Halsey Street and look to their left, they see a long counter. There, wisecracking deli men, armed with carving knives and forks, are at the ready to make a hungry customer one of Hobby's famous Over-Stuffed Sandwich Combinations, such as the Triple-Decker Special, with turkey, tongue, pastrami, coleslaw, and Russian dressing, on your favorite bread; or the Number 9, with corned beef and chop liver and tomato and onion.

Directly across from the counter, Marc or Michael can be found sitting at a table, surrounded by paperwork, greeting the customers who work in the many offices and municipal buildings in the area. Near the cash register, a visitor can buy a souvenir Hobby's T-shirt that proclaims, FROM BRIS TO SHIVA AND ALL THE BOLOGNA IN BETWEEN.

One of the old regulars was Samuel J. Alito, when he was a judge in the U.S. Court of Appeals, Third Circuit, in Newark, before he was named a justice of the U.S. Supreme Court. On the other side of the ideological fence, another frequent visitor is Frank Lautenberg, the senior Democratic U.S. senator from New Jersey. In 1999, when Lautenberg learned President Bill Clinton was scheduled to address students at Malcolm X Shabazz High School in Newark and later to join them for lunch, he suggested to the White House that Hobby's do the catering. The Brummers provided the president's VIP guests and members of the press with matzo ball soup and platters of turkey, roast beef, corned beef, and pastrami sandwiches, and salads.

(I can see why Hobby's has such a loyal following. After my interview with Sam, Michael, and Marc, I decided to get a sandwich to take back with me on the short train ride into Manhattan, where I was staying. I ordered the Number 5, which is the Over-Stuffed Sandwich Combination of corned beef and pastrami with coleslaw and Russian dressing on rye bread. It was about four o'clock in the afternoon and I was famished. As the train pulled out of Penn Station in Newark, I decided to take just a quick bite and then put the sandwich away. I grew up on sandwiches like this, but I restrict myself to having them only when I'm in New York or New Jersey— once or twice a year. The Number 5 was so good I took a second bite. And then a third bite. The seasoned briny brisket, the moist condiments, the authentic Jewish rye with caraway seeds—*heaven*. I was enjoying myself so much that I was almost embarrassed to be doing it in public.)

With its dark wood paneling, light brown tables, and red vinyl chairs, the Hobby's dining room takes a visitor back to the finished basements of suburban Jersey homes in the mid-twentieth century. Sitting at a table in the dining room with his father, his younger brother, and me, Marc Brummer, a friendly, thoughtful man, reminisced about the days "when we were kids, we'd come down here on Christmas vacation or spring vacation or summer vacation when we weren't at camp, just to spend some time with our father. We'd bus tables, wash dishes, sweep the floors. Growing up as a kid, I had such a pride in this place. Things were done the right way. If something wasn't right, it was corrected. That sense of pride stayed with me. It was difficult to find outside. It was our dad's. It was ours. It was very special. That was my draw. Growing up, I saw that our dad made time for us. We weren't rich, but we enjoyed a decent lifestyle."

It's clear when speaking to the brothers that their biggest hero is their father, Sam, who spent a good portion of his life working for personal and professional freedom. A quietly impressive man, who in 1962 took over Hobby's from its previous owner, Sam was born and raised in 1920s Poland in a farming village with no paved roads. As a Jew, Sam endured virulent anti-Semitism "that was probably worse than it was in Germany," he told me and his sons. "I couldn't go to a public school. People knew me, knew my family. But, I was still a Yid. They would throw rocks at me when I was three years old. So, my mother didn't let me go to public school. I went to private Hebrew schools; that's where I got my education."

Sam's practical education came from his maternal grandfather, who was "a pious Jew, who would get up at three o'clock in the morning, do his prayers, then his chores, including feeding his cows and chickens," Sam recalled. "I would follow him around, helping him do whatever I could, and he would talk to me about things. I learned more from him just walking around, doing his chores." When Sam finished relating these experiences, he turned to his sons and asked them, "Did I ever tell you these things?" To which Michael, deeply moved, replied, "This you never said."

After Sam arrived in the United States in 1939—three months before war broke out in Europe—"I went to night school, to learn the language," he said. "In 1940, I was a stock boy at a superette [supermarket] in Newark, making seven dollars a week—plus tips, when I delivered orders. I later got a job working in a factory where they were making salamis and bolognas. Eventually, the boss put me in front, where there was a deli store. I became a cashier, and helped the men working behind the counter. That's how I learned the business. From there, I got a better job. Before I left for the army, I was making fifty dollars a week. For a single guy, that was pretty good money in 1942.

"I wound up in the army. I had three months of basic training, and then I was shipped to England for training." As a member of the Twenty-ninth Infantry Division, he was part of the 105 mm Howitzer team. "On D-Day, we landed on Omaha Beach, France, as part of the Normandy Invasion."

After Sam told me this part of the story, his face turned grim. As I looked into his eyes, I got a hint of what this memory meant to him. He finished talking about the war with these words: "I'm not going to go into what took place or what I saw." Pause. "I was able to survive." End of discussion.

After twenty-seven months in the army, where he earned several medals, including the Bronze Star, Sam opened a deli in Lakewood, New Jersey. He was able to buy the business with a loan of five thousand dollars from an uncle, a retired baker living in the Bronx, who had brought Sam to America.

"I paid back my uncle with the same interest that the bank was charging—plus a box of cigars. For five years, I would travel from Lakewood to the Bronx [a journey of a couple of hours back then], with a payment, and a box of cigars. Later on, there was a delicatessen called Kartzman's on Bergen Street in Newark. I wanted to buy it. Now, I needed ten thousand dollars. I went to my uncle and he loaned me the money. I was there for ten years. Of course, I paid off my uncle, all the money with interest and the cigars."

Sam bought and sold a couple of other delis. At the end of 1962, he took over Hobby's, which was not doing well. He revitalized the eatery with a simple formula: "I gave people their money's worth. I was liked by the customers. If somebody is unhappy with something, don't ask questions, take it back and give them something else. The key to success in the restaurant business is you give them good food, good service, and be a mensch."

On the other hand, Sam is no pushover. "Some people you invite to stay out of your business. I've been known to do that."

Michael recalled, with a smile, the time that "a lady said her pastrami sandwich was too tough. My father is trying to satisfy her. He's bending over backwards doing whatever he could, but she doesn't want to be satisfied. She kept saying the pastrami was too tough. So, finally, he said to her, 'I'll tell you what. Go sharpen your teeth.' "

Although he enjoyed having his sons helping out, their father, Sam, "did everything he could do to keep us away," said Michael.

"I didn't want them to go into this business," Sam agreed. "I wanted them to be a lawyer or a doctor, anything but the deli business. There are easier ways to make a living. You don't make a fortune in this business. I didn't want my sons to be sold to their business, and not have a happy family."

Marc, a graduate of Brandeis University, and Michael, a graduate of Franklin & Marshall College, looked at other vocations.

"Let me tell you about my brief career in retail," said Michael, who once worked at a Macy's department store in Livingston, New Jersey, for three months through Christmas. "Two weeks before Christmas, they told us that the next day the president of Macy's North division was coming to our store. They made all the sales managers stay until midnight cleaning out the dressing rooms, which were travesties, and ordered us to be back at five o'clock the next morning, to finish. We had to make the place perfect because the president of Macy's North was going to spend five thousand dollars in the store. I said, 'What about the customer who comes in every week to buy at Macy's? Shouldn't the dressing room look good for her?' They said, 'We don't care about that. It has to look good for the president.' After Christmas, I walked in and said, 'Thank you very much. I'm leaving.' They said, 'But you'll be a buyer in four years, making a hundred twenty thousand dollars a year.' I said, 'This is not the philosophy that I believe in. I don't care if I make less, I'm not going to work for anyone. If I'm going to work twenty hours a day, I'm going to do it for myself. That's the last time I'm going to work for someone.'"

The brothers remember well the night in 1984 that they decided to make Hobby's their career.

"Marc was going to move to Florida," Michael recalled. "He

visited me at college, before taking a train down to Florida. We had a party at my fraternity house. Somewhere around one in the morning, we had a conversation. We remember it clearly. Everyone around us said we were talking gibberish. The gist of it was that Marc said, 'I'll see you in a year after you graduate, and we'll take over Hobby's.'

"But before we took over the business, my mother, Rona, sat us down and said, 'You're brothers and that's the most important thing. If the business comes between you two, I don't want that to happen. You will always talk.' We both turned to her and said, 'If we ever start having problems, we'll put the key in the door and walk away.' Because the friendship between us is more important than any business. I'm not telling you that we get along twenty-four hours a day, seven days a week. We'll have a fight, then we'll sit down at lunch and talk. A lot of it is blowing off steam from frustration, maybe from an employee. Who are you gonna pick on? We pick on each other."

Marc noted how close he and his brother are with their father because they've had the opportunity to work with him. One of the joys of working in the restaurant is that "I know my father better than ninety-nine percent of kids know their fathers." The brothers also worked closely with their mother and their grandmother, Helen Lalin, "who was here doing payroll until four weeks before she passed away at the age of ninety-four. You talk about rich. There is nothing in this world that makes you wealthier than what we have together. We don't make what others make in terms of salary or whatever. But everything's a trade-off. We run the business so that we can go home to our families. We'll work all week and still get together for dinner on Sunday night."

Sam remains a fixture in the store, a familiar face to people who have been coming to Hobby's ever since they were little. "They come in because they just want to see my father and say hi," said Marc. "Some he remembers, some he can't remember because there are so many. But they all feel like they know him."

Incidentally, Sam didn't receive his Bronze Star until 2006. He was reluctant to discuss with his family his heroic experiences on Omaha Beach, and the role he played in the liberation of the village

of St. Lo. But as his wife, Rona, began to coax some details from her
husband, she was determined to see that he received the medal. She
gave a copy of Sam's discharge papers to her sons, with the request
that they give the documents to Senator Lautenberg. A few weeks
later, at a ceremony at Hobby's, Lautenberg gave Sam his Bronze
Star and told the gathering of customers, friends, and family (including grandchildren) that people knew Sam Brummer "because of his
food. Now I hope they'll know him for his incredible courage."

THAT'S MY CUSTOMER!

FROM THE AGE of three, Steven Uyesugi, now in his thirties, loved
visiting his family's jewelry store in Orange County, California.
"My parents tell me that when people came into the store, I would
stand on a chair and say, 'That's my customer!' For as long as I can
remember, this is what I've always wanted to do. My parents figured I didn't know anything else, so they weren't sure that this was
what I wanted to do." Steve eventually convinced his parents, Allan
and Georgine, that the AA Jewel Box was exactly where he wanted
to spend the rest of his working life.

I found out about the Uyesugi family and AA Jewel Box, in the
town of Tustin, from David Fujita, who works for Centaurus Financial Corporation, a financial services company that hired me to give
a series of presentations on customer service. Because one of the presentations was going to be near Centaurus's headquarters in Orange County, I asked David if he knew of any nearby mom & pop
stores that were owned by Asian Americans. He immediately suggested the Uyesugi family and AA Jewel Box, where David as well
as several of his colleagues were longtime customers, including his
boss, Ron King.

AA Jewel box is nestled in a small upscale Southern California
strip mall with other tastefully decorated specialty mom & pop
businesses, including a gourmet sandwich shop, a women's apparel
store, and a florist. AA Jewel Box sits between an antiques store
and an art gallery. I arrived for my appointment with the Uyesugi
family just after closing time on a late Saturday afternoon. Steve

saw me outside and unlocked the door with his key. In that instance, I found myself oddly moved by the mundane gesture of a merchant opening the entrance to his business. There was millions of dollars' worth of merchandise inside, so you can't be too careful. At that moment it was clear that Steve had a natural affinity for his family's business. A few minutes later, we convened in one of the small private rooms in the shop (where customers make their buying decisions), where we were joined by Steve's grandmother, Mary; his parents, Allan and Georgine; and Steve's wife, Pua. Three generations of jewelers sat across from me, a family history in flesh and blood. The only one missing was Mary's late husband, Maseo Mark "Mas" Uyesugi. Because the room couldn't accommodate that many people, Allan had to sit on a chair out on the selling floor.

The jewelry store and the Uyesugi family are integral parts of their Southern California community. In an age of retail specialization, the Uyesugis still offer a variety of products and services—from unique engagement rings and wedding rings to watch restoration to anniversary gifts. In a retail environment crowded with mall-based chains and Internet discounters, AA Jewel Box is "still trying to be a family-oriented jewelry store, which is hard to do nowadays," said Steve.

The Uyesugi family has been in the United States since the late 1890s, when Mary's grandmother, like many other young Japanese women, arrived as a "picture bride," to be matched with a Japanese man who was already in America—scraping to make a living in a country that treated him like a second- or third-rate citizen. Mary's father worked on a dairy farm in Yuba City, in Northern California, eventually saving up enough money to buy his own orchard, where he grew peaches and prunes. The parents of Mas Uyesugi owned a restaurant. Both of those businesses and livelihoods were taken from them when they, along with 110,000 other Japanese nationals and Japanese Americans, were sent to war relocation camps after the Japanese attack on Pearl Harbor on December 7, 1941.

In 1944, twenty-year-old Mas was able to leave the camp by enlisting in the United States Army. Working in military intelligence in the Philippines, his duties included translating Japanese documents and helping to interrogate prisoners. Decades later, Mas was

asked what was the most important thing he experienced personally from his service. His answer was "This was necessary to reflect
my loyalty to my great nation by protecting her against any and all
enemies. Now we can no longer be judged by anyone as to what
country our loyalty is with. God Bless America."

After the war, Mas, Mary, and newborn son, Allan, moved to
Cleveland, Ohio, where Mas learned how to fix expansion watch-
bands. Taken under the wing of older Jewish jewelers "who were
good to him," said Allan, Mas was taught how to repair watches
and how to conduct business. "A lot of his negotiation skills came
from what he learned from those men." In 1957, the family moved
back to Orange County, where they bought the AA Jewel Box from
the founder, who had started the business in 1946.

During the transition of ownership, the store had to be closed on
a Saturday, which Mas lamented because he felt it sent the wrong
signal to the customers about the new owner. He reopened the following Monday "and never missed a beat," said his daughter-in-
law, Georgine. "One of Dad's mantras was 'never inconvenience
the customer.' Whenever we had a project to do in the store, whether
it was reconstruction or moving jewelry, we always did it on *our*
time, whether it be nights or weekends. We never closed or incon-
venienced the customer."

Back then, AA Jewel Box was located in Santa Ana, a quiet,
close-knit little community where orange trees outnumbered customers. "They say that Dad used to go to lunch, with the door unlocked, and leave a sign on the door with the time he'd be back,"
said Georgine. "When he came back, the customers would be there
waiting for him. He had a lot of faith in the community, and the
community had a lot of respect for him."

After a couple of relocations, the shop was moved to its current
twenty-four-hundred-square-foot location in Tustin.

Steve began working at the store through high school, and upon
graduation "I told my parents: 'This is what I want to do. I'm ready.'
They said I should go to college first." For every weekend during the
four years he attended nearby Chapman University, Steve continued to put in his time at AA Jewel Box.

Ironically, as much as Steve was attracted to the business—and working with the other generations of his family—Allan had been reluctant to join *his* father, Mas. When he was in high school, Allan used to help out a little, but he wasn't particularly interested in the business. "In college, I did real well in my major but the other stuff was kind of boring," he said. My dad suggested that I go to the Gemological Institute of America in Los Angeles. I thought, 'Why not?' Then, the business became very interesting to me. I got a graduate gemologist's degree. At the time I graduated in the late 1960s, there were less than twelve hundred graduate gemologists in the world. For about a year and a half, I taught at the Gemological Institute."

In 1971, with the business doing well, Mas said that he could use Allan's help in the store. "Teaching didn't pay very much, so I decided to come to work with my father," said Allan, who was reluctant because Mas "was a real strong person, who ruled the store with an iron hand. But I was used to that because I was used to him. Working with my dad was a one-way education. We listened to see what he would do. Living with a person is totally different from working with that person."

Allan knew what he was doing technically, but he was not comfortable waiting on customers. "I had been teaching people from all over the world, and yet when it came to a customer walking into the store, I'd find something else I could do. It took me a while, but I learned by listening to my dad and observing how he took care of his customers."

Years later, Steve learned by listening and observing how his parents and grandparents took care of their customers. That's how customer-service skills are passed on from generation to generation.

Steve's parents let him work in the store after he graduated from the Gemological Institute of America, his father's alma mater. It was not easy at first. And it was a bit frustrating. "No customer wanted to talk to me," said Steve. "They wanted to talk to my dad. They'd come in to the store and ask, 'Is Allan here?' I'd say, 'Sure. Is there something I can help you with in the meantime?' They'd say, 'No, not really.'" But Steve learned quickly, and soon he had many of his own customers. "My dad loves it. He goes over to wait on a customer and they say, 'I'm here to see Steve.'"

His mother, Georgine, recalled how naturally Steve would "take a customer by the hand at the doorway, sit the customer down at the counter, and get them jewelry. Just because you're exposed to the business doesn't necessarily mean you're a good salesman, nor does it mean that you're going to enjoy the business. The goal for our children [their other son, Matt, lives and works in San Francisco] was to go into an occupation that they were going to enjoy and wake up smiling every morning and looking forward to going to work."

After Steve graduated from gemology school, his parents thought it would be a valuable experience for him to work for another retailer so that he would be exposed to a business that was not family owned. He was all set to start work at another shop during the holiday season in December 1995, but four days before Christmas, Mas Uyesugi passed away at the age of seventy-one. Steve then changed his plans and came to work in the family store, where he was needed. "We continued to do the business according to the way Dad liked things," said Georgine. "We did exactly what he would want us to do. We kept the store open and did as much as we could do for the customer, and not let anybody know what had happened."

"That was the hardest thing," said Steve. "People would come in every day and ask for my grandfather, and we'd have to say he isn't here today. It just killed you every single day. But you can't tell that to somebody who's buying a gift for a loved one. We wanted everybody to have a wonderful holiday. You still go on, and that's the way it is."

One of the essential ways for family businesses to endure is to give increased responsibility for making decisions to the next generation. Steve told me that he is keenly aware that his father treats him differently from the way Allan was treated by Mas. "Whereas my grandpa said, 'This is the way we're going to do things,' my dad gives me the option. If it works, it works. If it doesn't work, it's my fault. He helped me and guided me. My dad has given me a lot more opportunities to succeed or fail."

When he was in his early twenties, Steve would attend jewelry trade shows "and try to do business," he recalled. He was frustrated. "I was the youngest person most of the time. No one's taking me seriously. I'm looking to spend money and nobody wants to help me. One time I went to a trade show in Las Vegas with my mom. Dad was at the store because not all of us could take time away. Dad wanted me to find a ten-carat diamond and buy it on my own for a particular customer. That was one of the biggest trials in my life. I had to (a) find the stone in the world market out of the thousands and thousands of vendors, and then (b) negotiate the right price. My dad said, 'If it's the right stone, then you need to get it.' If I'm not there, we miss the deal. If that vendor goes back to Switzerland, the opportunity is gone. Dad told me, 'You have to make the decision.' He's leaving it all up to me. I'm an adult, but I'm still fairly new to the business. He said, 'If this is a business you want to be in, these are the things you're going to have to do on your own, in order to succeed.' He trusted me to do it. The question was: Do I trust myself enough to do it? I knew that I needed to do a good job for everybody that works here."

Steve successfully acquired the stone. The price: $250,000. Now *that's* a big responsibility.

Steve remembered that episode as a rite of passage—the moment when he knew that his father took him seriously as a colleague. Howard Fink, who has a home-decor store in Perth Amboy, told me a similar story about his early days working full-time in his family's store on Smith Street. Only the price points of the items were different from those of Steve Uyesugi.

"My father and I were partners," Howard Fink recalled. "We would go into New York together to buy, and he'd ask my opinion about what we should buy, even though he knew the right thing to do. Normally, drapes come in single, double, or triple width. My father had always bought twice as many triple width as double width. On this particular buying trip, I said we should buy twice as many doubles as triples. My father asked why. I said, 'Sliding-glass doors.' Bam! There's the answer right there! At the time, most apartments were starting to have double windows in the bedroom, dining room, and den. The only triple window you'd have in your house might be in your living room. I told him, 'Go through some bills and see if I'm right or wrong.' That was a realization for him, a turning point so to speak. You gotta be open to suggestions and not fight it. Today, I listen to my sons, Robert and Daniel, when they have suggestions."

Over the course of several decades, Howard Fink has worked side by side with his grandfather, his father, and now his sons, so he's an authority on communication among generations in a family business. "It was easier for my dad and me to communicate on a one-on-one basis than it was for him to communicate with his father," said Fink. When I asked Howard which one he listened to— his father or his grandfather—he laughed and said, "Whoever was yelling louder."

"YOU CONTROL YOUR OWN DESTINY"

I LEARNED ABOUT Wassler's Meat Market in Cincinnati when eighty-two-year-old Gene Wassler contacted me after reading about this book project in the *Cincinnati Inquirer*. Gene, the grandson of the store's founder, Eugene "Pop" Wassler, sent me an e-mail, which read, in part, "Ours is truly a family business. All our wives and children, girls as well as boys, have worked at some time in the business."

Pop Wassler came to Cincinnati, from his native Alsace-Lorraine in 1880, at the age of fourteen. In 1894, with the birth of his son, Fred, and with an investment nest egg of fifty dollars, Pop opened his first store at the corner of Wade and Denman streets in Cincinnati's West End neighborhood, which is well known for its German American residents. He moved his business a couple of times, following the migration of his target customers to other German-centered neighborhoods, such as the city's Over the Rhine area. In 1970, they moved to their current location on Cincinnati's West Side. (For a time, the family had a second store in Findlay Market, which is considered Ohio's oldest continuously operated public market.) Gene's father, Fred, "never did retire," Gene wrote to me. "He worked every day until a week before his death in 1985 at the age of ninety-one."

When I pulled into the strip mall in the working-class section of

Cincinnati where Wassler's is located and parked out front, I immediately knew that the store was the kind of business I was looking for. Surrounded by simple, utilitarian houses, the strip mall, which the family owns, also includes a flower shop, a beauty shop, a music store, and an accountant's office.

I walked into the compact little shop, and looked around at the showcases and displays packed with Wassler's specialties: cold cuts, fresh brats, cottage hams, and fine beef cuts. Customers were being taken care of. Cuts of meat were being suggested. Friendly neighborhood banter was in the air. I was looking forward to meeting with Gene, with whom I had spoken by phone, but when I saw the expression on the face of Gene's eighty-year-old brother and business partner, Bob, I sensed something was wrong. Gene, they told me, had passed away suddenly a couple of days earlier. My heart sank, and I felt like an intruder. "This is probably the wrong time," I said. On the contrary, despite their grief the surviving Wasslers—Bob, Gene's widow, Gloria; his sister, Carol; Bob's sons, Kenny and David; and Ken's wife, Debbie—were eager to talk about their family's mom & pop store, perhaps as a way to salve their grief.

We drove in two cars, a mile or so, to Ron's Roost, a local fried-chicken restaurant, where everybody knew the Wasslers, who are pillars of this close-knit neighborhood. As we sat at the table, I said that I wanted to thank Gene for bringing us all together. I sat near his widow, Gloria, a strong woman who honored her husband by sharing their story with me.

Fourth-generation brothers Kenny and David Wassler are running the business today, along with their sons, Michael and Chris, who are in their twenties. When asked if they always wanted to be in the business, David said, "I don't think we had much of a choice"—an answer that made Kenny laugh. "You worked through high school and you stuck with it. It's been good. When I graduated from high school, I drove our delivery truck for about two years. Then my father said, 'We gotta get you off that truck so you can learn how to cut meat.'"

Kenny's story was virtually the same. After high school, "I didn't want to do anything else. It's all I've ever known. Other than cutting grass, I didn't have any other jobs. I like working for myself. You set your own hours, even though they are long. You control your own destiny."

For members of the Wassler family "as soon as you were tall enough to see over the counter, you went to work in the store. We were taught that you were in it for the long haul and you were honest with all the people that you dealt with," said Carol Wassler, a member of the third generation. "Today, we employ fourteen people—of which six are blood relatives. A Wassler was never able to do anything important on a Saturday, which is the busiest day of the week. You couldn't get married on a Saturday. A lot of us got married on Thanksgiving. We wouldn't give birth on a Saturday. Our dad died on a Saturday and Gene died on a Saturday. I thought, 'Boy, did they have their nerve. They should have known better.' "

Kenny confessed that this lunch at Ron's Roost was the first time he had ever had a sit-down lunch with David during a workday. "We always eat standing up. If my grandfather saw this, he'd be rolling over in his grave," Kenny said with a laugh. "Typically, I get up a little after five. I'm at the store by six thirty. We close at six, and leave at six thirty. Saturdays are the same. When I was younger, we used to get up at four, then stop at the store to load up and then go down to Findlay Market. Then we'd load up at six and take what we didn't sell back to the store."

His father, Bob, told me that when he was Kenny's age, he and Gene had the same kind of schedule. "We used to get up at five A.M., go to our old store at Findlay Market in a 1939 Chevy that cost seven hundred eighty dollars new, and we wouldn't get back home until ten o'clock at night. Sometimes, I'd crawl up the steps of our house to our bedroom, I was so goddamn tired. You rest up on Sunday and you're back at it again on Monday. But at least we had Sundays off."

Kenny picked up on what Bob said. "We figure that if we open on Sunday, we wouldn't have a day off. My grandfather and my uncle instilled in us that if you're going to make it, you have to work hard. You work until you're done. The whistle doesn't blow at four o'clock. That's pretty much standard in the retail industry."

Wassler's is well known for making its own *goetta*, which is a peasant family food of German origin that is similar to scrapple. Goetta, which is primarily composed of ground meat and pin head or steel-cut oats, can usually be found frying on a Sunday morning breakfast skillet in the German American households on the west side of Cincinnati. Almost every day of the week, the Wasslers prepare goetta in four-hundred-pound batches, which they sell in their store or wholesale to local restaurants.

"Last Saturday, we ran out of goetta," said Ken. "I thought we were going to have riots. People screamed, 'What am I going to do for Sunday morning breakfast?'"

As I interviewed the Wasslers, I was moved by the closeness that permeated their family and business relationship. The whole family celebrates together every Christmas Eve, but the festivities don't start until nine o'clock "because everybody has to go home and take a nap," said Kenny. "We do between a quarter and a third of our business at Christmas. Around here, everybody eats at home around Christmas."

While they spoke to me, I thought of my own family business, where there were many conflicts. When my uncle Sidney left to go off on his own, my grandfather gave the butcher shop to my father. When Sidney's business failed, he returned to Spector's Meat Market as an employee, working for his brother, who was six years his junior. My uncle's wife was always bitter about that, which created a constant undertone of tension and animosity. For years at a time, my mother and my aunt would not speak to each other. I also thought about the stories my older cousins would tell me about how tough it was to work with our demanding grandfather. By comparison, when Kenny Wassler talked about working with his grandfather, he'd smile at his memories. "Every once in a while, my grandfather would get his feathers ruffled. He'd speak his mind. But in all the years that I worked with my dad and my uncle I never heard them argue or raise a voice to one another. My brother and I are the same way. You have to be. You can't go home mad. It just doesn't work."

OF ICE CREAM AND INDEPENDENCE

IF THERE'S ONE thing the people that I spoke to share, it was an antipathy toward working for someone else. Their overriding desire for independence came through again and again. Typical was this response from Roger Bassett, who is a part of the fifth generation of his family to work for Bassett's Ice Cream Company in Philadelphia: "There was a short period of time where I was working for someone else and it was horrifying. I couldn't stand it."

Bassett's, a legendary institution in the City of Brotherly Love, has been located in the same four-hundred-square-foot space in the downtown Reading Terminal Market—eighty thousand square feet of unique food stands and shops—since 1893. That was thirty-two years after Roger's great-great-grandfather, founder Lewis Dubois (L. D.) Bassett, first began using a mule-turned churn to make ice cream in his backyard in Salem, New Jersey. A farmer and a teacher at a Quaker school, L. D. loved to experiment with fresh ingredients, which he either grew himself or bought from the farmers who sold their wares at Reading Terminal Market. He even made his own *tomato* ice cream. Today, Bassett's is easy to find at the market under its large painted overhead mural that proclaims L. D. BASSETT, INC., EST. 1861.

The shop features old-fashioned round stools, a marble counter, pitchers of water, small ceramic dishes, and thirty-three flavors of ice cream in as many combinations and with as many toppings as you can think of. (Bassett's vanilla, a blend of Madagascar and Bourbon vanilla beans, all grown on Madagascar, accounts for one third of all sales.) Because the product is produced in small quantities (compared to giant national ice cream makers), Bassett's is not legally required to include information on their deep blue containers about saturated fat or cholesterol. (And isn't it better not to know?)

The recipes they use today come from L. D.'s grandson, Lewis Lafayette (L. L.) Bassett, whose picture can be found on one of the walls of the shop. "Grandfather's only interest was the store. He didn't have aspirations beyond the retail side of the business," said Roger, who shares his grandfather's love of retail, despite the ups and downs of the Reading Terminal Market, which had fallen on hard times by the late seventies and early eighties. "The market was about ready to close. We were down to about twenty merchants." Roger's father, who had another job at the time, wanted to shut down the ice cream counter and concentrate on the wholesale side of the business. But Roger, who was a freshman at nearby Rider College in New Jersey, wanted to take over the counter and find a way to make it work. "My father said, 'I don't want you quitting school to scoop ice cream.' When I took it over, as a freshman, he said, 'That's it. You're paying for your own college.' I took morning classes and night classes and ran the store. There were days in January and February when I'd only do twenty-five dollars or thirty dollars in sales for the day. In a week, we'd do a thousand dollars."

By 1993, the Reading Terminal Market was slated to be torn down and replaced by a parking lot for the new downtown Convention Center. But the market merchants and their customers rallied to save the old building through fundraisers and good old-fashioned political maneuvering. "Luckily city hall is nearby, so we had a lot of help from customers who worked there," said Michael Strange, Roger's cousin, who runs the wholesale operation. Using some of the money that had been earmarked for the Convention Center, the market property was fixed up and today it is a vibrant renovated indoor bazaar, a beloved place among Philadelphians and a popular tourist attraction—thanks to stores like Bassett's.

Markets such as Reading Terminal survive only when enterprising entrepreneurs present a coherent, workable, customer-friendly concept. Roger, who also owns the Original Turkey, a hand-carved turkey sandwich stand in the market, felt that "the biggest challenge for the market is getting mom & pop operators who have some sense of retail. If you can't be successful here, you can't be successful anywhere."

The company ships hand-packed pints all over the United States to expatriate Philly natives who still have a yearning for their favorite Bassett's flavors. Bassett's has been featured on the cable television channel Food Network, and whenever that episode is aired, the company gets a new flood of mail orders.

But it's Bassett's space in Reading Terminal Market that is the public face of the brand, which is also sold in local restaurants, dipping parlors, supermarkets, hotels, and to caterers. Michael Strange often sends potential wholesale customers to the store in order to sample the ice cream. Roger said that the store, which he still manages, is "a major part of the mystique. People from all walks of life, from all over the world come here. We're a tourist attraction. A lot of people think that the ice cream tastes better here than anywhere else."

To Michael Strange, "the single most satisfying thing is when someone who has never heard of the brand before comes into the store, buys a cone, sits down at the counter, tastes the ice cream, does a double take, and says, 'This ice cream is *good.*' When you have a retail store you get that immediate feedback from customers. If our ice cream gets customers' attention, if they think that it's amazing ice cream, then we take a lot of pride in that."

There might even be a sixth generation of Bassetts. Roger's young son, Eric, helps out and "he's the envy of his friends," said Roger. "They think it's cool that he gets free ice cream."

WERE YOU GREETED WITH A SMILE?

Down the road from Cincinnati, in Dayton, Ohio, is Furst Florist, which has been at the same location on North Troy Street since its founding in 1905 by Joe W. Furst, an immigrant from Wiesental, Germany. Today, the shop occupies two acres, with three quarters of that space allotted for the greenhouse. The store's early history is illustrated on its walls, where a colorful mural features Joe W. riding on a delivery wagon pulled by his faithful horse, Mabel, clip-clopping through the cobblestone streets of early twentieth-century Dayton.

In 1925, Joe passed on the business to his son, Bill, who ran it for forty-five years. Current owner Bill Jr., who took over the business from his father in 1970, first started in the shop when he was twelve years old. He knew early on that this would be his life.

"At that age, I'd run over here and work for a few hours after school, and then all day on Saturdays and Sunday mornings," Bill fondly recalled. "I learned from the ground up—from the greenhouse to delivery. Back then, I was doing everything: answering the phones, writing the cards, doing the buying, sweeping the floors, making the planters. My dad was working in the greenhouses with my uncle. They were partners until my uncle died when he was fifty-six. After high school, I went to Hixson's Floral Design School in Cleveland. I came back and took over design. I was fortunate to have a God-given talent, and business began to boom."

It's obvious that Bill, now in his early seventies, takes pride in the family business, which includes his two sons and both of their wives, who represent the fourth generation.

Why do some mom & pop stores last for several generations and others don't?

Bill Furst, who knows something about multigenerational businesses, said, "The failure of most third-generation business comes when people get a big head. They say, 'I'm the boss's son or daughter and I don't have to do anything. I just have to come in and crack the whip a little bit, then I'll go to the golf course for the rest of the day.' Those are the businesses that go down the tubes. Most businesses don't last till the fourth generation because the kids don't want to work as hard as mom and dad did. The other day, my son Tom seemed stressed and I didn't think he was as bubbly as usual. I said, 'Tom, do you need some help? I could have someone help you.'

"He said, 'Dad, I'm just a hands-on person. I love doing my paperwork, the planting, the delivery. I love doing it all.' I allowed my kids to make decisions and now they are totally programmed."

Although Furst Florist is located in a part of Dayton that is more industrial than residential, the store attracts customers from all over town. "I look at the checks to see what zip codes we're pulling from," said Bill. "The other day, I saw a client's check in the cash drawer. I hadn't seen her when she came in. She's in her seventies, and she knew my father and my grandfather. I called her and told her that I was sorry that I missed her. We chatted for a while on the phone and we reminisced."

Furst admitted that these days he doesn't really need to come into the store every day, but there's no other place he'd rather be. "I love the business. I love the people. I love coming in here and seeing my family working here together and getting along. That's a reward that not very many people can appreciate. My [seventy] employees are as much a part of my family as my own family is. I'm thankful that the good Lord sent these people to me—friendly, hardworking people with great personalities. We don't want to be the largest; we just want to be the best. We have had slow, but regular growth. When you get a customer on board, you've got to make sure you can take care of them and take care of them properly. I've seen people who have gotten aggressive and done giant advertising programs to get the business rolling. But at holidays, they can't handle all the business, and they get everyone angry with them. That's when I get my little increase."

Even during our chat, Bill was keenly aware of how he wanted visitors to his store to be treated. As we spoke, he leaned over and softly said to me, "Let me ask you a question. When you came through the front door, were you greeted with a smile?"

I was. He smiled.

"I WANTED THE FREEDOM"

THE SAME LEVEL of care for the customer transcends race, geography, and product. I saw those qualities when I visited Tokyo, and called on Hiroshi Odsutsumi, who owns several tea shops in Kasukabe city, Saitama Prefecture, about twenty miles north of central Tokyo. I had previously met Mr. Odsutsumi, whose business is called Odsutsumi-en, when he visited Seattle on an educational business trip with other Japanese owners of small businesses, which was led by my friend and colleague, Yoshinao Sato. Mr. Odsutsumi is an open, friendly man with a big toothy grin and a playful demeanor.

In the 1970s, his great-grandfather brought tea to Kasukabe city from another part of the same prefecture.

"Originally, tea was not grown in this area," he explained. "They brought the tea here for economic reasons. Most people are rice farmers. Rice is planted in the spring and harvested in the fall. The tea is harvested later in the spring, in May, so tea represented another business opportunity for them. My grandfather continued the business and was active in the local cooperative of green tea producers, before the war. He made the transition from hand-picked to machine-harvested tea. After the war, my father increased the acreage of the tea farms and began selling to wholesalers."

Hiroshi began working with his father and grandfather at the store when he was in the first grade, packing boxes and doing small jobs. "When I was young, I wasn't really sure that I wanted to work in the family business. It was a difficult decision. But in my college years, I knew that I didn't want to work for someone else, for another company. I wanted the freedom." From his honored grandfather Hiroshi learned "the importance of honesty and straightforward dealings. I feel very thankful to my great-grandfather and my grandfather for the opportunity they gave me to do the things I'm doing."

After we conducted our interview in a spacious, rustic wooden cabin that he owns near one of his stores, Hiroshi took me upstairs because he had something special to show me. At the top of the stairs, we turned in to a small room where I was greeted by a sight that made me smile: a shrine to the great Japanese baseball player Ichiro Suzuki, who plays for my hometown team, the Seattle Mariners, after having become a legend in Japan. There were Ichiro pictures, uniforms, bats, and gloves in the room, which was Hiroshi's pride and joy. It made me laugh to see a successful businessman display such glee for his baseball idol.

Hiroshi and his business play important roles in his tight-knit community, and he considers his service to his customers and neighbors as part of a sacred duty and obligation. After meeting at the train stop at Kasukabe, we walked a couple of blocks to one of his stores in this bustling city of two hundred thousand. As we strolled through the urban landscape of retail shops, he casually mentioned that he sponsors a local annual jazz festival. A fan myself, I asked, "Do you like jazz?" With a complete lack of irony, he replied, "No, not really," and kept walking to the store. He was just doing what a neighborhood retailer does—promoting activities in his community.

A SENSE OF PURPOSE

OF ALL THE people I met on my retail journey, no one displayed more passion for his family business than Bob Margolin. Bob, a trim man of sixty, owns and operates Miller Lumber, which was started in 1921 on Division Street in the Bucktown/Wicker Park neighborhood of Chicago by his grandparents, Louis and Dora Miller, who emigrated from Russia.

Bob knew early on where his future would be: the store.

"My dad encouraged me to experience what was out there in the world," Bob said, in his quintessential Chicago accent. "I worked for the Chicago Metropolitan Sanitary District. I learned that I wanted to work hard. But I didn't want to work for anyone else."

Miller Lumber was originally a hardware store that catered to a community that was primarily Eastern European, Italian, Jewish, German, "and stayed that way for many years," said Bob. The business consisted primarily of selling home-improvement products, particularly paint and wallpaper to home owners. Miller's was an old-fashioned shop, where the merchandise was displayed in oak cases with clear glass fronts. Customers would point to the item they wanted to purchase and the store clerks would retrieve the goods from the storage cabinets on the walls by sliding from display to display on a ladder that was set on tracks. Miller's was the local source for chisels, screwdrivers, measuring gauges, plumbing, electrical products, and everything else a hardware store can offer. Nails, screws, nuts, and bolts were sold by the pound.

Bob, who was born in 1948, wasn't just raised in the business, it was all around him. "When I grew up in the neighborhood, we lived in a three-floor walk-up and my grandparents had the apartment next door. When we moved, we lived in a two flat, with my grandparents upstairs and my parents and me on the second floor. We all worked in the business. We drove to work together. There was a tremendous sense that this is our business; this money is the lifeblood of our family. I grew up having a sense of struggle and purpose within the context of my family. Even at a young age, I had an opportunity to contribute. I started working, at eight years of age, with my grandparents in the hardware store, and my dad and uncle in the lumberyard. I was a stock boy. I swept the floors. I learned the whole picture by doing all the jobs—threading pipe, glazing windows, cutting keys. I'd get a quarter an hour under the table from Grandma, plus whatever I could eat for lunch. When I got tired of having my uncle give me direction, I'd go hang out with my grandparents. My grandmother had a little kitchen in the back.

"My grandfather, the patriarch, was a very hard man, a hard guy to work for. In the old country, he supposedly was indentured to cut down trees. I remember him coming in one day, throwing the store keys on the counter, and telling my father, Abe, and my uncle Harry, 'When I die, throw these keys in my casket, because no one here's going to be smart enough to do this business.'"

Bob fondly recalled the day when he was working in the store as a stock boy, "and we had a ton of stuff to put away. We started at seven in the morning. It was hot. I was getting a workout, but I enjoyed it. I'm working and working and working. Finally, it was seven in the evening, and my grandfather said to me: 'That's enough. Let's go home.' For him to tell me to stop working, was, for me, the greatest compliment. It meant something to me to be part of that struggle. Even today, when I come to work, it's the same location and the same family. Although it's a different business today, we still do many of the same things we did in 1921. Every day, my mother brings me lunch, including homemade soup. I have a nice continuity in my life."

"I GOT INTO THE BUSINESS SAME AS YOU"

WHEN I WENT to London to visit my high school friend, the children's book illustrator Dana Kubick, she urged me to call on the local butcher shop, M. Moen & Sons, which overlooks lush green Clapham Common in the South London borough of Lambeth.

The business was started in 1971 in South Norwood (about ten miles from Clapham Common) by Maurice Moen, an Irish immigrant from Monaghan, which is not far from Belfast. Maurice's father, also a butcher, emigrated to London in the 1940s to start his own business. Today, the shop is run by Maurice's son, Garry, who told me over a cup of coffee that "as a teenager, I started to come to work on Saturdays. I got into the business same as you," a comment that made me chuckle. Garry and I differ in that his father envisioned his son taking over the business. "My father taught me in ways that I didn't know I was being groomed. He taught me bit by bit by bit. Over the course of four or five years, I learned the cuts of meat, how to cut them, the quality of the meat."

Garry's shop is one of the most beautiful high-end butcher shops I've ever seen. And to call it just a butcher shop is to say that Martha Stewart is just a caterer. In fact, if Martha Stewart were to design a butcher shop, it would probably look like Moen's, with its hardwood floors, tiled backsplashes, and high-end grocery items such as bread, crackers, sauces, pickles, mustards, chutneys, jams, and vinegars. Spread out on the counters and floor of the shop are abundantly filled baskets of walnuts, artichokes, carrots, lettuce, garlic, and other fresh offerings, looking like so many horns of plenty.

But it is the meat that is the attraction. Garry Moen stocks his cases with organic and free-range meats from some of the United Kingdom's best small suppliers, whom he carefully vets. In addition to the usual meat selection, Moen's carries seasonal game (pheasants, partridges, woodpigeons, hare, wild duck, venison, and wild boar); prepared fresh meat (stir fries, lamb marinated in olive oil, rosemary, garlic, and juniper berries); haggis and gulls' eggs; ox and lambs' hearts; and pigs' trotters.

"We're members of the Guild of Q Butchers, an organization of independent butchers who must submit to rigorous standards of hygiene and food preparation before being admitted as members," Garry said, while Bruce Springsteen's "Born to Run" blared out over his in-store speakers.

Moen figured out a way for an independent to compete in well-to-do Clapham, which is served by three major supermarkets. "As the area became more affluent I changed the cuts and quality of meat to appeal to the local customers. We put quality before price. Our grocery items have to be something that the supermarket doesn't sell, otherwise they will always sell it for cheaper than I can buy it."

Standing outside the shop, I noticed that Moen had set aside space in one of the window displays for a charitable project that had been initiated by one of his regular customers and her daughter. As part of the project, fair-trade cotton bags and aprons, made in Changarawe village, Tanzania, are for sale and all profits go to support destitute women, orphans, and grandmothers in that troubled African country.

"We subsidize it," said Garry, who admitted that he sold the items at a loss. "We do what we can for the local schools and that sort of thing, when all the mums come in for vouchers for everything, donations for barbecues, and such. There aren't enough hours in the day for me to do my own charity work. That's my contribution."

Will there be a fourth-generation butcher in the Moen family business? Garry's two teenage children help out around Christmas, but he said, "They haven't expressed interest, and I discourage it. There are easier ways to make a living." Asked what he would say if they insisted they wanted to join the business, Garry smiled. "I would try once more to talk them out of it, and then if they wanted to do it, I would let them do it. But they would have to understand this wouldn't be an easy ride."

When I asked Garry for his philosophy of how he runs his business, he shrugged his shoulders and said, "My father used to say that there are fifty-two weeks in the year, and you're in business in all of them. That's how we run our business: Buy fair, and always leave a little bit for the next man."

6

Independence

The four cornerstones on which the structure of
this nation was built are: Initiative, Imagination,
Individuality, and Independence.

—CAPTAIN EDWARD V. RICKENBACKER (1890–1973)

THE DECISION TO OWN A SHOP takes many different paths.
Some shopkeepers are born to it; others choose to combine
their passion and interests with a business. Some are looking for
meaning in their lives; others are looking for means.

In 2002, I read an op-ed piece in the *New York Times* about the
sad demise of Balducci's, the legendary family-owned gourmet grocery shop in Greenwich Village, which had been founded in 1946.
Family squabbles caused the breakup of the pioneering shop that at
its peak had annual sales of twenty million dollars. Balducci's was
sold to a company that had plans to roll it out as a national chain,
but the plan failed and the store ended up closing its doors. The name
has since been revived, but it's not the same business or the same
family.

The author of that *Times* article, Rob Kaufelt, wrote that he had
personally cautioned the people with the grandiose national plans
for Balducci's that "the specialty food business was not the supermarket business . . . supermarkets are driven by efficiency, while
specialty stores are about excellence of product and knowledgeable
service."

At the bottom of the article, Kaufelt was identified as the owner
of Murray's Cheese Shop in Greenwich Village. *Kaufelt.* His name
was familiar to me, but at first I couldn't place it. Eventually, I

remembered who he was. I think we might have met in high school. We were the same age, had grown up in the same area of New Jersey, and we had a mutual friend, who later gave me Rob's e-mail address. Rob and I set up an appointment for my upcoming visit to New York to talk about the importance of mom & pop stores—and his own journey.

Murray's is on Bleecker Street in the heart of the West Village, where I lived for several years. The store is small, but once you get inside, you are overwhelmed by the assortment of products. Murray's is the best-known cheese purveyor in the United States, offering more than 250 varieties of cheese of every taste and description, from all parts of the world; a wide selection of charcuterie meats such as cured sausage, chorizo, and salami; and a wide assortment of specialty groceries, olives, antipasto, fresh breads, crackers, toast, butter, oil, vinegar. You get the idea. Thanks to Kaufelt, who has built an international reputation as a cheese maven, Murray's has been named New York's Best Cheese Shop by the *New York Times* and the *Village Voice*, among many other publications.

Upstairs from the store is a conference room, where Rob and his staff have meetings, and where classes in all things cheese are taught. This is where we sat, overlooking the activity in the store below, while Rob told me how his path brought him to Murray's. His paternal grandfather, Irving, emigrated to the United States in 1914 from Poland, eventually settling in Perth Amboy, where he opened Kaufelt Bros. Fancy Grocers, just a couple of blocks away from my father's shop in the farmers' market.

In 1947, the year Rob was born, his grandfather and his father, Stanley, bought a 6,000-square-foot supermarket—one of the first in New Jersey, at a time in retail history when supermarkets were becoming an important new concept. A decade earlier, the first A&P supermarket—a 28,125-square-foot store—opened in Braddock, Pennsylvania. Over the years, A&P added stores and expanded its merchandising by introducing self-service meat and frozen-food departments, and promoting bakeries as "stores within the store." A&P eventually became the biggest retailer in the United States—the Wal-Mart of its day. By the mid-1950s, supermarkets accounted for 60 percent of all the grocery sales in the United States.

Rob eventually joined the family business, Mayfair Supermarkets, in the early 1970s, working with his father to create one of the most successful upscale independent supermarket chains in the country, and one of the first to offer high-quality prepared foods, salad bars, and to emphasize fresh products.

But by the mid-1980s, Rob left the thirty-store chain, which his father later sold to Ahold, the Dutch supermarket conglomerate, because, he said, "Supermarkets were not gratifying to me personally." Back then "supermarkets didn't have all that much interest in food. I was always interested in food and having some sort of contact with my neighbors." He opened a couple of specialty food stores in New Jersey under the name Kaufelt's Fancy Groceries, in honor of his grandfather. "I have a romantic vision of my grandfather's shop," he told the *New Yorker*. "I think I have a romantic vision, period."

By 1987, at age forty and divorced, he sold that business and moved to Greenwich Village, where he eventually came upon Murray's, which was then located on Cornelia Street. Founded by Murray Greenberg in 1940 as a wholesaler of butter and eggs, Murray's was a quintessential mom & pop store in what was then a predominantly Italian neighborhood, with stores such as Faicco's Pork Store, O. Ottomanelli & Sons meat market, and Rocco's Pastry. He later sold the business to his clerk, Louis Tudda, who ran it, said Kaufelt, "like a bodega or a Korean deli is today; not only cheese was sold, but also cheap oil and tomatoes for the locals."

In 1990, while standing in line at Murray's, Kaufelt overheard Louis Tudda tell a customer that he had lost his lease and was returning to his home in Calabria, Italy. Almost on the spot, Kaufelt decided to buy the six-hundred-square-foot shop for two reasons: It would provide him with (1) a job, and (2) an opportunity to rescue a longtime neighborhood store.

"I wanted to go back to some current version of what I assumed my grandfather had, which was as close as I could find in this neighborhood and that happened to be for sale. That's why I bought it," said Kaufelt, who has since moved Murray's twice (the last time in 2004). It is now at 254 Bleecker Street, near Leroy Street. One constant throughout all of the moves has been a photograph—an enlarged grainy black-and-white of Rob's grandfather's butcher shop in Perth Amboy, ca. 1920s—prominently displayed on a wall in the store.

As a neighborhood store owner, Kaufelt saw himself as a steward of his part of Bleecker between Sixth and Seventh avenues, where he has helped to spark the rise of luxury food stores such as Amy's Bread Bakery Café and the Lobster Place.

"I'm a finger-in-the-dike sort of guy, which is fine, having come from the other side of the supermarkets (at least a small version)," said Kaufelt. "Nevertheless, I'm not naïve. I'm not looking to go out of business. I'm doing something that's more modern. Wanting to do this individual thing may be quixotic. Neighborhood shops are the same sort of thing. They feed that community need. But having said that, the community will only support them if they deliver what the modern market wants."

As a refugee from big supermarkets, Kaufelt strongly believed that small independent food retailers "have some intrinsic value in and of themselves, if they can be viable and survive."

Sitting in his conference room, looking out at the commercial and community buzz in his store, Kaufelt confided that he was living "a wonderful life. It's creative. You can see it, touch it, and taste it. You can shuck and jive with it." As a wry smile crossed his face, he pointed to the front of his store, and said, "And you can stand over there by the window in the spring time and look at the prettiest girls in the world walking by."

LIBATIONS AND CONVERSATIONS

STARBUCKS HAS BEEN credited with popularizing the modern concept of the "third place"—the place in your life after home and work—where people enjoy spending time and partaking in libations and conversations.

Before the advent of coffeehouses, the favorite meeting places were pubs, alehouses, and inns.

The "pub," which is the Victorian abbreviation for "public house," has been around for a couple of millennia, dating back to when the Romans introduced one-room commercial spaces (*taber-nae*)—sidewalk cafes—where patrons enjoyed food and wine and people watching.

The alehouse came into being when brewers started to sell their wares informally at their houses. As the English began to incorporate pagan drinking rituals into the Christian church, they designated ales that were expressly brewed for church festivals or to generate contributions to the church as "scot ales." Clandestine brewers who avoided giving the church its monetary due were said to have been able to drink "scot free." The alehouse eventually became a place for the down-and-out.

The tavern, which initially sold only wine, was where the professional classes dined on good food, drank fine wines and ales, and consorted with their peers for both business and pleasure. As Samuel Johnson once said, "No, Sir; there is nothing which has yet been contrived by man, by which so much happiness is produced as by a good tavern or inn."

The coaching inn, a stopping-off point for traveling passengers in horse-drawn coaches, has been a part of English history since at least the fourteenth century. It was in the coaching inn where travelers found food, drink, lodging, conversation, and sometimes companionship for the evening. Probably the most renowned was the Tabard in the Southwark section of London. Geoffrey Chaucer began his 1388 classic *the Canterbury Tales* with this line: "In Southwark, at The Tabard, as I lay / Ready to go on pilgrimage and start / For Canterbury . . ."

Coaching inns became popular in the late seventeenth century with the start of the Industrial Revolution, when it became more and more important to safely move goods and people. The inns were places of trade, as well as food and lodging, with as many as sixty bedrooms, and stable facilities for several dozen horses.

One such place was the legendary George Inn. Located in Southwark, on the south side of the River Thames near London Bridge (which for many centuries was the only bridge across the Thames), the George dates back to at least 1542. Rebuilt in 1676, after a fire gutted Southwark, the George is London's only surviving galleried coaching inn. Nestled in a cobbled courtyard near Borough High

Street, the inn has two floors: an upstairs, where the lodging quarters once were and where there are now private meeting rooms, and a ground floor that today is partitioned into a series of adjoining bars. The Middle Bar, known as the Coffee Room, was frequented by Charles Dickens, who wrote about the inn in his novel *Little Dorrit* when the character of Tip goes into the George to write "begging letters." Dickens was writing from personal experience. As a youth, he trekked every Sunday from Camden Town to Southwark to visit his father in Marshalsea Prison.

I walked in Dickens's footsteps on my own visit to the George. I ordered a draft of ale from the bar in the center of the inn, and fresh hand-battered cod with chips, citrus salad, and homemade tartar sauce directly from the kitchen in another part of the inn. When I placed my order, I was instructed to take to my table an open wooden box with a handle, which was loaded with utensils, napkins, Sarson's Malt Vinegar, and HP Brown Sauce. While I dined, I read a little of the colorful history of the George Inn, which today shares its brick courtyard with the London School of Commerce and the School of Technology & Management. William Shakespeare lived and acted in Southwark, and, to this day, Shakespeare plays are regularly performed in the courtyard. In the 1920s, the George was run by a Miss Agnes Murray, who entertained many prominent diners, including Sir Winston Churchill, who usually brought his own port—and was charged a corkage fee by Miss Murray.

The George is now a part of a chain of corporately owned London pubs, inns, and taverns, and is a popular place for lunches, dinners, and private parties. Although the coach inn belongs to a bygone past, the necessity for all of us to have a "third place" to meet and break bread with friends and business associates is—and will always be—as natural as breathing, and schmoozing.

FINDING A "SOCIAL CENTER"

THE COFFEEHOUSE HAS been a part of our social life since the fifteenth century. Coffee historians cite Kiva Han in the Turkish city of Constantinople (now Istanbul) as the first public place where coffee (strong and black) was served, in the year 1475. The Turks have always taken seriously their coffee, which was known throughout the Muslim world as the "wine of Apollo, the beverage of thought, dream and dialectic." Back then, a husband's failure to provide his wife with a sufficient amount of coffee was grounds (no pun intended) for divorce.

The Turks helped to spread the popularity of coffee to Europe in the early sixteenth century when they invaded Vienna. They later retreated in defeat, leaving behind a large quantity of coffee beans. An enterprising citizen named Franz George Kolschitzky (who claimed to have once lived in Turkey) used some of those beans to open the continent's first coffeehouse, which featured filtered coffee with milk and sugar. Flavored syrups would come later.

Britain's first coffeehouse was opened in Oxford in 1650. Two years later, London's first java place, the Turk's Head, was started by two men who formerly had worked for an importer of Turkish goods and were familiar with Turkish coffee. Soon, hundreds of such establishments spread out all over the city. "For persons much concerned in the world," they were superior "to taverns and alehouses where continual sippings, tho' never so warily, would be apt to fly up into their brains and render them drowsy and indisposed for business," according to a 1675 article entitled "Coffee Houses Vindicated." Explained a newspaper account from 1698, "These houses . . . are extremely convenient. You have all manner of news there. You have a good fire that you may sit by as long as you please. You have a dish of coffee. You meet your friends for the transaction of business."

Conducting business has long been a part of the coffeehouse scene. In the United States, at the dawn of the nineteenth century, some say, the seeds for the New York Stock Exchange were planted at the Tontine Coffee House, at the northwest corner of Wall and Water streets. Other historians believed that the NYSE originated in 1792 at the Merchants' Coffee House at the southeast corner of Wall and Water, when twenty-four stockbrokers and merchants consented to regulations for securities transactions, popularly known as the Buttonwood Agreement.

A century earlier, in 1688 London, Edward Lloyd opened on Tower Street a coffeehouse that was popular with people involved in maritime trade—particularly sailors, merchants, and ship owners—where they could get the latest and most dependable shipping news. The conversation invariably got around to insurance, and eventually a new company was formed to help underwrite the perilous maritime industry—Lloyd's of London.

THE MOM & DAUGHTER SHOP

TODAY'S MODERN COFFEE shop follows in that tradition. On a visit to Savannah, Georgia, I came upon one of them—Gallery Espresso. The day I arrived in Savannah, to give a speech, I left my hotel to check out the downtown streets of this enchanting city. Strolling through Chippewa Square past the statue of James Edward Oglethorpe, who founded and established the colony of Georgia, my eyes were immediately drawn to Gallery Espresso, with its bright red table umbrellas that splashed some color on the corner of Bull and Perry streets, not far from Savannah College of Art and Design (SCAD). When I walked into the coffeehouse, I was immediately impressed and amused with its quirkily eclectic interior: exposed brick walls and wood beams, white tile floor, overhead fans, showcases and displays filled with colorful tea sets, crystal glass, dinner plates, chopsticks, greeting cards, and assorted tchotchkes. Trendy young SCAD students plopped on cushy sofas or high-back easy chairs, or sat with their laptops at wood tables scattered throughout the space. On the walls were paintings from local artists, hence the name, Gallery Espresso.

At her regular table, perusing her paperwork and casting a mother hen's eyes on the proceedings was Judy Davis, an attractive woman with red hair styled in a bob.

"Accidental entrepreneur" might be an apt description for Judy, who was born in Pittsburgh, and grew up in Bradenton, Florida, where for thirty-five years she trained Thoroughbred racehorses on her farm. In the early 1990s, her daughter, Jessica Barnhill, a student at SCAD, was friends with the owner of Gallery Espresso, which was then located on nearby Liberty Street in a one-thousand-square-foot space, with barely enough room to sell coffee beverages and toasted bagels.

"When I was making trips here to visit with Jessica, we would go to that coffeehouse," Judy recalled. "The shop had changed hands twice in six months. It was obviously a struggling business." In 1994, Judy, who was going through a divorce and a midlife change, relocated from Florida to run the business. Two years later, she became the owner.

Like Rob Kaufelt from Murray's Cheese Shop, Judy bought the business "to create a job for myself." It wasn't easy. "I had moved to a brand new area, where nobody knew me. I didn't have a lot of money. Plus, I'm a woman and divorced." She was able to get a loan from the Small Business Administration for fifty thousand dollars, which got her on her way. "I put everything I was making back into the business, so I could make a good presentation. For a while, we were the only coffee place in town, and we had a line going all the time. But then four more independent places opened in town. I guess it looked like I was making too much money. They must have thought, 'Wow, all you have to do is make that pot of coffee.' Little did they know that I drove the same car for eleven years.

"I'm here a lot. I'm not an absentee owner. In a town like this, a huge part of this business is me and my personality. I have people who walk in every day who just want to say hi. Or we exchange a look. It's part of their day. They don't want to walk in and have somebody different look at them every day. Lots of people have coffeemakers at home. They are still coming here every day. It's not just about getting their cup of coffee.

"Some people view their success as when they don't need to be in their store. That's when their business falls apart. A few years ago, a guy would come into my store and take notes. Then he opened up his own store, but he was not active in the business. He hired managers to run the business for him and it failed."

In 2003, after quickly paying off the bank, Davis decided to move to her current space, which is much larger. Needing to buy some additional equipment, she said she "went back to the bank for a second loan for seventy thousand dollars. By that time, I had such a good track record, I had three banks fighting to get my deal. I was able to negotiate on interest rates, on a ceiling on interest rates, and other terms. Back in the day, I was thankful that they loaned me money. I didn't even care what they charged me for interest."

The new location was in an area with considerably more traffic.

"Everybody in town comes by this street, comes through this square, and comes around this corner," said Judy's daughter, Jessica Barnhill, a redhead like her mother. "It's a very social area that has an interesting dynamic of different walks of life—business owners, doctors, lawyers, churchgoers, SCAD faculty members who have meetings here. There are many customers, where we don't know them by their names, but by their drink. We say, 'Here comes the double-cappuccino-with-skim-milk guy.'"

When her mother moved into the new space, Jessica joined her "to bring new ideas," including expanding the food menu, which had been limited in the original space. "We added a light lunch for people at work who want to come in and out fast. Salads, sandwiches. We could do more in-house baking without having to outsource, which made things more cost-effective."

Jessica curates the in-shop art exhibitions that change once a month. "There are a lot of young artists who can put together a show," she said. "When people go to these art openings, they get ideas themselves, and become more ambitious to take on art as a hobby or a moneymaker." Gallery Espresso takes a percentage of the sale of any work that is sold.

Working with her mother, Jessica noted with a laugh, "We'll get a little nitpicky with each other, but we make each other laugh. We go to lunches, dinners, social events, art openings: the mother-and-daughter team. It's definitely a team effort between me and my mother. She's the anchor holding this place together." Jessica will be eventually taking over the business. "I'm entrenched here. I'm devoted to it. There's a lot of me invested in this place. Just hearing the compliments on a daily basis is, by itself, a reason to continue. I like putting my little touches into the business—finding new [art] pieces and new furniture, adding some new thing to sell, coming up with a new drink. Being able to make those kinds of changes is a good feeling."

The centerpiece of the coffeehouse is the Nuova Simonelli espresso machine (price tag: eighteen thousand dollars), considered the Cadillac of espresso machines, which adds to the authenticity of the coffee drinks. Although the Nuova Simonelli was a huge expense, Judy made the kind of creative, calculated business decision that entrepreneurs must do. As she explained to me: "The technician who does all my maintenance started selling the machine. To help him get off the ground, I bought the best machine he had. I also knew, in turn, that I was going to get the best service."

When Judy hires a new barista, the first big test is the ability to operate the Nuova Simonelli. "I will never get a fully automated machine because I think that whoever is preparing the drinks should at least have certain talents, such as being able to create good froth. We have one customer, Steve, who has been my customer since I opened. He gets the exact same drink, mochachino, every time he comes in. He's had over six thousand of those drinks. I use him as a tester when I have a new employee. If there is anything that's not up to standard, Steve will let me know."

MAKING BOOK

CHUCK AND DEE Robinson own Village Books, one of America's great independent bookstores, in Bellingham, Washington, north of Seattle. When I thought about people to interview for this book, Chuck and Dee were at the top of the list. I first met the Robinsons in 1995 at the Pacific Northwest Booksellers Association Spring Conference in Spokane, Washington, where I gave the first-ever presentation of my book, *The Nordstrom Way*. We've been friends since that day.

Sitting with them in the small restaurant on the lower level of their store, they talked about how all this got started. They met in 1965 at a skating party during freshman orientation at Sioux Falls College in South Dakota. By their sophomore year they were engaged, and by their junior year they were married. For the next decade they lived in the Midwest, working as special education teachers. By 1979, ready to do something different with their lives, they liquidated their house and possessions, bought a motor home, and hit the road. After going through a self-described period of "values clarification," they decided to open a bookstore. The one remaining question was where to do it. Chuck and Dee had already established the criteria for their ideal location: a community with a population of between 40,000 and 100,000, near a college or university, and a major city. That's the perfect description of Bellingham, population 69,260, which is eighty-five miles north of Seattle, and forty-five miles south of Vancouver, British Columbia. Located on picturesque Bellingham Bay with snow-covered Mount Baker as its backdrop, it is also the home to the progressive Western Washington University.

In 1980, they opened Village Books in the folksy Fairhaven neighborhood in about fifteen hundred square feet of rented space. Over the years, the Robinsons have expanded Village Books to ten thousand square feet of retail selling space, which is complemented by two cafés (which they do not own) on different levels of the store. Adjacent to Village Books is another Robinson enterprise, Paper Dreams, which specializes in paper products, greeting cards, etc. Chuck and Dee own a condominium at the top of the Village Books building, so they literally live above the store.

Chuck, who is past president of the American Booksellers Association, and a luminary among independent book people, described Village Books as "being in the business of connecting people with the information and entertainment they are looking for—mostly, but not entirely in book form. That's not just semantics. We are not in the business of selling books. The grocery store and the drugstore are in the business of selling books. We would like to sell the books on our shelves. But our business is your coming into the store looking for a certain book or idea, and our ability to connect you with that book or idea."

Building their business to such a degree was never really part of a grand plan. "We thought we would open a mom & pop store, with a few part-time people to help us out so that we could take our vacations," said Dee. "We never thought about it long-term. It rolled along and suddenly thirty years have gone by."

MOM & MOM

WHEN CARLA COHEN decided to become a bookseller in the early 1980s, she took a course in the business that was led by a new bookseller: Chuck Robinson. Soon after taking that course, Carla and her business partner Barbara Meade opened their "mom & mom" bookstore, Politics and Prose, in the northwest Washington, D.C., neighborhood of Forest Hills, on Connecticut Avenue NW between Fessenden and Nebraska.

While I already was familiar with Politics and Prose, I got my entrée to Carla and Barbara from Alan Cheuse, the novelist, short story writer, and professor of creative writing at George Mason University, who is best known as the book reviewer for the *All Things Considered* program on National Public Radio. Alan, who lives near Politics and Prose, is an old family friend from Perth Amboy, where his maternal grandparents ran a candy/tobacco store on Smith Street. "I never worked there," Alan once told me. "I just lived off the candy bars."

Carla Cohen, who was born in Baltimore, earned a master's degree in urban planning, eventually becoming a city planner. During the Carter administration, she was a political appointee at the Department of Housing and Urban Development. When the White House changed hands in January 1981, Carla was forced to find something else to do. In 1984, she decided to open a bookstore in a northwest Washington neighborhood where "people were in consonance with us," she said. "I knew from my city planning background that this was an area with a lot of two-income families and a lot of graduate degrees."

To raise capital, Carla and her husband, David, refinanced their home and borrowed money from friends and relatives, with this caveat: "Lend me no more than you can afford to lose if, God forbid, it doesn't work."

When Carla advertised in the *Washington Post* for a manager, the first person to respond was Barbara Meade, a Washington, D.C., native with a master's degree in literature. Barbara had previously owned and operated a small bookstore in the Washington suburb of Potomac, Maryland. Coincidentally, her college roommate was married to the brother of Carla's former boss. (Washington, D.C., really is a small company town.) Barbara started out as an employee and soon became a partner in the store.

In 1984, they opened their fourteen-hundred-square-foot store. Six years later, firmly established, they moved across the street to another store with double the space. Helping to lug the books to the new location were hundreds of loyal customers, who assembled in front of the store on a hot Sunday morning in July. Everyone who participated was given a T-shirt that posed the question: "Why Did the Bookstore Cross the Road?" The current store has ten thousand square feet of selling space and a coffeehouse, another four thousand square feet of offices and receiving, and, most important, a hallowed place in the neighborhood. Politics and Prose is one of the best-known independent bookstores in the country, and past winner of *Publishers Weekly*'s Bookseller of the Year award.

As business partners, Carla and Barbara—who between them have six children and thirteen grandchildren—are a fascinating combination of opposites. As Barbara wrote in the bookstore's newsletter on the store's twentieth anniversary:

Carla is Jewish and I am a WASP. I am always early for an appointment. Carla is always late, convinced that nothing of importance happens until she gets there. Carla tends to be impulsive and unflaggingly enthusiastic; I am more reflective and usually have one foot on the brakes. Our events coordinator, Jana Kollias, describes us as like a cat and a dog. I, the cat, walk unobtrusively into a room and sit quietly on the periphery intently watching everything that is going on. Carla, the dog, joyfully bounds in and jumps up on everyone. I think we both have the wisdom to share our strengths and compensate for each other's weaknesses.

Why has our partnership flourished? Our age has worked well in our favor; both of us believe that at an earlier time we did not have the maturity that would have allowed the relationship to thrive. We seldom quarrel, though we often disagree, which is then resolved by whoever has the most persuasive argument.

During my interview with the two women, they discussed what it takes for a mom & mom store to work. Carla said, "Look, we don't make a lot of money. I couldn't have done this if my husband hadn't been earning a living. Barbara couldn't do this if she weren't single and her kids were grown up."

Barbara expressed the belief that if she and Carla were men, "we would each have our own secretary and wife, with all the services they provide. We still answer the store phone, type our own letters, and leave in the middle of the day to meet repairmen at home. We have also been well served by our gender. We have a flexibility, an openness to change, and a pragmatic approach that I think are more female attributes than male.

"In a male partnership, there is a tremendous emphasis put on money—making it, keeping it, and divvying it up. I can't remember a single quarrel that Carla and I have had over money. From our female perspective, the money is less important than the quality of relationships we have with each other, with our customers, and with the staff, and we have always felt that that is where our energies belong."

THE NEIGHBORHOOD HARDWARE STORE

SEVERAL MILES AWAY from Politics and Prose is Frager's Hardware, the quintessential neighborhood hardware store, which was recommended to me by Etta Fielek, an old high school friend of mine and a longtime resident of Washington, D.C. The store is currently owned and operated by John Weintraub and Edwin Copenhaver, two longtime friends and business partners.

Despite the onslaught of the Home Depot and Lowe's, Frager's is a survivor. Located on Pennsylvania Avenue within sight of the Capitol, Frager's has combined knowledgeable, friendly service and convenience to become a local institution. It's the place where people who live in the Capitol Hill neighborhood go to find hardware, garden supplies, and advice in the midst of a labyrinth of rooms clogged with every home-repair or home-improvement item you would need—as well as things you didn't even realize that you needed, such as natural geranium-scented floor wash or multicolored magnetic bag clips. Despite the narrowness of the aisles and the crowdedness of the displays, Frager's is as comfortable as your favorite shoes, and the employees are as reliable as your best friend.

Frager's is an icon in D.C. A customer once told store manager, Nick Kaplanis, what he learned when he called the telephone directory-assistance operator for Frager's number. The operator informed the customer that Frager's is the second-most-asked-for number in D.C.—after the fire department.

In May 2006, when President George W. Bush's staff wanted to stage a photo opportunity to illustrate positive news on the economy, he made a brief appearance at Frager's, where he toured the store and bought some treats for his dog.

The store was founded in 1920 by Fritz (Frank) Frager, an immigrant from Russia, who was trained as a carpenter. Fluent in Russian, Italian, Yiddish, and English, Frager was named foreman at the Washington Navy Yard because he was the only man who could talk to everybody. But despite his linguistic skills, Frager was laid off. Soon after, he opened the hardware store, and lived above it with his wife. His fluency in languages helped him do business in his ethnically mixed neighborhood.

His two sons eventually took over the business, but in the mid-1970s they decided to search for a buyer. Around that time, John Weintraub and Edwin Copenhaver were looking for a business to get into. The men had been roommates and fraternity brothers at the University of Virginia in Charlottesville. After college and military duty in Vietnam, they both returned to Washington, D.C., and did graduate work at George Washington University—Weintraub in business administration and Copenhaver in engineering administration. For a while, Weintraub worked in sales for National Cash Register, and Copenhaver worked in construction for the Charles Tompkins Company, which has built many large projects in the District of Columbia, including the headquarters for the International Monetary Fund and the Federal Reserve.

Why buy a hardware store? Weintraub called it "a process of elimination. We looked at a bunch of other businesses. When we first took a look at this place, we weren't impressed. Then, we looked at other businesses, and came back to this."

In 1975 they bought the three-thousand-square-foot store and its inventory for sixty-seven thousand dollars. The Fragers, said Weintraub, "allowed us to work here for thirty days prior to buying it, so we could see everything was legitimate. They showed us everything. We rented the entire building, and we subrented the upstairs apartments, to help defray costs."

The closest big-box store, Home Depot, is just four miles away, but because of the way the streets are laid out in the District, and the preponderance of block-long government buildings, monuments, and parks, it could take thirty minutes to get there.

"If you want lumber for a deck, if you want drywall, then you go to Home Depot. But if your faucet malfunctions, your toilet breaks, your lights don't work, you go to Frager's. You don't go to Home Depot—unless you know exactly what you want," said Weintraub. He and Copenhaver have made sure that Frager's has succeeded by offering good old-fashioned customer service. "Sometimes, in hardware, people will ask for the wrong thing. When it doesn't ring true, you ask them additional questions. What's your project? What are you trying to do? You can solve their problem."

When you walk into Frager's, an employee will actually talk to you. "We have people here who are capable of answering questions, having an intelligent conversation, and getting you to where the merchandise is," said Copenhaver. "You can buy it, and get out—without spending twenty minutes roaming cavernous aisles. That's one of the big appeals. The more than fifty people who work here know what they're doing, and know how to give customer service. The important thing is to get to know your customers by their first names. They are your bread and butter. You should be down there talking to them, asking them what they need. If you're doing that, you'll know what products to carry, because they'll tell you. People are not shy about telling you what they want. That's the heart of the business. If you sit in the office and stare out the window, it doesn't work."

Frager's reach extends into the Maryland and Virginia suburbs, where many longtime customers have moved. "They go to their local home center, can't find something, and they remember, 'I know who'll have this. Frager's.' So, they'll drive into the city," said Weintraub.

The Capitol Hill neighborhood, which endured riots in the 1960s, was considered "a downscale, working-class neighborhood on the fringes of some bad neighborhoods," said Weintraub. "After the riots, everybody was a little gun-shy" about moving into the neighborhood. "This area was considered a little far out. Hardware stores do better when they're not in the higher rent country. They need to be low rent and they need working-class people."

As the neighborhood has evolved, with many homes being bought and renovated, Frager's has responded by adapting to the changes. "We're always trying to remerchandise, to look at products that don't turn," said Weintraub. "We bought the building next door seven years ago, and moved better quality paint over there. Today, paint and garden are our biggest departments." Frager's remains a neighborhood fixture, and in Weintraub's words, "a beloved institution. People here are committed to the neighborhood and to buying locally."

SAVING A NEIGHBORHOOD INSTITUTION

WILLIE EARL BATES wasn't laid off from his job. He wasn't looking for new meaning in his life. He didn't have lifelong plans to become an entrepreneur. But in 2002, in his early sixties, after a successful career selling insurance, that's exactly what he became. That year, he rescued the legendary soul food restaurant the Four Way Grill, in the Sugar Hill neighborhood in the southern section of Memphis, Tennessee, where it was the center of the community.

When I learned that I was going to be giving a speech near Memphis, I sought out a classic Southern soul food eatery. I called the Black Business Association of Memphis, and they recommended the Four Way. At first, I had considered another famous soul food restaurant, which had become a local chain. The husband and wife who ran the chain had become prominent cooking celebrities with their own television show. But they weren't quite what I was looking for. I wanted something more modest, not as polished, but just as soulful. In the Four Way, I found what I was looking for—and a whole lot more.

The Fourway (its original spelling) first opened its doors on the corner of Walker Avenue and Mississippi Boulevard (an intersection known as the Corner) on October 1, 1946, under the ownership of Clint and Irene Cleaves. Clint was the longtime chauffeur for Mayor E. H. Crump, who encouraged his fellow citizens to patronize the restaurant. With Irene Cleaves running the kitchen, the Fourway—with the slogan "Rightly Seasoned"—became one of the most popular soul food restaurants in town, and the center of the South Memphis community. "There were several reasons that made it extremely important," said Willie Earl. "It was the centerpiece of the times when the musicians from Stax Records and around the world would visit here." Stax Records, just a few blocks away, at the corner of College Street and McLemore Avenue, was one of America's most influential record labels, particularly in the 1950s and 1960s, with the music of legendary artists such as Otis Redding, Isaac Hayes, Sam & Dave, Booker T. & the MG's, the Staple Singers, and Ike & Tina Turner, who would all eventually find their way to the Fourway for house specials such as chitterlings, neck bones, black-eyed peas, fried chicken, and sweet potato pie.

"There were not many other places for black people to eat out," said Bates. "The Fourway had soul food that was second to none. Dr. King ate here. This was his favorite place. Elvis Presley ate here. Wilson Pickett ate here. David Porter of Sam & Dave still comes here to eat. We've served Dr. King, B. B. King, Don King, and Aretha Franklin, the Queen of Soul. That's why we say that we always strive to provide royal service."

Willie Earl has lived in and around Sugar Hill since 1947, the year "my mother, Magnolia Gossett Bates, brought me and three pretty sisters here, without a father. She cooked in people's kitchens. I went to the Metropolitan Baptist Church in this neighborhood. I was a Cub Scout, Boy Scout, Explorer Scout. My pastor helped me develop principles. He taught me discipline. I went on to graduate from Booker T. Washington High School, which is down the street from the restaurant, and from Tennessee State University, where I earned a degree in business management. My drive came from those basic fundamentals that were developed as a child in this neighborhood. I developed the love and appreciation for this historic site, the Fourway. That was the motivating factor."

Willie Earl's soul is rooted in this neighborhood. A lean, wiry former football player, he smiled and pointed to a little red child's wagon that sat in the patio behind the restaurant. When he was a small boy, he used that wagon to haul groceries to the homes of neighbors for twenty-five cents a load. As he got older, "I worked cutting grass. I started developing muscles, pushing that lawnmower. I remember the day I made my first paycheck. There was a dime store down the street. I went down there and bought my loving mother a gift. When I got older, and I wanted to play football in high school, I needed to work. I got a job delivering the morning *Memphis Commercial-Appeal* newspaper, using that red wagon. From 1955 to 1959, I would pass the Fourway Restaurant at four thirty each morning, deliver my papers, then go home, get dressed, and go to school. I never had any idea that one day I would have the opportunity to become the steward of this historical facility."

After the original owner, Clint Cleaves, passed away in 1979, the Fourway changed hands several times within the Cleaves family. By 2001, the restaurant was in receivership and was fated for demolition. When Willie Earl learned it was for sale, "I knew I had to try for it." He and his partner, Tyrone Burroughs, were initially outbid, but when the other party didn't come up with the money, they "picked it up on the courthouse steps" for seventy thousand dollars. Bates's portion of the money came from an annuity that he had built up after thirty-seven years in the insurance business. Bates and Burroughs bought part of the northeast corner of Mississippi and Walker, which included a pool hall, a beauty salon, a shoe repair shop, and the restaurant. "It was ordained. This place meant so much to the neighborhood. It would have been a great disaster to let all this history within this facility go down."

Willie Earl put on his hardhat and went to work with Tyrone on the renovation. They eliminated the pool hall so that they could expand the seating in the restaurant. They replaced the beauty shop and shoe shop with a garden and landscaping in honor of his mother. The landscaping includes cactus and rocks from her garden. A plaque with her likeness watches over the proceedings.

Then, of course, there was the matter of the food.

"When we first started, the chef told my wife that if I didn't stay out of the kitchen, he was going to quit," Willie Earl said. The chef eventually did leave. "I didn't know anything about the restaurant business so I had to learn fast. I had to organize, plan, direct, and find someone who could cook the type of soul food that the restaurant was accustomed to."

Chef Kathy Watson oversees the kitchen, and Willie Earl credits her for carrying on the tradition that was started by the previous ownership. By continuing the kinds of offerings that Mrs. Cleaves was famous for—pork chops, fried catfish, baked chicken, fried green tomatoes, black eyed peas, sweet potato pie, and crumbly cornbread—Willie Earl has been able to maintain the reputation of the place, which was once known as the Fourway Grill, but is now known as the Four Way Restaurant, with the slogan "Your kitchen away from home. Every bite's a delight." And as a recent review in the *Frommer*'s travel guide declared "The soul food remains the tastiest in town."

To which Willie Earl Bates smiled and added, "We are here to spread the good vibes."

7

Passion and Persistence

Perseverance brings good fortune.
— I CHING

THE PASSION AND PERSISTENCE of Willie Earl Bates is typical of the entrepreneurs I met on the road. Without passion and persistence, there's no reason to open the doors of the shop; there's no reason to get up in the morning.

"For us, the passion about what we're doing is important," said Chuck Robinson, the co-owner, with his wife, Dee, of Village Books in Bellingham, Washington. "We see that in other businesses. The good restaurants that we know of are certainly run by people who are passionate about what they do and who throw themselves into the work. It would be impossible for a mom & pop to survive if somebody looked at it as just a job. This business gets in your blood.

"Like most liberal arts graduates, Dee and I had romantic notions about the book business. We were told the highest mortality rate was in restaurants; the second-highest mortality rate is bookstores. The message we heard over and over from people in the book business was: 'This is no way to get rich. But it's a great way to make a living if you can make a go of it.' That's the same thing I would say to someone today. If this is your passion, it's a great way to make a living. But if you're opening a bookstore because you love reading books, then become a night watchman because you'll be able to read more books that way."

Dee Robinson called owning a bookstore "a lifestyle choice. You don't ever leave it behind. You think about it in the morning when you wake up and when you go to bed at night. It's who we are. We agree not to talk about the business for a certain period of time, although we don't view talking about the business as an onerous burden. Sometimes we talk about problems. But sometimes we talk about ideas. Other times, we just want to shut discussion down. We know couples who have an agreement not to talk about business at home. I'm not interested in having that kind of division in my life. We don't have children, so we don't have that element of family. Our dog doesn't care what we talk about."

Echoing the Robinsons is Alan Robson, who, with his wife, Linda Sutherland, owns the Great British Pine Mine in suburban Kensington, Maryland. The eight-thousand-square-foot warehouse is chock full of antique armoires, cupboards, buffets, bookcases, desks, and other items imported from Great Britain and Europe. A lover of antique furniture could easily spend a day or two closely examining all the pieces that Alan and Linda have assembled.

"The work itself has been my passion," Alan told me, as we sat in his office. "I could never have done it if I didn't love it. I talk about my product with genuine enthusiasm." Every piece of furniture is personally bought in Europe by Alan and Linda, who speak eloquently about the differences in finishes, workmanship, and carvings among pine from various countries. Quoting from the *I Ching*, the five-thousand-year-old Chinese Book of Changes, Robson believed that " 'perseverance furthers.' If you stick at it, if you like what you do, if you believe in what you do, if you have a good product, and if you treat people honestly, like they really matter, then you should prosper."

The passion and perseverance for independence have been keystones to Robson's life. He's a slim man with red hair with traces of gray, who graduated from Cambridge University in England in 1972 with a master's degree in history and social and political sciences. Early on, he realized that he "couldn't imagine taking a regular job, joining a corporation or even a profession."

At that time, Robson met Linda Sutherland, whom he described as "a beautiful American hippie girl." After they married, Alan and Linda, who had recently graduated from the University of Iowa, teamed up with some other friends and moved to Exeter, Devon, in England's West Country, where they opened up a vegetarian cooperative restaurant, called the City Ditch. "This was a time when vegetarianism was a political statement. We felt that you could change the world by changing the way people related to food. Our idea was to provide reasonably priced food for the people. We asked people to spend more time in their kitchen, cooking red beans, so there would be less factory farming."

Buying and selling "seemed to me to be a way that I could be independent and true to myself; not selling my labor power for forty hours a week to someone else and having my life the rest of the time," said Robson, who was born in 1950, the second son of a working-class family from East London. The family had been coal miners, but in the 1930s, when the pits were closed, they got factory jobs in London, where Alan grew up. When Alan was nine his father died. To support the family, Alan's mother worked for a neighbor, Ron Ross, who had just opened a small drugstore in Walthamstow Market, selling toiletries and household goods such as shampoo and hairspray. At age ten, Alan began working in Ross's stores. "I don't remember any great lessons from those early days, other than that it could be done. But, at the time, it didn't look like I was going to be a shopkeeper."

Over time, while still in England, Alan and Linda, who eventually had three children, developed a love of antique pine furniture. In 1982, they decided to set up a business in the United States in what would turn out to be several temporary locations in Virginia and Maryland.

"When I first arrived here, other dealers questioned the idea of selling just antique pine," Alan recalled. "They said that it was like owning a clothing store and selling all the suits in the same color and the same size. But I believed there was a market for antique pine. Most people who did this were a married couple where the husband was a lawyer and the wife did the business on the side. It wasn't something that young people would go into, thinking that you could make a living out of it. At first, we struggled. Linda sold Herbalife [nutrition and weight-management products] until the late eighties. We couldn't have made those first couple of years without that income."

In 1990, the Great British Pine Mine moved to its present location on Howard Avenue in Kensington, in an area that has become one of the mid-Atlantic's premier sources of antique pine furniture.

"We do custom finishing and adjustments, to improve on whatever we buy. Working with customers, we adapt pieces for modern functions, for example, making wardrobes suitable for office use. We take antique armoires and convert them for use for TVs. If someone comes back to me with a table that they have a problem with after five or six years, I take care of it. I don't necessarily see it as my responsibility and there is no guarantee, but it's important to me that my customer is satisfied and that she tells as many other people as possible that I'm obliging and helpful and that I stand by my product. That's always been key to my business philosophy and what I teach my kids: We want to end up with happy customers."

The passion for the business extends to all three of their children—daughter, Abbie, and sons, James and Charles—who have helped out in the business through their high school and college years, and are now working full-time. As each child has joined the firm, Alan has told them, "The job description is that which needs to be done."

Alan emphasized that theirs is truly a family business, and that a customer is always greeted and served by a family member. All the pieces have been chosen by Alan and Linda, who have taken each of their children on European buying trips. The whole family has had the opportunity to travel and to learn the business from its very source. Any changes or restoration will be performed or supervised by Alan or one of the boys. Not only that, any piece purchased from the Pine Mine is delivered by James and Charles, who will also offer advice on interior design, if requested.

"My brother and I have been delivering furniture together for many years," said James. "I know while walking backwards carrying a piece of furniture which way we're going to have to turn it to make it fit through a doorway. There's a comfort level with family and with people you've worked with for so long. My parents were always my example growing up. In high school, when I wanted to make extra money, it was either work at the pizza place, which was terrible, or come in here a few days a week to work on furniture.

I found it much more satisfying to be here, mainly because of my dad. There's no one I would rather work for than him."

Alan reflected on his children's involvement in the family business with a combination of satisfaction and bemusement. "When it's good, it's really good. There's no one who has my interest more at heart than my kids. It's in their self-interest, too. We have three siblings working here and there can be times when things get a little bit iffy. It's more than sorting out the staff problem. We have one employee who's not a family member. I don't love that guy like I love my kids. So, it's very easy to be straightforward with him. But, sometimes, with family members there are a lot of vicissitudes that come into play, and we have to remind ourselves that this is primarily a business, and we have to leave a certain amount of that at the door."

Nevertheless, "I find that a lot of people envy what we have, although it can be very difficult. Sometimes, Linda and I think, 'Our kids are all around thirty and they're still receiving so much and our lives are so involved. We're still worried if someone has a sore throat. When I was their age, I left my home and went thousands of miles away. It's great that we can be all here eating pizza together. Whenever I wonder why the kids want to be in the business, I then answer, 'Why not?' It's the most natural thing in the world."

Alan and Linda are in their late fifties, and Alan readily admitted that they are "in no position to retire and we have no intention to retire. We may not ever do so. I still work in much the same fashion as we have over the past twenty years. Now, there are these new opportunities, but I'm not the one to seize on them. That's for this next generation, who are now selling to the children of customers who have been loyal to us for over twenty years."

Reflecting back on the last three decades, Robson said, "We've had the good fortune to be able to make a living from something that we believe in and enjoy doing. That's the key: We wanted independence. We wanted to do our own thing. I'm no tycoon. Here I am, still in my one shop, and that's not really an accident. Eight thousand square feet is a lot of space to rent and a big overhead. If I had my wits about me twenty years ago, I should have tried to buy a building. But twenty years ago I was hoping I could sell that chest of drawers over there to cover the check I paid for groceries yesterday. You had to take baby steps."

THE BARBER POLE

GARY FOUST KNOWS what it's like for a job to get into his blood. The owner of the Barber Pole in Savannah, Georgia, is from a family of barbers. It's a joy to hear him wax eloquent and romantic about the sensory experience of a classic old-time barbershop.

The Barber Pole certainly is on its way to becoming a classic. When I walked past it on my first visit to Savannah, I was captivated by its red and white striped awning, barber pole stencils at its entrance, and shoe-shine station, which is manned by shoe-shine master William Boyce, who has immodestly proclaimed, "I think I'm the best there ever was." I wasn't able to find the time to interview Gary on that trip, but even after I returned home to Seattle, I kept on thinking about the Barber Pole. When I found out that I was going back to Savannah a few months later, I called him and we were able to get together for a chat early in the morning before the shop opened for business.

The Barber Pole offers traditional haircuts, hot lather shaves, and razor cuts for men only. "Regular customers come in and don't have to say a word. They get the same haircut every single time. You know exactly what to do," said Gary. "To work with the tools that we work with, and use them in the way that we do, that's art. I feel that I'm practicing my craft. People walk in here and they see the razors and the hot lather, and it takes them back to a place in their memory. People from all parts of the country come by here, and they take pictures of the shop," which is decorated with pictures of barber products and replica signs from the nineteenth and early twentieth century, from the William Marvy Company, which manufactures barber poles. "They say there isn't a place like this anymore."

While Gary loves the sights and sounds of an old-fashioned barber shop, he gets almost dreamy eyed when describing the shop's inimitable bouquet. "When you walk through the door of shops that have been around for thirty years, you smell those aromas. Oh my gosh, that smells fantastic," he said, with a big smile on his face. "When I tell that to people, they wonder what I'm talking about. I say, 'You just have to know.' Even though we've been open for only ten years, when I walk through the door first thing in the morning, I can smell the shine stand, the hair, the tonics that we use. It's starting to resonate for me."

Foust, a forty-something man with a shaved head and a soul patch on his chin, comes from a family of barbers. His grandmother's brother still has a barbershop in West Texas. His grandfather, originally from Wanette, Oklahoma, spent twenty-two years in the military. His father started cutting hair at the age of fifteen, in the early 1960s, and also worked on military bases. "Back then, you didn't need a license, like you do now," Gary explained. "You needed a scissor and a comb and you were taught by a family member. It was passed on from father to son."

Gary's father, Dewey, has owned and operated barbershops for decades. "He used to cut full-time, every single day. I remember living in Oklahoma City, when he opened Dewey's Night Owl Barbershop, which stayed open late. Everybody else closed at six P.M. He's still at it, one day a week, in Asheville, North Carolina, and totally enjoys it.

"My first job in a barbershop was shining shoes for a quarter. It was pretty cool. But becoming a barber was the last thing on my mind. When I was sixteen, I dropped out of school and went to barber school. Pretty soon, dad had me working weekends at the training base. I remember the first time I had a four-star general sitting in my chair. I was so dang nervous, I couldn't cut his hair."

With a twenty-thousand-dollar investment, Gary and Dewey Foust opened the Barber Pole in 1998, right after downtown Savannah's best-known barbershop suffered a fire and did not re-open. "We're still the only barbershop downtown," said Gary. The shop's ideal location is on busy Bull Street (a couple of blocks away from Gallery Espresso), with street traffic, tourist trolley tours, and lots of local office workers passing by every day. Today he works with his brother and two women, who are not family members, in a four-chair shop. The Barber Pole accepts only walk-ins. You sign in and you wait your turn. "There's no difference between the bank president and the guy who's servin' up sandwiches."

Despite the presence of the women barbers, the place definitely has, in Foust's words, an "all-male vibe." But don't look for copies of *Playboy* magazine here. "*Maxim* is the most risqué. I know when I have the mothers in here instead of the fathers, because *Maxim* and those other magazines are all turned around," he said with a laugh.

Proof of the popularity of the Barber Pole can be seen all over the walls: snapshots of many of the community's young boys who got their first haircuts in Foust's chairs.

"We have so many dads who are adamant about bringing their sons in for their haircuts. You watch them grow up, graduate college, get married. I'm looking forward to fifteen or twenty years down the road, when I look back on all these photos, and say to them, 'Here's your first haircut with your dad.' It's pretty cool. When I talked to the landlord about leasing this space, I told him that barbershops don't usually go out of business. They close because the guy gets old and doesn't want to stand up all day. I told him that we were a twenty-years-plus business, and that's turned out to be true."

PASSIONATE ABOUT THE PRODUCT

MOST MOM & pop store owners are passionate and thoroughly knowledgeable about their products—and the best way for their customers to consume them or use them. For example, Wassler's Meat Market in Cincinnati today serves many more prepared ready-to-eat and ready-to-heat meals because "a lot of working women don't know how to cook the meat," said Debbie Wassler, the wife of co-owner Kenny Wassler. "My husband calls me for recipes and cooking tips."

Rob Kaufelt, owner of Murray's Cheese in Greenwich Village, has noticed that among today's younger customers "there is a need for education about food. Their grandparents had the knowledge, but with passing generations, that knowledge has been lost. For example, the customers I inherited in the 1990s were the little old ladies from the neighborhood who knew everything about the cheeses and the San Marzano tomatoes that we carry—even though those women were not sophisticated and didn't have any money."

Kaufelt enjoys educating his customers because "I have a passion for cheese. The small retailers who do survive still insist on a direct connection with their products and the people who supply them. The main thing is to let the customers see our passion, that's what it's all about. Turn them on to whatever we've got going. Taste it yourself. My grandpa always said, in that [Russian] accent of his, 'Go on, take a taste.' Nothing's changed, I suppose. We tell our customers, 'Here, take a taste.' "

A major part of his job, he said is to travel the world for different kinds of cheese and bring them back to Bleecker Street for his customers to try.

"Sameness is what the larger market is about," said Kaufelt, who is married to Nina Planck, a food writer and expert on farmers' markets. "Clearly, what we're celebrating is not sameness. The cheese that you're buying today is not going to be the same next week as it was this week, because the seasons are changing. The cows are eating something different. You go to a McDonald's or Starbucks for the same thing. That's what you're there for. You come to us for the opposite experience of going to Starbucks."

Roger Bassett and Michael Strange, who run Bassett's Ice Cream in Philadelphia, wax poetic about the subtleties of their product.

Their passion for the ice cream comes from their grandfather, Lewis Lafayette ("L. L.") Bassett, a Renaissance man, an artist, and a gourmet, who studied the art of making of ice cream, and, who, like his father before him, enjoyed spending hours and hours in the basement of the Reading Terminal Market playing around until he found the perfect formula. (All of Bassett's ice cream was produced in that basement until the early 1970s.) The cousins credit their grandfather with their ice cream's inimitable taste. "He really studied the making of ice cream," said Roger. "He loved experimenting with unusual flavors. In the 1960s when Nikita Khrushchev, the premier of the Soviet Union, visited Philadelphia, they asked L. L. to make fifty tubs of borscht sherbet."

L. L. was thoroughly versed in the chemistry of ice cream. Like every other member of the Bassett family (through five generations), L. L. took the world-famous ten-day Ice Cream Short Course at Penn State University's Creamery. (Ben Cohen and Jerry Greenfield of Ben & Jerry's took Penn State's correspondence Ice Cream Short Course.) Initially taught in 1892, and given continuously since 1925, the ten-day course covers every aspect of ice cream making.

"At Penn State, they didn't believe grandfather's formula. They said it couldn't be done," Roger said with a laugh.

"As a superpremium brand, our ice cream is sixteen-and-a-half percent butterfat, compared to most premium ice creams, which are ten to twelve percent butterfat," explained Michael Strange. "The higher the butterfat—up to a point—the better the mouth-feel. Our ice cream also features a low 'overrun,' which means that less air was injected into the ice cream. Less air makes the ice cream denser and creamier. Roger and I could tell our vanilla from anyone else's from eight or ten feet away by the look and the tex-ture. We see the fat in there."

Roger picked up on that thought from Michael, noting that "the other main difference, which our grandfather worked on in devel-oping the ice cream, was the solids"—nonfat milk solids and sugar. "That's the 'secret' part of it. With more solids, the ice cream feels warmer. With less solids, the ice cream is closer to a popsicle."

Roger felt that the best part of his business is "not about the money. It's about the satisfaction of the generations who come here. We have regulars who started coming here with their grandparents, such as 'Irish Coffee Bob,' who visits several times a week. He doesn't need to order. When he sits down at the counter, we give him two scoops. As soon as he finishes that, he gets a second plate. We take a lot of pride in our product, and that's where it starts. It makes you keep going and trying to make it better. I like it when someone says, 'You've got the best ice cream in the world.' "

THE RHYTHM OF THE NEIGHBORHOOD

IN MY TRAVELS, I didn't find anyone who enjoyed what he was doing more than Pedro "Pete" Hernandez. Along with his parents, Angel and Guillermina, and his brother, Angel Jr., Pete owns and operates Los Pinareños Fruteria, an open-air fruit and flower stand on Calle Ocho (Eighth Street) in Little Havana, in Miami, Florida.

When I drove up to the shop, I could hear through the speakers a recording of Benny More, the Afro-Cuban performer, singing the Afro mambo tune "Dolor Carabali." Pete offered me a plate of the family specialty—*arroz con pollo ale chorea*—chicken and wet rice with a huge slice of avocado, which was just what I needed after my drive from Ft. Lauderdale. Sitting inside his shop, among open boxes of bananas, papaya, oranges, guavas, and coconuts, curly-haired Pete, wearing a white T-shirt with the word LOVE in large block letters, is a bundle of affable energy—loquacious, articulate, passionate.

With the open garagelike doors (just like Spector's Meat Market), the store spills out onto the sidewalk and helps define the neighborhood. From a tiled counter open to the street, while the blender steadily whirrs in the background, customers can select from an assortment of natural fruit drinks that are listed on a white board. The house specialties include *remolacha* (beet), *coco frio* (cold coconut milk), *naranja* (orange), *zapote* (sweet tropical fruit), mango, and melon. The shop's *guarapo* (sugar cane juice) is considered by many to be the best on the street. The coffee is the real deal—strong, robust, eye-opening. If you're not in a hurry, the counter at Los Pinareños Fruteria is a great place to watch the passing parade on Calle Ocho.

Pete's parents, Angel and Guillermina Hernandez, were both born in 1941 and raised in nearby towns in Cuba, in an area called Pinar del Rio, Cuba—Pines of the River (the source of the name of their shop)—that is best known as the source of some of the choicest tobacco for Cuban cigars. Both of their families were farmers.

"My mom was in a university movement, one of the many movements for democracy in Cuba," said Pete. "They were both anti-Batista [the dictator Fulgencio Batista] and anti–Fidel Castro. They wanted a third way. The way it was going with Batista was no good. But they definitely knew that what was coming [Castro] was going to be no good. They came to the U.S. around 1958. Fidel took power in 1959. My father came with friends. My mother came with her grandfather. They were not from wealthy families. They were noneducated farmers. My father washed dishes, and later opened up a cafeteria on West Flagler Street in Miami. My grandfather and my mother were renting an apartment on top of the cafeteria. That's how they met."

Angel and Guillermina and Guillermina's brother bought the store for eighty-five thousand dollars in 1968—with a two-thousand-dollar down payment and a handshake—from the heirs of Indian River Fruit, then the biggest citrus producer in north Florida. Pete and Angel Jr. both started to work as small children. "As soon as we could walk and pick fruit, we were picking. When I was five or six, I was picking avocados off the ground and putting them in a bushel. We've always picked a lot of our own fruit: mango, avocado, yucca, or malanga—all the tropicals . . . lychee nuts. There used to be mango groves around here. Now there are five-million-dollar homes. Today, we get the fruit from people's backyards, small farms, and wholesalers. A few come from abroad—pears, apples, whatever can't grow here in Southeast Florida, which is the only subtropical climate in North America."

When it comes to knowledge of the products that his family sells, Pete proudly said, "My brother and I have one hundred and fifty years of purchasing experience, through the eyes of all of our ancestors—from my grandfather, my six uncles and aunts, and my parents, who all worked here. That is the key. That's why I can guarantee the fruits to my clients. Our clients are the owners, We are here to serve the owners. If it wasn't for them walking through the door, we're gone; we're history. If there's something wrong with the fruit, bring it back. I'll give you your money back. Guaranteed. No problem. Do you get that at supermarket chains? That's our pride and our reputation. That's why we're still standing."

It hasn't been easy. In 1995, after Pete bought out his uncle's interest in the business, the wooden fruit stand caught fire, and was totally destroyed. With no insurance, it took the family three years to rebuild the store.

How did they survive? Like all successful owners of small businesses, they did what they had to do.

"We fenced up the burned property and worked in the back [of the property] by selling flowers on the corner and picking fruit for our wholesale business. We'd buy and pick, buy and pick, rebox and sell, and move around—and survive. We reopened in March 1999 with the same aesthetics, but the building is made of concrete, not Florida pine. Everybody thought we were foolish for not putting glass windows in, and sealing it up. Look around you. There are no doors here. It's like your house. You can come in and out at your will. We've held on to the roots of this part of the community, to the humble way of life."

When I asked Pete Hernandez what he liked best about working at Los Pinareños Frutería, he replied with a smile, "I don't have to wear a shirt and tie. I wear flip-flops and shorts. People ask me why I don't go into a business where I wear a shirt and tie. I worked at a law firm for seventeen years, starting as the mail carrier, and ending up assistant senior administrator and business manager of the Miami office," while still putting in hours at the fruit stand. "I'm here with my parents and my brother. The people who ask me why I'm here are people who wish that they were in this position. We are humble. We have our feet on the ground. We are living closer to the earth. Where you are standing is the earth, and that piece of land is your neighborhood. So, stick to it," he said with emphatic finality. Then he turned to a customer, and began to extol the taste of a luscious ripe mango, with the passion of a man who loves his produce and loves his customers.

8

Reinvention

The best way to predict the future is to create it.

—PETER DRUCKER (1909–2005)

Mom & pop stores are not *owed* survival because they are filling some noble purpose. There are fewer more competitive businesses than retail, which is in a continuous state of change. As William Knudsen, a twentieth-century industrialist, once said, "In business, the competition will bite you if you keep running; if you stand still, they will swallow you."

The shopkeeper receives a report card every day in the form of the daily receipts. Those stores that survive are the ones that find ways to adapt, to reinvent themselves. Every successful enterprise must adapt to change. Mom & pop stores stay in business by constantly tweaking what they do.

Bill Furst, the owner of Furst Florist in Dayton, Ohio, comes across as a mild-mannered man, but he has a steely determination that served him well in the 1980s, when he was faced with stiff competition from the large chain stores.

"One day, my supplier of foliage plants and small plants told me he wouldn't be able to service me the following week—just before Mother's Day, when I really needed him—because he was going to be busy servicing the Kmarts," Bill recalled. "Needless to say, that got me angry. But it planted a seed. I thought that independent florists deserved better service than this. So, I decided to start a wholesale division and compete with the big suppliers. I bought a box truck, and sent my son out with product to our competition, telling them, 'We are your supplier. You will have specialty product. We're not going to sell to basement florists, garage florists, or box stores.' I broke that chain."

Furst's wholesale business extends to a 125-mile radius of Dayton and has grown to be as large its retail operations.

"We're large enough to buy direct from South America," Furst said proudly. "Big-box stores get their flowers into a distribution center, and by the time they get processed and out to the field, there is a day or two along the line that is taken away from the original consumer. So, that has helped us tremendously. We used to have that cash-and-carry business. Now, we get all the specialty orders— the arrangements that have to be made by hand. Today, we deliver the majority of what we sell. When business slows in one area, you learn how to expand into other areas, to compensate for the loss. That's how you survive."

KEEP YOUR HAT ON

FURST FLORIST HAS been in business since 1905, but it's a mere babe compared to Lock & Co. Hatters, the United Kingdom's oldest family-owned—and best-known—hat shop, which has been trading in London since 1676 and is still going strong, because its owners have made sure to adapt to changing times and tastes.

Since 1765, Lock & Co. has been in the same location at 6 St. James's Street, in central London in the City of Westminster, bound to the north by Piccadilly, to the west by Green Park, to the south by the Mall and St. James's Park and to the east by Haymarket. Here's proof of Lock & Co.'s fame: Years ago, a customer from abroad mailed a postcard to the store. Not knowing the shop's location, he addressed the postcard "to the best hatters in the world, London," which ensured that it would be delivered to Lock & Co.

This warm and charming shop is a delightful example of what is known in Britain as a Grade II listed building, which means that it has special architectural, historical, or cultural significance. Tracing its origins to Elizabethan times, Lock & Co.'s fine regency shop front has a dark green door between two small, modest windows tastefully filled with merchandise. The second floor features a narrow balcony that looks out onto busy St. James's Street. The interior has the understated elegance of one of the neighborhood's many gentleman's clubs, such as Boodle's, Brooks's, and White's.

The neighborhood, where St. James's Palace is located, is close to Jermyn Street, the shopping thoroughfare renowned for its custom shirtmakers, and Savile Row, the home of the City of London's world-famous bespoke tailors. Adding to the charm of St. James's Street are neighboring establishments of high quality and repute, including Berry Bros. & Rudd (founded 1698) at No. 3 St. James's Street, which is London's oldest family-owned wine merchant; John Lobb, the boot maker (founded 1849) at No. 9; and two upscale cigar merchants, Davidoff and J. Fox.

"Our customers rely upon our knowledge of companies in St. James's and the surrounding area. We know each of our neighbors well and are therefore able to recommend their services and products," said Janet Taylor, the shop's marketing manager. "We cherish our heritage. It is the foundation from which we have grown and developed to be the company we are today."

Lock & Co. offers every conceivable type of gentleman's headwear—trilbies, fedoras, bowlers, top hats, wool and tweed caps, cashmere beanies, panamas, travel hats, riding, and sports hats. Throughout its colorful history, the shop has attracted customers from all walks of life, including officers and gentlemen from the military, politics, literature, and the arts, with such well-known names as Admiral Lord Nelson, the Duke of Wellington, Beau Brummell, Lord Byron, Rudolph Valentino, Sir Winston Churchill, Sir Laurence Olivier, Oscar Wilde, Salvador Dalí, Frank Sinatra, and Jacqueline Kennedy Onassis. Douglas Fairbanks Jr. once had a flat above the shop. There is a framed picture in the shop of Edward the Duke of Windsor in 1921, wearing his Lock & Co. Turnberry tweed cap.

The shop holds the royal warrants of H.R.H. the Prince of Wales and H.R.H. the Duke of Edinburgh. Royal warrants are issued to individuals or companies who have supplied goods or services for at least five years to royal households. Royal warrant holders are granted permission to display the relevant royal arms and the legend "By Appointment."

On my visit to Lock & Co., I was given a tour by Ms. Taylor, a fount of history behind the display of vintage bowlers, silk top hats, and military naval hats, which complement the contemporary selection of headwear and accessories such as bags, umbrellas, walking sticks, and ties.

For much of its early history, Lock & Co. specialized in military hats and caps. The "cocked fore and aft" that Wellington wore at Waterloo was made by Lock & Co. as were the hats of many of his officers. From 1800 to 1805, Admiral Nelson was a customer. His bicorn hat incorporated a unique feature—a green silk eyeshade to protect his eyesight, which had been damaged when he suffered a shrapnel wound to his forehead at the Battle of the Nile. The green silk peak was requested by Nelson's doctor so the admiral could protect his good eye while at sea.

"Our ledgers show that in 1803 a drawing was made of the bicorn indicating the position and dimension of the peak," said Ms. Taylor. "Admiral Lord Nelson never wore an eye patch, although he is often depicted with one, but whilst at sea, he did use the eye peak. His last order [which is on display in the shop], made on ninth September 1805, reads: 'cocked hat, cockade and green shade, 7 full.' He settled his final bill on thirteenth September before he left for Portsmouth and the Battle of Trafalgar against the French and Spanish. This hat can be seen on his effigy in Westminster Abbey."

Today, Lock & Co. is still family run by the descendants of the company's founder, James Lock, and a later business partner, James Benning. Two generations of both families sit on the board and are active in overseeing the direction of the business.

Taylor credited Lock & Co.'s longevity to adapting to change. "We continue to do what we've always done, which is to provide quality headwear, a high standard of personal service, and to adapt to the changing headwear requirements of customers today."

For example, in recent years Lock & Co., which was formerly a male bastion, now includes a ladies' department on the remodeled second floor of the shop, where colorful, fashionable female headwear is displayed in light and airy surroundings that form a fitting backdrop to the ladies' collection. Lock & Co. offers three different collections of ladies' hats: a couture collection by in-house designer Sylvia Fletcher, where hats can be purchased from the department or made to order and dyed to match or complement an outfit; a "Hât-a-porter" label of stylish midrange millinery; and casual headwear including trilbies, shower-proof hats, classic panamas, and sun hats. Lock & Co.'s hats are seen in the fashion shows of British designers such as Stella McCartney, Vivienne Westwood, and Bruce Oldfield.

"Today, as well as welcoming our many traditional, loyal, and regular customers, we also see a steady stream of new and young ones," said Ms. Taylor. To that end, the shop has benefited from the cool appeal of personalities and young celebrities from television, film, and music, such as hip-hop music stars Pharrell Williams and André Benjamin.

After three-and-a-half centuries in business, Lock & Co. is testimony to the truism that survival hinges on adapting to change.

THE YODA OF SODA

JOHN NESE OF Galco's Old World Grocery in Los Angeles hadn't planned on reinventing his business. Sometimes life just works out that way.

In the late 1990s, he was running a traditional, conventional Italian grocery store in a neighborhood that had lost much of its Italian residents and flavor. The store is a flat-roof building on York Boulevard, a busy four-lane street in the Highland Park neighborhood of Los Angeles. Galco's carried produce, meats, and all the other necessities, and like every other food store the usual brandname sodas such as Coca-Cola and Pepsi-Cola. But Nese simply couldn't compete on the price of soft drinks with the big supermarket chains. It was a losing proposition.

"It was cheaper for us to buy Coke or Pepsi off the shelf at the supermarket than it was to get a case delivered to us," said John. "In supermarkets, the soft drink giants dominate the shelf space and try to keep small bottlers out."

One day the Pepsi-Cola salesman came into the store and told Nese that he was going to give him the best buy he was ever going to get on a one-hundred-case pallet of Pepsi cans—$5.59 a case.

When Nese asked how much profit he was going to make, he was told it would be thirty dollars. "Thank you, but no thank you," he informed the salesman, who answered back, "But Pepsi-Cola is a demand item and your customers are going to demand that you carry Pepsi-Cola." Nese replied, "My customers are going to be happy that I was honest with them and that I told them to buy Pepsi at Ralph's Supermarket, where it is cheaper. Why would they buy Pepsi from me? For my good looks?"

The next day, the salesman returned, but this time he was accompanied by his regional manager and his area manager. "They looked around and walked out. They didn't say anything," said Nese. But after two weeks of being upset, he had a moment of clarity. "Why am I upset? I should be thanking Pepsi-Cola for reminding me that *I* own my shelf space, and they don't, and I can sell anything I want."

Even before all this happened with Pepsi, Nese's business was in deep trouble. "I was taking money out of my pocket and charging things on my credit card to keep the business going. We were right up against the wall." Desperate times called for desperate measures. Inspired by the popularity of beer from microbreweries, Nese decided he was going to start selling soda pop from small bottlers. He had always been passionate about soda pop. "When I was a kid, we went on vacation in Northern California, in a tiny logging camp called Happy Camp, near the Klamath River. It's beautiful there. There was this naturally carbonated water bubbling up from the spring. I tasted it, and I thought, 'If I could put a pipe in here, I could pipe it right to my school, and open up the water fountains, and have soda pop coming out of the fountains,'" he recalled, smiling as he savored the memory.

"When I graduated from college, my father's best friend, a man named Ben Binder, was bottling Dad's Root Beer here in Los Angeles. He had been instrumental in my getting a scholarship to the University of Southern California. Ben's business was really struggling." Before going to work full-time in his father's store, John had set up a meeting with Ben. "I had so many ideas for what we could do. I said, 'Ben, we could do a lot of things to help your business. I'd really like to work for you.'

"This was at eight thirty in the morning. He said, 'John, I'm selling my business. I'm going into escrow today. But, thank you very much.'"

But Nese never abandoned his soda pop dreams. So, when he was ready to take on Pepsi and Coke, with his business already failing, he felt liberated enough to say to his father: "Pop, if we're going to go down, let's go down doing something that I enjoy doing."

Nese was the kind of person Ralph Waldo Emerson had in mind when he wrote, "Good luck is another name for tenacity of purpose."

Nese became an expert on the micro-soda-pop industry and began a search for small bottlers from all over the United States who shared his passion and vision. A purist, he had his own strict criteria for the kind of product he would stock in his store. The pop must come only in glass bottles and must be made from natural ingredients such as pure cane sugar rather than corn syrup and essences, which are used in today's mass-produced sodas. He soon found twenty-five small brands that were still available in glass bottles; many of them had been famous in their regions of the country. When Nese first put them on the shelf of his store, they were just curiosities. "Customers would ask me why I'm carrying all these old brands that don't sell anymore. When I got up to two hundred fifty brands, people started asking me where I was finding them. Now, we have five hundred brands."

The store is known online as Soda Pop Stop, with a Web site (www.sodapopstop.com) that has helped to spread the word—and the soda pop—all over the country.

Nese actively seeks out small independent bottlers and has helped to create a network for the bottlers to help one another. As examples, he cited Plantation Style Mint Julep and Red Ribbon Original Cherry Supreme (made from real cherries), from Natrona Bottling Company, near Pittsburgh; and Manhattan Special, an espresso coffee soda that's been around since 1895, on Manhattan Avenue in Brooklyn. "The soda has the orange pulp, sediments from the vanilla beans. People see that stuff floating around and wonder if it's OK to drink."

The shop carries sodas of every conceivable flavor, formula, product, and presentation, including cucumber and rose, which is pressed from rose petals. In fact, when I visited the store, John offered me a taste of Mr. Q. Cumber, which I politely declined. (I don't like cucumber in natural form, much less carbonated.) But John thought so much of cucumber and rose that he commissioned a run of them, which he carries exclusively.

Today, many people come into the store to find regional soda pops, such as Sun Drop (complete with fruit pulp) from Tennessee, Green River from Chicago, Cheerwine from North Carolina, Fitz's Grape Pop from St. Louis, and hundreds more, which they haven't tasted since they were kids. They take a swig of the pop, close their eyes, and remember life from way back when.

"Some people said we were selling nostalgia," said Nese. "Yes, early on, the grandparents would bring their grandchildren, and point out what they used to drink. Now, it's the young people who are coming in, bringing their parents. If it was about nostalgia, it'd have been over in five years. It's about freedom of choice. Five hundred choices. Mom & pop stores disappeared because the big chain stores bought up all the distribution channels and raised the prices. In my store, it's not a situation where just two kinds of cola and two companies are controlling the entire shelf. I tell the little [soda] guys: 'Your enemies are Coke and Pepsi. They are out to destroy you. They want to close you down. As soon as they close you down, it's too expensive for anyone else to get back in business.' I tell them that their friend is the little tiny guy who sells his soda on my shelf next to theirs."

Proof that what Nese is selling is not about nostalgia are the vast array of soda pops from new companies that appeal to today's young people, with names such as Black Lemonade (with a skull and crossbones logo), Love Potion #69, Jack Black's Blue Cream Soda, and Leninade (as in Vladimir Ilych Lenin), a slightly carbonated version of pink lemonade, with the slogan "A taste worth waiting in line for."

Nese is the consummate expert. When a customer asks him, for example, for the best root beer, Nese will tell them that " 'that decision is yours. We have forty-two of them. Where do you want to begin? I have one that's the driest and the highest carbonated, and

I have one that is the creamiest, and everything else falls in between. They are all seasoned differently. Some have licorice in them, and some have vanilla, and some are this or that. What do you want?' Everybody has a different idea of what the best is. Other stores may have thirty or forty different kinds of sodas, but they don't know what they're selling."

Because he's offering such a specialty product, Nese can't match the low prices offered by mass-market bottlers. "Some people complain that it costs too much. I say, if you're buying for price, you can buy cans of soda pop for thirty-five cents in a twenty-four-pack . . . Here, you can buy a single bottle. A lady came in and said she went to Vons Supermarket to buy water and they told her that she couldn't buy a single bottle; she had to get a twelve-pack. Here, she bought single bottles of different kinds of water. I encourage single-bottle sales. It's just like going to a hardware store and the guy working there doesn't know what you need to have in order to fix something. So, what good is a cheaper price if the guy doesn't know anything?

"I want them to taste the pop first, and not have to buy a six-pack or a twelve-pack, and then stare at it six months later because they don't like it. Buy one bottle, and if you like it, you'll be back to buy another one. And if you don't like it, you never have to buy it again. People appreciate that. I feel so good when people come in here and smile. Almost everybody leaves here with a smile. Over the years, we've received letters, phone calls, and e-mails from people relating their stories of where they were and what they were doing when they had their favorite soda for the very first time."

Nese phased out of the grocery business to specialize in soda pop as well as another object of nostalgia: candy. He said, "Candy was my daughter Noelle's idea. She's responsible for a lot of what's happened here. She said, 'Dad, you should really have all the old candies.' I said, 'I know where to get them.' "

He got rid of all his produce, and replaced it with old-fashioned regional candy that is still made today, such as Abba-Zaba, Charleston Chew, GooGoo Clusters, Idaho Spud, and Clark Bars. In many cases, an entrepreneur secured the original recipe, packaging, and trademark, and started a mom & pop candy company—just like the suppliers of Nese's unique soda pops.

With his passion for the product, John Nese is not a man who spends his time in the back room of the store. He loves talking to anyone who's interested about the nuances of his soda pop. "I'm out on the floor most of the time. I want to meet the customers and I want to talk to them. I will give them as much information as they need, so that they know what they're doing. People come in and feel overwhelmed with five hundred sodas. I want people to be happy. Soda pop makes you happy."

Soda pop certainly makes John Nese a happy man. Take that, Coke and Pepsi!

GRANDFATHERS, FATHERS, & SONS

THE STORY OF Sanford Restaurant in Milwaukee, like the story of Galco's, begins with a neighborhood Italian grocery store. It takes a decidedly different turn, but with an equally happy ending.

Chef Sandy D'Amato and his wife and business partner, Angie, have run Sanford, a fine-dining restaurant, since 1989. I was intrigued with the D'Amatos' backstory, which epitomized the often complicated dynamics between and among three generations of a family-owned mom & pop store.

Sandy's paternal grandfather, Joseph, came to the United States as a young boy early in the twentieth century from Sant'Elia, a small fishing village in Sicily, outside of Palermo. Eventually, Joseph and his two brothers made it to Milwaukee, where the family opened a neighborhood grocery store around 1917. In that era, thanks to improvements in transportation of goods, consumers from all over the United States were able to find virtually everything they needed at neighborhood grocery stores like D'Amato's or Galco's. Serving their primarily Italian clientele, D'Amato's sold cheeses, olives, meats, bread, fruit and vegetables, and a wide variety of delicacies and staples. Joseph and his wife, Katherine, eventually bought a nearby building, set up shop, and moved into an apartment upstairs, following a tradition of "living over the store" that dates back hundreds and hundreds of years, when work *was* life, and took up most of the shopkeeper's waking hours.

Sandy, who was born above the store, began helping out at the age of five years with his father, Sam, and his grandfather. "I spent many of my younger days working at the store," he fondly recalled. "After school, I would take the bus from school and arrive at the store around four P.M., which gave me enough time to eat dinner at four thirty at my grandparents' next door and then help my dad through the five thirty to six thirty rush, before the store closed at seven. Not quite a full day of work. If I was tired, I'd sleep on top of the beer cases. Saturdays were a bit different as I would get to the store around nine A.M. It would take about an hour to stock the shelves with the newly arrived products, then I would wait for the noon rush."

Although a tough, prickly taskmaster, Joseph D'Amato knew food. "As miserable a person as my grandfather was, he was an incredible cook, always bringing over the freshest artichokes or fennel or whatever was in season. I was the only child in the family that he liked because I got involved in cooking. He didn't have any use for kids at all, unless they could work. But he liked that I was interested."

Joseph was constantly pushing Sandy's father, Sam, who enjoyed working with his hands and who had once been employed as a machinist. Joseph forced Sam to work full-time in the store. Although Sam liked the social part of the shop, he never fully enjoyed it. It was a grind working seven days a week and never taking a vacation. He was also a victim of bad retail timing. By the time he and his brother took over the store in the late 1960s, independent neighborhood grocers were in a downward spiral, unable to match the prices and selection of the big supermarkets. Some retailers like John Nese of Galco's found a way to adapt; others closed their doors. Sam D'Amato held on for as long as he could.

After graduating from high school, Sandy told Sam that he planned to take fine art courses in drawing and design at the University of Wisconsin–Milwaukee. Sam was pleased. "That's great," he told his son, "I always wanted to draw. I don't care what you choose to do with your life. I just want you to be happy." One thing he did not want his children to do was to work in the store. Sam couldn't have been more definitive on this point: "Don't think that the store is something you're going to do in the future. You can do anything else, but you can't have the store."

Sandy's love of food, nurtured by his father and grandfather, eventually led him to a cooking career. After graduating from the Culinary Institute of America in 1974, he worked in various New York City restaurants throughout the 1970s before moving back to Milwaukee in 1980. As a chef at a restaurant called John Byron's, he gained his first national attention in 1985 when *Food and Wine* magazine selected him as one of the top twenty-five "Hot New Chefs" in the country.

By that time, Sandy had met Angie Provencher, who was a cocktail waitress at the restaurant and later managed the place. Angie's food background matched Sandy's. Her grandmother owned her own grocery store, Martha's Foods, and was a butcher who cut her own steaks, ground her own beef, and made her own kielbasa. Angie fondly recalled working in the store when she was in high school, and going to the farmers' market in West Allis, Wisconsin, "which is the same farmers' market we buy from today."

In October of 1989, Sam D'Amato closed his store. By this time, Sandy and Angie had married, and they knew they wanted to open their own restaurant. What better place for their new enterprise than the old family grocery store? Sandy would technically be following his father's edict. He wouldn't be working in the store, but he would be working in the space.

First they had to secure financing, which is never an easy sell for a small business under the best of circumstances.

"We might as well have had a skull and cross bones on our Small Business Administration loan because we were small, nonethnic fine dining. Ethnic restaurants can get money. If you're a diner you can get money. Fine dining, the odds are horrible," said Sandy. "We had sold our house because we were going to do whatever we had to do to open the restaurant. Everybody puts together a business plan thinking of their best scenario. We put together a business plan thinking of our *worst* scenario. We went to twelve or thirteen different banks to get a loan." Finally, the loan was approved. "Luckily, this was a couple of years before the first Gulf War. Our banker later told us that if we had applied for the loan during the war we wouldn't have gotten it."

The day the banker called with the approval "I told my dad that we were going to be able to open the restaurant. Then I turned to Angie and began talking to her about something. A few minutes later, I hadn't noticed that my father had disappeared. As I went looking for him in the back of the store, I heard this loud BANG! BANG! BANG! I went to see where the noise was coming from. There was my dad. He was wielding this sledgehammer and was breaking through the back wall. He was immediately starting the demolition. He was so ready. The store is gone! The store is gone! He loved it."

Sandy's grandfather's spirit remains within the walls of the building, particularly in the cellar where Joseph D'Amato made his own wine and olive oil, and cured his own raw olives. "The smells down there were amazing," said Angie. "We put our wine cellar there because the temperature was so right for wine."

Sanford's became one of the America's great restaurants, and over the years it received national accolades from publications such as *Food and Wine*, *Bon Appetit*, *Wine Spectator*, *Chicago Tribune*, *New York Times*, and *Esquire*. *Bon Appetit* has called Sandy "One of the finest seafood chefs in the country." In 1992, he was one of twelve chefs in the nation to be personally chosen by Julia Child to cook for her eightieth birthday celebration in her hometown of Boston. After being nominated for six consecutive years by the James Beard Foundation, Sandy won the Perrier Jouet Best Chef Midwest award in April of 1996. In 2007, Sandy and Angie were given the honor of cooking for the Dalai Lama at the Madison Club in Madison, Wisconsin. Sandy, who was one of five chefs asked to prepare a special luncheon for the Benefit of the Deer Park Buddhist Center, presented slow-cooked Strauss veal breast with scalded Wisconsin morels and escarole, rhubarb essence, and warm bittersweet "intentional chocolate" tart with coffee ice cream. Certainly a meal fit for any man (or woman)—holy or sinful.

How did Sandy and Angie accomplish all this? Like everyone else represented in this book, they worked their asses off.

"The whole idea of Sanford when we opened up—and how we sold it to the bank—was that we didn't need any staff," said Angie. "In the beginning, I was everything in front of the house; he was everything back of the house. We had no overhead, no bills, no house, and we could eat there. We lived above the restaurant for the first four years. There were days when we didn't even leave the building. Sunday, the only day we were closed, we would lay in bed and watch TV. Then at six o'clock, we'd go to another restaurant and have a special meal and bottle of wine. Then we'd go home, put on the TV, and pass out. Then we'd get up and do it all over again. We had no life. Running a business, the pressure never goes away. We quit a lot. We'd say, 'I can't take this anymore.' After four or five years, we decided to take Mondays off. Having two days off gave us a life. That's why we started hiring people. Slowly, we added a person here, a person there. To this day, we know that if we need to fire someone, one of us can jump in and do that job. After twenty years, we don't want to do that, but we can if we have to."

Because the more formal Sanford's restaurant doesn't have a large enough dining room "to make hay on Saturday night," said Angie, she and Sandy diversified their business by opening a second restaurant, Coquette Cafe, which features authentic bistro fare in warm, casual surroundings. Located in the Landmark Building in the Historic Third Ward in Milwaukee (considered the SoHo neighborhood of the city), Coquette "is a place where guests could pop in any time of day for everything from French onion soup and flatbread pizza to crisp provincial roast chicken."

Their philosophy for their restaurants centers on "the product." Working in the grocery store "we had access to almost anything— and in season," said Sandy. "It gave me an understanding of what every product's season was. We'd look forward to when pomegranates were coming. At Sanford's, we don't use tomatoes unless we can get them locally and in season because the best tomatoes are those that are homegrown. When I was a kid, I remember the Italian women asking my father, 'Sammy, when's the *finocchio*—the fresh fennel—coming in?' Finocchio always held a prize place at their household holiday entertaining tables.

"My father would barely start trimming the fennel for stocking the vegetable bins before they were quickly snatched up by the faithful. During the trimming he would pick out a perfect specimen to slice up and eat raw. He handed me a slice and as I crunched into its sweet texture I was quickly repelled by the anise flavor (never being a big fan of licorice). This was at seven years of age but by the age of nine, I started to look forward to the arrival of fennel as much as I did chestnuts."

After Sandy's mom, Kathleen, passed away, Sam moved back above the store, where he had lived as a kid, and was an integral part of the restaurant—personally, professionally, and emotionally—for the rest of his life.

"He did the maintenance. He watched everything that was happening. If he didn't think a new person was working out, he would say so. And he was usually right," Sandy recalled with a smile. "He came in to the restaurant every day, until the day he died."

"YOU DO WHATEVER IT TAKES"

WHEN JACK WEISS'S father died in 1941, eight-year-old Jack became the man of the house. In order to become a contributor to the household, he began delivering the local *Pittsburgh Press* newspaper and taking jobs babysitting kids in the neighborhood, while his mother sold dresses in a women's store. When Jack graduated high school in 1951, he needed to get a job because "I had no hope of going to college," he said.

He wanted to work for the *Pittsburgh Press* as a route man on a delivery truck. The job paid $124 a week, which was pretty good money in those days. "But they hadn't hired a Jew in fifteen years," he recalled. Jack tried his luck at the local Jewish employment agency, which placed him as a shipper and packer at the Modern Carpet & Rug Company, which was owned by Norman Arluck, a fifty-one-year-old Russian immigrant. Arluck, who started out as a peddler, also owned a dry goods store in the Squirrel Hill neighborhood, where he sold sheets, blankets, pillowcases, rugs, and bath mats to small stores and peddlers.

Although he was running a mom & pop capitalist business,

Arluck, said Weiss, was involved in Labor Zionism, which was the left wing of Zionism, the international political movement that pushed for the reestablishment of a homeland for the Jewish people in Israel. Zionism had grown out of the historic Jewish labor movements of Eastern and Central Europe. Labor Zionists established local groups around the world where there were significant populations of Jews, including Pittsburgh. Arluck was a member of the Pittsburgh unit of Histadrut, a trade union that tried to organize the economic activities of Jewish workers. "His philosophy was that no one who came into his store got turned down for anything," said Weiss. Local Histadrut members held meetings of the group in the store "to discuss world affairs. It was Socialism bordering on Communism." The discussions "became my education. I was not educated to be religious. They weren't religious, but they had such a zeal for Israel. When David Ben-Gurion [the first prime minister of the state of Israel] came to Pittsburgh, I picked him up at the airport."

To look at Jack Weiss today, in his midseventies—with a neatly trimmed white beard, and dressed in a natty beige blazer, pale yellow dress shirt, and red bow tie—one wouldn't guess how hard he had to work to be in his position of prosperity, both materially and spiritually. Sitting next to Jack were his daughter, Stacy, and his son, Lou, who have been in the business since they were children. The four of us were gathered in the family's elegant, new, beautifully lit home furnishings store, surrounded by lovely woven area rugs, stylish wall hangings, and chic furniture.

But that's getting ahead of the story.

In 1951, after working at Modern Carpet & Rug for nine months, Jack (who was not yet eighteen) was left to run the business by Mr. Arluck, who went to Israel for three months. (The only other person working there was Arluck's daughter, who was the bookkeeper.) "He didn't like business," said Jack. "He really wanted to be an actor on the Yiddish stage." It didn't take long for Jack to face his first test, when a supplier brought in half a dozen short rolls of carpet, which, the supplier claimed, Mr. Arluck had bought. After Weiss paid the supplier, he discovered that he had been had. Arluck had never agreed to buy the carpet. To make matters worse, the merchandise was shoddy. Jack didn't find out that little detail until after he had sold the carpet to several people in the neighborhood. Then the phone started to ring.

"I began getting calls from customers [who had bought the carpet] that there were some tufts missing. I would go to their homes at night after work, with a crochet hook and fix the carpet myself. In those days, carpet was all woven. At the time, I didn't know that there was a special needle to fix the tufts. By the time Arluck had come back, I had sold them all. That put me in the business," said Jack.

When business was slow, Jack would travel to stores in the small towns around Pittsburgh, selling rag rugs that were made at the Allegheny County Work House. On one of those sojourns, the owner of one of those stores offered Jack a good job, but Jack didn't want to leave while Arluck was in Israel. When Arluck returned, he promised Jack a partnership in the business. In 1953, Weiss left to serve a two-year stint in the army. When he came back to Pittsburgh, Arluck, being a man of his word, took Jack in as a partner. The two men had always had an affinity for each other that transcended business. Arluck's only son, also named Jack, had been killed in World War II. Weiss had lost his own father at an early age.

Since Arluck hated business so much, Jack told him that he did not have to work anymore, and that Jack would send him a check every week for his share of the profits.

"But he came in every day and the two of us went to lunch," said Jack. "Believe me, those lunches with him were worth their weight in gold. A super guy. He and his wife were almost like grandparents to my three children."

Eventually, the partners purchased a large building in the heart of the Squirrel Hill neighborhood of Pittsburgh. They sold off the dry goods part of the business and concentrated on wall-to-wall carpet. In 1967, when Arluck moved to Florida, Jack bought the rest of the business from him. He initially catered to the large Jewish population (some thirty-five thousand people) in the Squirrel Hill neighborhood. As his reputation grew, he expanded to the rest of the city. It was a long, hard slog.

As an independent shopkeeper, Jack learned early on that "you do whatever it takes. I was so desperate to make this business work. I stayed open late and made appointments in the store with customers who couldn't come in during the day." Soon his carpet was in many Pittsburgh homes. "The women would be sitting around their mahjongg table and one would ask another: 'Where did you get your carpet?' Even though they bought the carpet from me, they'd say, 'Wayne & Weil,' which was then the prestige store in town. Eventually, *we* became the prestige store in town, and people who bought their carpet at Wayne & Weil would say they bought it at Modern Carpet & Rug Co."

Jack eventually gathered a small, loyal group of employees. "I would tell my drivers, there's nothing that you are going to do that I haven't done."

Early on, Jack started a pension and profit-sharing plan for his employees. This commitment to the people who worked for him reflected Jack's core belief in simple fairness. "I've always preached to the kids: 'There's an entitlement there for employees. You're not doing the employees a favor; they are creating a business for you.' If they had to work until ten o'clock at night, no one said a word. They didn't get paid extra for it. The next day, if we weren't as busy and they could leave at four o'clock, so be it. If we had a party at the end of the year and one of the guys got a little drunk, I would personally carry him home. I'd put him in the car and deliver him to his wife. They were a part of our family and they helped to make the business. In the same respect, we benefited. When the Soviet Union fell, my son, Lou, joked, 'I have the only remaining communist sitting across the desk from me.'"

Lou joined the business the day after he graduated from Kenyon College as a drama major. As a teenager, he had worked at the store for a couple of summers—sweeping the floors, hanging up samples, and finding ways to keep busy. "When I came full-time, we didn't have offices in the store, so for the first year, I sat at the same desk with my dad, which is where I learned the business. We have the salesman gene in our family."

On the other hand, Jack's daughter, Stacy, described herself as "least likely to come into the business." She had dropped out of the University of Pittsburgh to become a photographer and helped start a gallery with other photographers. "One day, my brother called me up and said, 'Do you want to run the blinds business?'

I didn't really. But not having a job, I said, 'OK.' That was 1982. After two years of running the blinds, I moved into carpet. I learned how to sell carpet by watching what was going on. "My father and brother were concentrating on our commercial real estate, so people got used to me waiting on them." She also began dealing with local interior designers who were shopping the store for their clients. This aspect of the business proved to be a great outlet for her design creativity and vision.

Lou and Stacy eventually became partners. (A third sibling, Ellen, is not active in the business. She became a lawyer and founded a nonprofit organization.) In the mid-1990s, when they completely took over ownership, they began to totally transform the company.

In 1997, "We were going to paint one of our stores," Lou recalled. "We thought while we're painting it maybe we should replace the sign. And then we thought maybe we should change the name. By this time, we had a different business. We were still selling wall-to-wall carpeting, but it was better goods." Lou and Stacy rebranded the store Weisshouse (*weiss* means "white" in German), which proved to be a great stroke of marketing. They created their own line of souvenir coffee cups with the simple black-and-white Weisshouse logo and commissioned the making of chocolate bars—made of crisped rice in milk chocolate—called "weisskrispie treats." (The Weisses are notorious for their love of puns.) "We'd go to trade shows and give people candy bars. Those vendors would be standing all day at their booths, so these candy bars were gold. Soon, we were on the map in the trade papers."

They eventually added area rugs, draperies and blinds, floor coverings, home accessories, and high-end furniture from vendors such as Ralph Lauren, Mitchell Gold + Bob Williams, B&B Italia, and Odegard. They moved to a new, larger, more open space, with lovely natural lighting on Highland Avenue, in the exclusive Shadyside neighborhood. Although the new store was geographically close to the old one, by all other measures, it was a long way from Jack's original business.

Today, Weisshouse has a national reputation. The company employs about twenty people, including a team of in-house designers, who create total interior looks for their clients. The store's "community" has gotten very large, thanks to local clients who are furnishing second homes in places such as Washington, D.C., New York City, and Arizona. A job they did for the North Carolina home of Bill Cowher, the former football coach of the Pittsburgh Steelers, was featured in *Coastal Living* magazine.

Although the prices of the merchandise they sell is higher than the old days, the Weisses' work ethic remains the same. "I go out to the homes to supervise the installations," said Stacy. "I'm dragging stuff in. It's a very hands-on business."

Jack is not involved in the day-to-day affairs of Weisshouse. He is often in the store, but not on the sales floor. A talented painter, he has a studio in the corner of the store, which receives the kind of natural light that an artist yearns for. His work has been shown in several galleries and museums.

Asked how their father has handled all the changes, Lou—who has left the business to devote his time to philanthropic pursuits and the family's real estate interests—said, "We've been very lucky because my father would give us our own free reign. I felt like the company was totally mine. Even in big decisions, he would generally defer. In a lot of family businesses, the passion is squashed by the founder. As a result, the next generation tends to be dispirited and not be anxious to go to work."

Stacy agreed. "What stops family businesses from growing is that the founder doesn't want to let go. You need to cultivate the ability to make decisions. We learned by stepping in and making decisions. You learn from your failures. Failure is a good teacher."

Especially when you're reinventing your business.

9

There Goes the Neighborhood

It is not the strongest of the species that survives,
nor the most intelligent, but the one most
responsive to change.

—CHARLES DARWIN (1809–1882)

CHANGES IN THE NEIGHBORHOOD inevitably force a mom &
pop store to reinvent itself. It's one of the laws of (retail)
nature.

"The neighborhood has changed" is a familiar lament. So, what
else is new? The neighborhood is *always* changing—sometimes for
the bad, sometimes for the good. Economies change. Old ethnic
groups move out; new ethnic groups move in. Neighborhoods are
affected by new commercial and housing developments, gentrification, the exodus of industries of long standing, changing tax bases,
competition from other neighborhoods and other towns. The list
goes on and on.

When I moved to Greenwich Village in 1970, it was still very
much of an Italian neighborhood, plus an assortment of hippies, a
smattering of beatniks, and students from New York University. The
newly dubbed SoHo neighborhood was just beginning to develop into
a hip area. Before it became SoHo (taking its name from its location
south of Houston—pronounced HOW-stun—Street), it was called
the Cast Iron District because of the hundreds of buildings and warehouses that featured cast-iron architectural elements. When industrial
companies abandoned the neighborhood, they left behind the spacious buildings that were filled with natural sunlight (thanks to large
windows), and were dirt cheap to rent. The whole neighborhood was

inexpensive. In 1971, a friend of mine rented a sixth-floor walk-up studio apartment on Prince Street, across from the famed Vesuvio Bakery, for the princely sum of ninety-seven dollars a month.

Artists were naturally attracted to the spaces, which were converted to lofts, and the neighborhood began to change. It didn't take long for SoHo to begin to gentrify and for loft prices to shoot through the proverbial roof. Tourists flocked to this new hip destination. Entrepreneurs opened cool shops, which added value to the real estate. Retail is the most visible component of neighborhood renewal because it generates activity on the street. Eventually there were new art galleries, hip bars, trendy restaurants, and chic boutiques. Later the area began to fill up with branches of uptown art galleries and stylish stores, such as Bloomingdale's, Prada, and Chanel. When the artists were priced out of the neighborhood, they moved to other parts of downtown Manhattan, and created new neighborhoods such as Tribeca (triangle below Canal Street), Nolita (north of Little Italy), and Dumbo (down under the Manhattan Bridge overpass) in Brooklyn. And so it goes.

Whether it's downtown or uptown, New York is in a constant state of change. Little Italy, a longtime neighborhood in downtown Manhattan, has only about a thousand Italian Americans still living there, and has been engulfed by its neighboring ethnic community, Chinatown. Today so-called Little Italy is more a state of mind than a reality. Nevertheless, the famed Feast of San Gennaro, a New York institution since 1928 that salutes the Patron Saint of Naples, continues to be one of the city's best-attended street festivals, drawing more than one million people every year. (San Gennaro also evidentally doubles as the Patron Saint of Tourism.)

Uptown in Harlem, the historically African American–dominated area at the north end of the island of Manhattan is also changing its ethnic identification. The gentrification of the neighborhood, where former president Bill Clinton has his offices, has been picking up steam over the past few years with the arrival of young urban professionals of many races, including African Americans. This new demographic is attracted to the lovely turn-of-the-century brownstone apartments (just perfect for interior renovation) as well as pricey new condominium apartments.

Harlem's main drag—the famed 125th Street—has been rezoned to permit high-rise office towers and thousands of new market-rate condominiums. In the name of "progress," dozens of small businesses were closed and many residents displaced. Low-priced, family-operated soul food restaurants, for which Harlem has long been famous, are disappearing. These eateries, which had been operated by African Americans who migrated from the South, are closing because the neighborhood's dwindling number of older African Americans are being replaced by a younger clientele (of many races) who are more interested in healthier foods or more exotic cuisine, such as Thai or Indian. When the city of New York outlawed the use of artificial trans fat for preparing food, it scored a direct hit on many of Harlem's traditional soul food restaurants that offer fare that is generally fried, salty, and fattening.

"The majority of the stores, the 99-cent stores, they're gone," Gwen Walker, a longtime resident, told the *New York Times*. "The Laundromat on the corner is gone. The bodegas are gone. There's large delis now." Instead of the inexpensive beer such as Old English or Colt 45, stores are selling more expensive imported beers. "The foods being sold—feta cheese instead of sharp Cheddar cheese. That's a whole other world."

This has been distressing for Harlem old-timers, who long for the days when they were comfortable with the faces on the street, when they knew the owners of the mom & pop shops, and the owners knew them. This feeling of dislocation, this anxiety over the loss of community identity, has been dubbed "root shock" by Dr. Mindy Fullilove, a professor of clinical psychiatry and public health at Columbia University, which is right next to Harlem. Dr. Fullilove compared this feeling of displacement to what happens to plants when they are pulled out by their roots. But in the case of the people in Harlem or other neighborhoods, they are in the same place; it's the surroundings that have been altered.

"The old order changeth," wrote Alfred Tennyson, "yielding place to new." Whether we like it or not, this is the natural flow of life, particularly urban life.

Consider Southwest Eighth Street—Calle Ocho—between Seventeenth and Twenty-Seventh avenues in Miami's Little Havana, where brothers Angel Jr. and Pete Hernandez run their open-air fruit stand, Los Pinareños Fruteria. The street is home to the Little Havana to Go souvenir shop, where tourists can buy dominos or maracas or panama hats. Visitors can stop by the pocket-size Bay of Pigs Museum, which honors the people who participated in the ill-fated attempt to overthrow Fidel Castro in 1961. Looking for a good cigar? Ask the elderly gentlemen covered in billows of smoke, playing dominos and chess in diminutive Maximo Gomez Park— named after the military commander in Cuba's War of Independence (1895–1898)—which is known locally as Domino Park. Although these days people of Cuban heritage currently account for less than half the local population, Angel and Pete Hernandez nevertheless insist that Little Havana is still "the real thing." I couldn't argue the point with Pete, as we watched a group of tourists—cameras draped around their necks—filing out of their bus to soak in the local atmosphere. From the vantage point of their open-air shop, the Hernandez brothers see this scene played out several times a day, every day.

Before the Cubans, this area had been home to—at one time or another—whites, Bahamians, Jews, and immigrants from all over the Middle East. The Bahamians, who came as laborers to help construct the city of Miami, started a farmers' market on this property, which was later acquired by a white Southern Baptist family, who later it sold it to Jewish businessmen. Cubans began migrating to what would ultimately become Little Havana in the 1940s and 1950s.

Succeeding generations often measure their success by how far away they can escape from the ghetto of their parents and grandparents. As I drove away from the Fernandez's shop down Calle Ocho, and observed all the mom & pop stores, I was convinced that this will always be a vital urban center. It already has the highest residential density in the city. But I did ask myself one question: What will they be calling this neighborhood in twenty-five years?

"It is not necessary to change," wrote W. Edwards Deming, the famed professor of management. "Survival is not mandatory."

Not mandatory, but preferred. In order to survive, mom & pop stores have learned to adapt to changing times and evolving neighborhoods—good, bad, or just different.

Newark, New Jersey, has gone through difficult times over the past several decades, but Hobby's Delicatessen has made the adjustments in order to keep going. "Newark is not what it was when my dad bought the place and when we were growing up. Many of the shops were owned by Jewish people," conceded co-owner Marc Brummer. "The nature of the neighborhood has changed. Thus the nature of our business has changed. You can't stay the same. You have to see who your customers are, and find out what they want. It's a constant, yet interesting, battle."

Marc pointed out that Hobby's workforce has radically changed over the years, reflecting the diversity of Newark.

"When you have Francisco Lopez making your matzo balls, Mohammed Hissin making your strudel, Sidney Hatcher making your salads, and Deeowhatee Moolchan filling orders for coleslaw, you know you're running a diversified organization. When I was growing up and working at what was then my father's delicatessen, the countermen I knew were named Lou Tannenbaum, Natey Diamond, and Benny Friedman."

Even though the community and neighborhood have changed, the Brummers and Hobby's Delicatessen continue to be a very big part of it. Marc and Michael were selected as the 2009 Humanitarians of the Year by the Essex County Chapter of the American Conference on Diversity. The business is busier than ever. They've adjusted to the slower foot traffic by emphasizing catering. The Brummers are famous for putting together trays of sandwiches and other delicacies, such as Hobby's Unbeatable Delicatessen Buffet, which is an array of meats and cheese, fresh rye bread and rolls, side salads, sours, and condiments, or the Hot Delicatessen Buffet comprising hot corned beef and pastrami, choice of side salads, potato chips, rye bread, and rolls.

As the population and the workforce has become more diverse—religiously and culturally—Hobby's menu has changed accordingly. Now, at this pillar of Eastern European delicacies, some of the Brummers' more popular sandwich items include eggplant, roasted pepper, and fresh mozzarella; and grilled rosemary chicken with avocado, arugula, fresh mozzarella, and tomato on twelve-grain bread.

Hobby's delivers to businesses in all the skyscrapers in Newark. They serve law firms, government offices, and the local campuses of Rutgers University and New Jersey Institute of Technology. They even have a concession at the Prudential Center where the New Jersey Devils of the National Hockey League play their home games. That's how you keep a business vital.

WRONG SIDE OF THE TRACKS

NEIGHBORHOOD DISRUPTION IS endemic all over the developed world. I saw this firsthand when I got off the train at Akishima, a city west of the central Tokyo downtown core. I was in Akishima, with a population of one hundred thousand, to visit Mr. Shinichi Nagatsuka, the forty-something owner of Nagatsuka Shoten, a general neighborhood grocery store.

Disembarking from the elevated train and walking down to the street, I was aware immediately that the Nagatsuka Shoten store, which was once on the right side of the tracks, is now on the wrong side. The "right" side is a complex of some 140 specialty shops called Moritown/ESPA, featuring a lovely and lively promenade with a cinema, a Harley Davidson store, restaurants, candy stores, several restaurants, Baskin-Robbins ice cream, Starbucks, Toys "R" Us, and the ESPA department store, which is comparable to Sears.

The development is credited with bringing more life and economic opportunity to Akishima. But the neighborhood revitalization hasn't extended to the "old town," where Nagatsuka Shoten is located, where the venerable shops used to be before the neighborhood started to change in the 1990s. Walking to the store, I was struck by how different the town became from one block to the next, in terms of the shops and the shoppers. This was the old part of town in more ways than one.

Nagatsuka Shoten has been in this location since it was founded in 1925 by Shinichi Nagatsuka's grandfather, who passed away when Shinichi was twelve years old. Ever since, it has been a pure family shop that Shinichi owns and operates with his father, mother, and sister. There are no nonfamily employees.

"From the time I was a small child, I was always working around the shop," said Shinichi. "When you have a family business, there is no such thing as a vacation. We are always working. That is good and bad. That's why I want to spend as much time as possible with my children [ages thirteen and ten], because my father didn't have the time to spend with me. The children have grown up in the store. They love eating and drinking in the store. I'm hoping that one day they will take over."

To find a way to survive, Shinichi differentiated himself from other small grocery shops by evolving into a specialty purveyor of sake, Japan's fermented rice-based beverage, which is about 15 percent alcohol. The store still carries many grocery basics, but the draw is its vast collection of local sake, which are as varied in taste and style as wine. Sake plays an important role in the rice culture of Japan and its predominant Shinto religion. As Shinichi explained, "For celebrations, sake is very important. We see our customers for happy occasions, and at funerals. Japanese food and sake always come together."

Shinichi's effort to specialize in a beverage product is not unlike John Nese's decision to concentrate on soda pop. In both cases, the owner of a mom & pop store—one in Los Angeles, the other in Tokyo—arrived at the same conclusion: As the neighborhood changes, I've got to find a way to survive.

"LUDICROUS SERVICE"

BOB MARGOLIN, WHO owns and operates Miller Lumber on Division Street in the Bucktown/Wicker Park section of Chicago, figured out how to stay alive as he saw the changes both in his neighborhood and in the very nature of the independent hardware/lumber business. "We used to be the friendly neighborhood lumberyard," said Margolin, the third generation of his family to run the store, which was started by his maternal grandparents. In the early days, the neighborhood was predominantly Eastern European, like Margolin's family.

"My grandparents spoke five languages. I learned how to swear in Polish or Russian or whatever. I learned the language of the business in those ethnic languages. There was a loyalty in the neighborhood. Ninety-five percent of my client trade was walk-in; only five percent from small factories in the neighborhood. But that equation went out the window in the 1970s when the big home centers came in, and in the 1980s with the big-box category killer retailers like Home Depot and Lowe's. I realized that customers weren't going to walk through the doors anymore."

As the neighborhood became predominantly Puerto Rican, so did the ethnicity of the contractors that Margolin was dealing with. So, he learned the language of the business—colors, numbers, names of tools, cuts of lumber, etc.—in Spanish. Still, he was perceptive enough to know that learning a few Spanish words would not be enough to sustain the family business over the long haul. Because Miller's was no longer the "friendly neighborhood lumberyard," Margolin expanded beyond the neighborhood and began focusing on generating business from more small factories.

"I saw the adversity as an opportunity. As a young kid, I read in *Grimm's Fairy Tales* about the little boy who puts his knapsack on a stick over his shoulder, and goes off into the world to save his family and seek his fortune. I never thought I'd have that opportunity. Around this time, when I turned twenty-seven, my dad, Abe, passed away. He was my best friend, my mentor, and my hero, who brought this business into a larger format, taking it to the next level. He told me, 'I would rather go out of business than have anybody lose a dime here.'

"Now I had a wife, mother, and two younger siblings and not a lot of resources. This was my opportunity to get my 'knapsack,' and start making cold calls to commercial accounts. I had once worked for a hose-and-rubber company, where I had to learn to do cold-calling, so I wasn't afraid to do that. I went to the local factories of Morton Salt, Oscar Meyer, and other big companies. I walked in to one plant and the guy said, 'Look at these terrible two-by-fours we have here. Can you do better?' I said I sure could.

I came back with fifty two-by-fours, loaded them all myself, and they were perfect. I got their business."

From there, Margolin began expanding with commercial accounts all over the city, including hotels, hospitals, schools, the Art Institute of Chicago, the Major League Baseball parks (Wrigley Field and U.S. Cellular Stadium), the United Center (home of the Chicago Bulls of the National Basketball Association), and the University of Illinois's Chicago campus. When theatrical movies are shot in Chicago, the material to build the sets is usually supplied by Miller Lumber.

"My blessing in disguise were the big-box stores. The category killers made me a ton of money. I want to get as far away from them as I can, and find guys who feel the same. We had to find our niche market where customers needed service—more than the price. I give what I call 'ludicrous service.' I tell my customers everything but no. You create customers who are spoiled. They want Miller's service.

"I find it more enjoyable to work with corporations with deeper pockets, who are willing to pay more for the ludicrous service. And you need to cherish your vendors as much as your customers because they provide you with goods and services that are invaluable. You better believe that if you are a good and loyal customer, you're going to get materials when no one else can. Those relationships are essential. In some cases, thirty years after I first called on these accounts, I'm still selling the same guys. Word of mouth is so important."

Margolin looked at his accomplishments with understandable pride, and refreshing clarity about the ways of business.

"You can't change the world. You can't say it's not fair. It *is* fair. To claim it's unfair, then you become a victim; you've lost the game. It was either find something else to do, sell, or die. We've made adaptations to that idea over the years. My greatest blessing is that I was able to continue our business, what my dad worked so hard for."

Margolin's neighborhood is in the midst of change—again—with the arrival of young, affluent urban professionals, and the hip shops, restaurants, and bars that attract them. But even as the neighborhood begins to gentrify, Margolin holds on to some basic, old-fashioned community obligations.

"There is still a minority community here with kids who don't have a lot, amidst affluence. We donate theater tickets to the local school so that the music director can take them to a play every year. When they have a cleanup project, we give them brooms and rakes. When they do plantings outside, we give them lumber for the landscape timbers. Anything they need. They are our adopted school."

The neighborhood may change, but Bob Margolin's commitment to the neighborhood and his business remain steadfast.

"A LITTLE BUSINESS NEEDS A LOT OF LUCK"

A FEW MILES away from Miller Lumber is Dinkel's Bakery, on Lincoln Avenue, where owner Norm Dinkel has been around long enough to have witnessed his north central Lakeview neighborhood go downhill and then come back up again.

Norm is the third-generation owner of the German bakery that has been in business since 1922. The shop was started by his grandfather, master baker Joseph K. Dinkel, who in 1905 emigrated from Bavaria to Chicago, where he got his first job with the Schulze and Burch Biscuit Company, which is still in business. A classic entrepreneurial immigrant, Joe, with his wife, Antonie, opened Dinkel's Bakery at 3329 North Lincoln Avenue, at a time when there were about thirty-seven hundred retail bakeries in Chicago—compared to about two hundred today, according to Norm Dinkel.

In 1926, Joe Dinkel moved his business from the east side of North Lincoln Avenue to the sunnier west side. "Everybody told him that he was going to go out of business because nobody was going to shop the west side of the street on a summer day," said Norm. My grandfather's answer was, 'Well, if they want good bakery goods, they're going to have to walk across the street.' He had a simple business model: Make the best baked goods at the cheapest possible price. High volume and hand labor. It was a German bakery, with German salesgirls, who spoke German. On Saturdays, we would have twenty-seven salesgirls. Our competitors would have meetings, and ask themselves, 'How can we beat Joe Dinkel at this game? He's selling coffee cakes at twenty-nine cents; we're selling them for forty-nine cents.'"

In 1932, Joe's son, twenty-three-year-old Norman J. Dinkel, joined the business; Norm Jr. began working there full-time in the 1960s. "When I came in, it was the same philosophy: to make it as cheap as possible."

When I arrived at the bright, spacious bakery to interview Norm late in the morning on a hot Chicago summer day, I immediately gravitated to the showcases crowded with every manner of pastries, breads, and rolls, stollen (a breadlike cake), cakes, cupcakes with thickly spread icing on the top, cookies, croissants, doughnuts, chocolate brownies, and Danish. (Many of them are still made from their original 1922 recipes.) I watched a five-year-old with brunette ringlets, holding tightly to her grandmother's hand as she gazed longingly at the cookies at her eye level. She pointed to a cookie decorated with the logo of the Chicago Cubs baseball team. A young lady behind the counter handed it to her, and she immediately ran over to a table and took a big bite. Her mouth was a smile of crumbs and icing.

When Norm met me on the sales floor for the interview, he offered me anything I wanted from that treasure trove of baked goods. Unfortunately, I had already consumed a large breakfast and wasn't the least bit hungry. Plus I could hear my wife, Marybeth, whispering in my ear: "Remember your cholesterol." When I asked for just a plain donut and a cup of coffee, I thought I saw a flash of disapproval on Norm's face, but perhaps it was my imagination.

Norm Jr. has seen all the ups and downs of this neighborhood over six decades of his life. In his grandfather's and father's day (the 1920s to the 1940s), it was "a vibrant ethnic community of working-class people who had factory jobs and jobs in the community. In the late fifties to early sixties, they built expressways, and a lot of middle-class people moved to the suburbs. By the seventies, this place was depressed. Buildings were boarded up. The homes were run-down. It was a bad scene. I wrote an article in the local paper about how important it is for the residents here to trade locally, to keep the dollars in the community. My experience has been that when things get tough, the large chains are the first to close up shop and let people go, and screw the neighborhood. They don't have any staying power. I consider ourselves as a vital link to the community."

The neighborhood began to change for the better in the late 1980s, when young people, who had been born and raised in the suburbs, wanted to experience city life. By this time "we had gotten rid of all the manufacturing, at least in this community. So, we had people doing office-service jobs. This has become a very affluent area," said Norm, who noted that Starbucks is one of his neighbors, but that they peacefully coexist.

The buying habits and requirements of the new residents forced Dinkel's to alter the way it did business.

"The family unit has changed. A bakery is geared to selling to families to share." Previous generations of customers with large families used to shop the bakery two or three times a day during the week, and work in or near the neighborhood. Now, many customers are single, couples, or families with one or two children, and don't work in the neighborhood. "Today, we're busiest on the weekends because during the week customers are working out in the suburbs or working downtown. Forty years ago, bread and rolls were forty percent of our business; now they're about three percent."

Thanks to the Internet, Dinkel's has expanded its community beyond the neighborhood and beyond Chicago.

"In the early eighties, we had people who wanted to get baked foods by mail. That was a real problem. We would get a letter every year on September thirtieth from a customer who wanted us to send two fruitcakes to his son and daughter in Australia. The cakes would go by boat and take six to eight weeks to get there. That was the catalyst for us getting in the mail-order business. Today, the Internet has been a godsend for a little family business like ours. Without increasing overhead or staffing, we have increased our sales by focusing on a limited line of products, and shipping them. We counter slow weekday sales with our Internet business. We will take orders from literally around the world to deliver cakes. That keeps us going Monday through Thursday. At lot of the customers are people who are from Chicago, but are living all over the world. I'm selling nostalgia and stability in a very unstable world. Bakery goods is a comfort food. There used to be a lot of small family bakeries in small towns all across America. They're gone. Because there are fewer retail bakeries, lots of people in this country want to buy from us, therefore the advent of the mail-order business."

Norm is a tough, no-nonsense Chicago guy, who is proud of the fact that his family bakery is still around almost ninety years after his grandfather started it. "I could list you a number of stores on Lincoln Avenue that are all gone. I don't know why or how we're still in business. In my lifetime, we've had serious survivability issues in this bakery that I'll never want to go through again. If I wasn't here, I don't think we'd be in business. The bakery business is a hands-on business. You never quit. You have to hang tough, you've got to be tough. You have to demand respect. You've got to work hard. You need a lot of luck; a little business needs a lot of luck. You have to work on the quality of the product, because that's my identifying feature. It's the product that they're buying."

As we sat in the store among all the goodies, Norm described himself as "demanding and intense. I take pride in what I'm doing. This is my business. Somewhere along the line, with my crabby attitude, I've made stars out of several young women who worked for me and who today run their own successful businesses. I tell my salesgirls to treat this business as your own. Over all the years, how many people have we employed? How many have made their living to send kids to school, to retire on, to keep the community going?"

Norm likes to give tours of the bakery to classes of young kids. "I tell kids that the bakery business is a magic show. You take flour and water and yeast and you make a loaf of bread. You take flour, eggs, and sugar, and you make a cookie. You take flour, eggs, and sugar, and a little butter, and you make a cake. We're taking basic ingredients to come up with different products. My philosophy is that you've got to make it good, so that people want to come into our store."

THE PEDDLER'S PRESCRIPTION

ABBY FAZIO, THE owner of New London Pharmacy on Manhattan's West Twenty-third Street, saw the changes that were happening in her neighborhood at the beginning of this century, and figured out how she could make an independent drugstore survive in a city where there seems to be a chain drugstore on every corner.

Fazio, a licensed pharmacist, never went to business school. She didn't have to because she learned everything she needed to know from her father and mentor, George Mouzakitis, an immigrant from Greece, who was once a street peddler. From his vantage point on the streets, George kept a keen eye on the evolution of Lower Manhattan, and filed away every bit of information and insight to make himself a success, and to inspire his children to do the same.

Peddling is really Practical Business 101. Because every culture and country has had their peddlers, they've been known by many different names. In Great Britain, they were called pedlars, petty chapmen, and hawkers. In France, a peddler was a *colporteur* (one who carries goods literally on his neck); in Germany, *hueker*; in Italy, *merciajuolo*; in Spain, *bubonero*; and in Turkey, *seyyar satici*. These peripatetic entrepreneurs roamed the open road, hawking the wares they carried on their backs or carried by horses, to consumers who lived far from the markets and shops. One advantage to traveling the countryside was being able to sell to a vast array of customers who were geographically distant from each other.

For the most enterprising of people, peddling was a stepping-stone to shopkeeping. In the seventeenth century, most of the unpretentious village shops were opened by former peddlers. In the late nineteenth and early twentieth centuries in America, immigrant peddlers and street vendors were able to get their first foothold in the economy with a modest investment in a pushcart and merchandise. In 1910, over half the peddlers in the United States were immigrants. Pushcarts could be springboards to even greater accomplishments. Bob Dylan's grandfather, Zigmond Zimmerman, was once a street peddler in New York before becoming an insurance salesman. In 1881 in Pottsville, Pennsylvania, Moses Phillips, a Polish immigrant, and his wife, Endel, sewed shirts by hand and sold them from pushcarts to the local coal miners. Twenty years later, their son, Isaac, joined forces with the Dutch-born John M. Van Heusen to form the apparel company Phillips-Van Heusen Corporation, which today owns a wide variety of labels, including Calvin Klein and Michael Kors.

The men and women who sell ice cream or hot dogs or pretzels or gyros on the street are the direct descendants of such peddlers.

Abby Fazio's father, George Mouzakitis, was a hot dog vendor with a pushcart in Washington Square Park in Greenwich Village. Mouzakitis and his wife, Theodora, moved to the United States from Greece in 1966, uneducated and unable to speak English. "But they worked hard," said Fazio, echoing a familiar refrain. "In the busy hot days of the summer, my brother, Speros, and I would carry ice and sodas to them. They used to work at the art shows around Washington Square Park, which introduced my brother and I to the creative side, the melting-pot side of Manhattan."

With the money that Mr. Mouzakitis made selling hot dogs, he bought a coffee shop inside the main Midtown Manhattan post office on Eighth Avenue, where Fazio and her brother worked part-time.

"My father had made enough money," said Fazio, "to build a small eighteen-room hotel on the Greek island of Corfu, which is where I'm from. He had a gut feeling to buy the property, which is by the sea. My father's dream was for all of us to eventually move back to Greece, run the hotel, and live happily ever after. But that hotel wasn't big enough to support us all. My brother, who graduated Hunter College with a chemistry degree, went to Corfu to expand the hotel. He added more rooms, a bar, a swimming pool, and he built the family a house. My parents retired there."

Fazio is a neighborhood girl who started working as a cashier at the New London Pharmacy when she was sixteen. The original store, which took its name from the nearby London Terrace Apartments, opened in the Chelsea neighborhood in 1961 at 300 Eighth Avenue and moved to its present location at 246 Eighth Avenue in 1976. She gradually rose up the ranks, from prescription clerk to technician to pharmacist, and eventually became a partner.

By 2000, Chelsea was experiencing gentrification, and the rents were going up for both residential and commercial space. As the neighborhood began to be inhabited by designers, artists, stockbrokers, both men and women, "I knew that Chelsea was going to go up," said Fazio.

At the time, New London was, in Fazio's words, still "a typical, independent drugstore." As more and more chain drugstores started to move into the neighborhood, New London's other two partners retired early. "They thought the competition would be the end of us. They didn't see the upside, only the downside."

Fazio drew upon the lessons her father had taught her. Although he reached only the sixth grade, "he coached me on business. He has good business instincts. That's where I get my customer-service skills. My father was aggressive and ambitious. I have those qualities. The best advice he gave me was to think big. In order to make money, you have to spend it. My ambition and ideas in changing this store all come from my father. He always took little risks. For example, with the hot dog stand, he started out at another location, not in the Village. He talked to different people, mainly Italian, who coached him to go into Washington Square. He was networking, even if they didn't call it that back then."

Armed with that knowledge, Fazio did not back down from the competition. "We competed," she said. "We had good wholesalers. We tried to bring in the customer by having a lot of things on sale. Once they're in here, we can show them our service, fill their prescriptions. We saw good sales volume in our business."

Early on, Fazio made her thirty-eight-hundred-square-foot store an integral part of the neighborhood by responding to the concerns of the local residents.

"When the AIDS epidemic hit, we started taking courses about medication for AIDS, so we could talk to doctors and patients. We affiliated with different clinics," she said. Through word of mouth, people learned that New London's staff was knowledgeable about the disease and that New London was carrying the first major drug, Retrovir, an anti-HIV medication that prevents HIV from altering the genetic material of healthy T-cells. "Even though the AIDS epidemic was obviously a terrible thing, it helped us."

In 2003, Fazio and her co-owner husband, John Fazio, decided to change New London from a traditional American neighborhood drugstore pharmacy to a European pharmacy "where you can get service on every end." Fazio and her team "gutted the store and renovated it during the night so that we wouldn't close the store.

I was too afraid of losing the patients, which we still did, but they eventually came back."

The handsome-looking store has hardwood floors and a sleek look. Although there are many products on display, it doesn't feel crowded, and customers don't feel hurried to get in and out. Upstairs from the pharmacy is a three-thousand-square-foot luxury home emporium, which is called New London Luxe. With its sleek, classic furniture and wall coverings, the space resembles a private, elegant European designer sitting room or pied-à-terre, where customers can buy unique home and lifestyle products such as handmade Murano glass stemware.

The New London staff is composed of twenty-six full- and part-time employees, including three full-time and one part-time pharmacists and a full-time nutritionist, as well as a makeup artist and a perfumer. To help her customers find their best course of treatment, she offers consultations with the nutritionist and herbalist in a private room off the selling floor. Fazio travels the world on a regular basis to find organic tinctures and creams, phytonutrients, homeopathic remedies, herbs, supplements, and natural skin-care products that are not widely distributed. "I'm always hunting for great little brands. I believe in the small vendors. I have one line that consists of four products that a woman makes in her kitchen. My competition is not the chains. They've tried and failed to bring in European products and natural products. They don't have the counseling to be able to speak to the patient, so it doesn't work. Very few people just pick up an item that they don't know. But with the help of our nutritionist and our homeopath, our customers will pick up not one thing but five things. Once they see success and they can go off their prescription medicine, they come back for more, and they spread the word." Fazio and her staff work to educate their customers on their nontraditional products. "In the beginning, we had to convince people not to take Contac or Co-Tylenol, but to take something that I brought in from Germany or London. I became more of a buyer, counselor, and manager."

Her faith in alternate treatments came from her father, who "believes in herbal and natural medicine, and that you don't have to go to a doctor for a prescription," said Fazio. "You can go to a pharmacist and he'll aid you for your cold before you try an antibiotic. When he was working in Washington Square Park, my father would go into Chinatown and meet with Chinese doctors. He had a book about herbs. He would boil anything and drink it because he believed in it. He took care of his diabetes for twenty years without a pill, just herbal medicine."

With its location near the famed Chelsea Hotel on West Twenty-third Street, New London gets its share of prominent artists and performers. One day, the actor Ethan Hawke came into the store "and he looked horrible," Fazio recalled. "He was performing in town and he was losing his voice. I gave him Vocalzones, a throat lozenge, which makes your voice clearer. It's good for anybody who talks a lot. I helped him regain his voice. I didn't know who he was until after he left, when the girls in the store told me."

As its fame has spread, New London has been getting more and more business from the Internet. "We're sending packages all over the world, which is amazing to me. Why do they pick New London in Manhattan? I'm sure they can probably find the product in Europe or Australia." Fazio answered her own question by pointing to the increasing popularity of her Ask Abby column on www.newlondonpharmacy.com, where she answers e-mail queries about skin care, medication, even love triangles. The store and Fazio have been featured in many publications, including the *New York Times*, *Elle*, *New York* magazine, and *O, the Oprah* magazine.

Despite her store's international renown, Fazio knows that the most important customers are her loyal regulars from the neighborhood. She has never lost sight of the fact that New London Pharmacy helps make the Chelsea community what it is, and she believes in doing what she can to help the community.

"We have a longtime customer whose dog, Audrey, had cancer," Fazio told me. "Her expenses for the drug treatment for the dog were going to be twelve thousand dollars, which was more than she could afford. The customer was a photographer. We asked her to take a picture of Audrey, and put it on a poster to ask for donations. Whatever she got, New London would match. Chelsea is a dog place. We gave biscuits to the dogs of the owners who come into the store. The campaign raised almost five thousand dollars, which I matched. Later, Audrey and I were the official ribbon cutters of the New York Dog Walk for Cancer. The publicity and enthusiasm, for the dog being a survivor, gave people hope. That was so good."

Fazio, whose daughter, Eleni Argyros, has joined her in the business, still works the sales floor, to stay connected to her neighborhood. Her father told her that it's important for the customers to see her in the store.

"Sometimes, I ask people why they purchased a product here, when I know they work uptown and can buy it there," she said. "They tell me, 'Because I can come in my sweats and you don't give me an attitude.' "

THE CHANGE IN A CHANGING NEIGHBORHOOD

MARCIE TURNEY AND Valeria Safran, who own five businesses on the street where they live in downtown Philadelphia, represent the change in their changing neighborhood, which had previously been a run-down area that was rife with prostitution and homelessness. These two thirty-something life partners and business partners—like so many young entrepreneurs all over the United States—are helping to change and revitalize their neighborhood block by block.

Safran, a native of Lancaster, Pennsylvania, had taught eighth-grade Spanish for three years, but "I didn't see myself doing it for very much longer," she said. In 2000, she took a part-time waitressing job in a Philadelphia restaurant, where she met Turney, who was born in Wisconsin and grew up in the Pocono Mountains region of Pennsylvania. Turney, the restaurant's chef, attended the Restaurant School at Walnut Hill College in Philadelphia, and had helped to open several eateries in town.

"At that time, the restaurant we were working in was in a bad part of town," Safran recalled. "But people still came to the restaurant. We saw that if you have something to offer and people like it, they will come to you.

"When I was trying to figure out what I was going to do, a friend asked me, 'What do you imagine yourself doing five years from now?' I said I would have a cute little shop. I'd be getting out of my Land Rover with my baby and checking on the shop and making sure everything was fine. I didn't know how to put together a shop, so I started doing research. I called Marcie, who had been involved firsthand in starting up small businesses. I knew she was good at design and I knew I would be good at organizing it. I said I wanted to open a store and asked her if she wanted to open it with me. She said, 'Sure.' She's a risk taker. I ended up giving my notice to the school, and I then began waitressing full-time."

Over the next year, they worked together in the restaurant, saved their money, and looked for a location for a shop. "We started going to shops in every city that we could, and see what we liked. I had worked at Crate and Barrel and the Gap, where I learned a lot about customer service and other aspects of business," said Safran.

Meanwhile, a developer whom Safran had known of started buying up buildings and revitalizing the South Thirteenth Street area. Part of that revitalization included recruiting aspiring entre-preneurs who wanted to open up boutiques on the narrow, cozy street. Safran and Turney fell in love with a space that was available.

"We couldn't afford Rittenhouse Square or Old City [the upscale neighborhoods of Philadelphia]. This area was in the center of the city. The rent was cheap and the developer helped you build it out, to do the things you don't really know about the first time around."

They wanted to open a unique home furnishings shop with well-designed and affordable furniture and accessories for every room in the house. But when they tried to get money from the Small Business Administration, the reaction was, " 'Oh, you want to open up a trin-ket shop,' " Safran recalled. She decided to do a little creative financ-ing. "I was getting these zero percent interest cards in the mail. I have perfect credit. I figured out that I could get fifty thousand dol-lars in credit cards at zero percent and not have to pay it off for a year. So, I did that." She and Turney kept working at their jobs in the restaurant, so they could pay off the credit cards within a year. They did it in six months, and didn't have to pay any interest.

In October 2003, they opened their store, called Open House. It was such an instant success that by February 2004, they doubled their size by taking the space next door. "The people who live in the area were so happy that we opened up a shop like that," said Safran. "There was nothing like it in the neighborhood at that time."

Philadelphia Style magazine praised Open House's "hip collection of contemporary designs from around the world . . . [that] perfectly matches the tastes of city dwellers with a penchant for elegance."

By 2005, they were ready to add new challenges. They both love Mexican food and wanted to open their own Mexican restaurant. They found a space across the street from Open House and launched Lolita, a fifty-eight-seat contemporary eatery. "Val came up with the idea of selling traditional and flavored and seasonal margarita mixes by the pitcher for BYO [bring your own]," said Turney. "People bring their own tequila. We call it BYOT. [A Pennsylvania State Liquor Store is conveniently located around the corner for customers to buy tequila.] We've got eighty-year-old women, on their way to the theater, bringing their own bottles of tequila, and we supply the margarita mixes. I love the intimate settings of small restaurants. I love the open kitchen, so you can see the people making the food."

Lolita's margarita has been called the best margarita in Philadelphia by *Philadelphia* magazine.

Gradually, their neighborhood on South Thirteenth and Chestnut streets in Center City Philadelphia started to change. It even has a new name: Midtown Village. Another restaurant opened, with a big splash of advertising, which brought even more people into the neighborhood. Other stores and restaurants began to open.

The two women were hardly done with their entrepreneurial efforts. In August of 2006, they added Grocery, a prepared food and catering market on the corner of South Thirteenth and Chestnut.

"I'd always say, 'I just want some good soup or salad,'" said Safran. "That was the inspiration. We always ask ourselves: 'What's the void?' If there's something you want, and it doesn't exist, you do it. Grocery was meant to be the opposite of a supermarket. The same people come in every day. Prepared food is more expensive, but that's our customer. They know that it's all made here. It's all going to taste good. We establish that kind of relationship with people. We've had the same staff there for a long time. We have a staff that has been with us opening all these businesses. They don't leave. We take care of them and they take care of us."

In 2007, they opened Bindi, which they describe as "a modern Indian BYOB restaurant." It is located across the street from Lolita and next door to Grocery. Bindi is named for the brilliant red powder that Indian women dab on their foreheads in celebration of their energy and strength. "We love Indian food," said Turney. "Around this area, there are only traditional buffet Indian restaurants. No one said anything when two white women opened a Mexican restaurant. But here, opening an Indian restaurant, people would ask, 'Who is your Indian chef? What's his name? How much is your buffet?' All the stereotypes. It's none of that. It's modern, upscale Indian."

The couple continue to add to their retail collection on Thirteenth Street. In 2009, they opened their fifth business, Verde, which is an urban flower, garden, and chocolate shop, with a chocolate kitchen in the rear of the store where customers can watch artisanal chocolates being made by hand.

"We enjoy opening things and creating new things. That's why we have five totally different businesses," said Safran, who said they take pleasure in the challenge of creating shops that "you wouldn't find in other parts of the city."

The couple credited the support from the community with their success.

"We will see some people two times a day," said Turney. "They'll shop at Open House in the afternoon and then we'll see them for dinner that night. People want to be in this neighborhood. All of our little dreams are right here on this street. It's become more than we ever expected."

Sitting at a table with Safran and Turney in an empty Bindi, before the restaurant opened for dinner, it was easy to see that the two women complement each other well. They each pick up on what the other says, and often complete each other's sentences. The easygoing Turney, with her round face and ready smile, called herself "the chef, the plumber, the maintenance person. I'm the dreamer."

Safran, more angular and intense, picked up on that comment

and said, "I do everything else: organizer, manager, businessperson, worrier. It's a good balance. We do different things. I feel that if you're in business together—whether personally or professionally—it's better that you aren't interested in the same things. You fight less. She doesn't worry about the business end of this because she knows I'm taking care of it. Both of us get frustrated at different times. We rarely fight, but every once in a while. I can't worry about her issues. I have to worry about all these other things."

Turney added, "We need to pull ourselves away and trust other people, so we can relax. We pick each other up."

The couple share an apartment on South Thirteenth Street, so they are literally living above the store(s). That proximity can be a challenge because "the customers expect you to be everywhere at all times. We both work really hard. People who open businesses don't realize how much you have to work. It's your life. You're not going to just sit at the bar and drink with your friends," said Safran.

"If there's a problem, someone calls one of us," Turney said with a smile and a what-are-you-going-to-do shrug. "After all, it's a mom & pop business."

PART III

STORIES FROM THE COMMUNITY

10

Connection

I am of the opinion that my life belongs to the
community, and as long as I live, it is my privilege
to do for it whatever I can.

—GEORGE BERNARD SHAW (1856–1950)

Rᴇᴛᴀɪʟ ᴍᴀʀᴋᴇᴛꜱ have always been the social and economic
center of the community because they're places to see and be
seen, to buy and sell, to talk and listen, to be entertained, to taste
something new, to hear something new, to mingle with friends
and business associates, to debate civic life, and to find out the
latest skinny on the community.

"Local gossip is what wakes me up in the morning," said Pete
Hernandez, with a grin. The co-owner of Los Pinareños Fruteria in
Miami's Little Havana neighborhood added, "I love being here in
the morning and seeing my clients, hearing their stories, finding out
what happened yesterday. This is priceless."

Maya Angelou, in her autobiography, *I Know Why the Caged
Bird Sings*, wrote movingly of her grandmother's country general
store in Stamps, Arkansas, which was formally called the Wm.
Johnson General Merchandise Store, but everybody just called it
"the Store" (with a capital S). Until she turned thirteen and "left
Arkansas for good, the Store was my favorite place to be. Alone
and empty in the mornings, it looked like an unopened present
from a stranger." The Store, which was located in the heart of
the black area of Stamps, "became the lay center of activities . . .
On Saturdays, barbers sat their customers in the shade on the porch
of the Store, and troubadours on their ceaseless crawlings through

the South leaned across its benches and sang their sad songs of The Brazos while they played juice harps and cigar-box guitars."

The agora in Athens, sixth century B.C., was the beating commercial heart of the center of the city (the acropolis was the religious center), and the barbershops in the agora were the "center of the center," where news was exchanged between customer and *tonstrina* (barber), along with a haircut, and the occasional dentistry and bloodletting, just as they are today—except, of course, for the dentistry and bloodletting.

Gary Foust, owner of the Barber Pole, relishes his shop's location in the heart of his downtown Savannah community. "It's so nice to see the same people that walk by and wave. They stick their head in the door and say hello. Everybody stops in my shop to find out what's going in the neighborhood, which is pretty cool. People want to know what businesses are moving in or moving out. They stop in for recommendations for restaurants, or driving directions, or even computer repair. I don't know how I know all the things I know. How did I remember all this stuff? If you get me outside this shop, I don't remember diddly. But, when I'm behind that chair, and they come in and ask, I'm a different person."

When it comes to barber-chair discussion, Gary enforces just one rule: no religion or politics, because "it helps to keep things on an even keel. If someone asks me about a political race, I'll say, 'I haven't really been following it too closely.' I steer the conversation to the weather, or what you've been up to, or how your family is doing."

For a couple of centuries, the country store was the social center of the United States. The reasons were many, but one of the big ones was a lack of refrigeration in homes. Because people couldn't store much food, they made frequent trips to the store, which had the extra benefit of enabling them to stay in touch with the neighborhood. Bob Wassler of Wassler's Meat Market in Cincinnati recalled seeing "local people in the store almost every day to get their meal for the day, and then go home, because there wasn't that much refrigeration. You knew everybody in the community." With Wassler's, that connection to the community continues to the present day. Not long ago, a young girl came into the store and noticed a picture on the wall of Bob's father waiting on a customer in the 1940s, and remarked, "I think that customer is my grandmother."

As Gerald Carson wrote in *The Old Country Store,* "Other methods of distributing goods came along to serve better the needs of the motor age. None ever equaled the original Pa and Ma store as a social [and] commercial institution." Some country stores had a fireplace for people to gather 'round, to read the local newspapers, and to just hang around. Sounds nice, but there were some storekeepers who were not thrilled with hosting these often nonpaying habitués. Consider this lament from one exasperated merchant in nineteenth-century America: "I am a storekeeper and am excessively annoyed by a set of trouble-some animals, called Loungers, who are in the daily habit of calling at my store, and there sitting hour after hour, poking their noses in my business, looking into my books whenever they happen to lie exposed to their view, making impertinent inquiries about business, which does not concern them, and ever and anon giving me a polite hint that a little grog would be acceptable."

You won't hear that kind of complaint from the wonderfully named Misty Morningstar, the proprietor of Morningstar Coffee House in Glendale, a central Oregon town with a population of nine hundred. Misty told me that she and her husband, Paul Farnhan, "know and/or are related to almost everyone that we see every day."

Misty and Paul, who moved to town from Los Angeles in the 1980s, operate two businesses in a three-thousand-square-foot former hardware store. Morningstar Coffee House occupies the front half of the store; W-P Capital is in the back part. W-P is the home of Paul's company, Commander Board, which provides aluminum changeable signs for small, independent businesses all over the United States—including five in Glendale.

In 2003, Misty saw a need in Glendale "for a nondenominational, smoke-free place that was comfortable and homelike for people who didn't go to the bar or the church. We wanted to reestablish those community feelings. Before, when we would walk around in the evening, there were always televisions on in everybody's living room. Nobody was talking to their neighbor."

In response, she opened Morningstar Coffee House, which is more than a coffeehouse. It's a place where "all day long, there are groups of people—some churchgoers, some not—who just love to come in and talk to each other around our little wood stove, which is a central place to gather and try to solve world problems." Misty added a free book exchange, where people who bring in two books are allowed to take one new one. The store offers live music, including the use of five pianos. A local brass ensemble occasionally plays for the town on a warm summer night. "We put chairs on the sidewalk and have a lot of fun." All of these attractions "completely changed the environment of this town. It was a logging town. There was no real elevated thinking. We provided a place for that to happen."

Every Friday morning, a creative writing group meets at the coffee shop for lessons from the wife of the pastor from the local Presbyterian church, who is also a junior-college-level writing instructor.

"One time, one of our women, Alice, didn't show up for the class. We all said, 'I wonder where Alice is.' After the writing group meeting was over, some people went over to check on Alice. Turns out, she had had a stroke that night. They would not have found her had we not had the writing group. That was pretty cool."

Misty continues to work part-time as a registered nurse, and her medical experience comes in handy in her shop.

"I got a telephone call at home last week from a customer who told me about a lady friend of hers who was traveling from California to Washington state. The lady friend had run out of her blood pressure medication and couldn't get a refill unless a nurse checked her blood pressure and contacted a doctor. The next day, she came to the coffeehouse and I took her blood pressure, so she could get her refill. While she was in the store she bought a book."

Misty gets phone calls that cover a vast array of questions. "People will ask, 'Is it OK to burn in our yard today?' 'I can't breathe, can you come check my oxygen breathing machine?' I love the fact that the people in the community know we're here, that we're meeting this wide variety of needs. It's given me a great opportunity to minister to the local community that I love. I don't make a lot of money doing it, that's why I work part-time as a nurse. But it's just the funnest thing I've ever done."

Morningstar Coffee House is also a distribution point for deliveries from the Costco Warehouse store in Eugene, Oregon, which is about ninety-five miles away. Some sixty-five families (as well as the high school, churches, and fire department) place their orders for groceries and other products—such as washers and dryers and refrigerators—with Morningstar, who then faxes the information to Costco for delivery the following week.

"We have big 'grocery store day' at the coffeehouse, when the big Costco truck arrives. We divvy up the orders and charge ten percent on top of what they buy. It's been a wonderful thing for Glendale. I tell some of my customers, 'You have a business, you could do this, too, and have it brought to your business.' They say, 'No Misty, we like going through you.' "

Misty has five employees, including two daughters, Laura Brady and Emily Morningstar-Brady, and a son, Jacob, who are all in their early twenties. Laura and Jacob are volunteers for the Glendale Rural Fire Department and Glendale Ambulance, while Emily is the fire department photographer. Misty told me a story that encapsulates all the roles that her family and her mom & pop store fill in their community. A group of motorcycle riders had stopped at Morningstar for some coffee before taking a back road to the town of Riddle, about forty-five miles from Glendale. Twenty minutes later, Laura and Jacob answered a call about a motorcycle accident on that back road. When they arrived at the scene, Laura began giving medical treatment to a fallen rider. When the injured biker opened his eyes, he looked up, saw Laura, and said, "I know you. You just made me a latte."

CONNECTING WITH YOUNG PEOPLE

MOM & POP shops serve many purposes within the community, including employing young people. How many of us got our first job working for a small independent retailer? A good owner must know how to be a good boss.

Judy Davis of Gallery Espresso quipped that her previous career as a trainer of horses has been a great help in scheduling her two-dozen part-time employees, who are also students at the nearby Savannah College of Art and Design. "I used to have to do the training charts on the two-year-old horses. I equate scheduling a bunch of students with keeping a bunch of two-year-olds on track. I know which students not to schedule for Friday morning, because I know that they are going to go out on Thursday night, which is the last day of classes every week. I know they will be worthless on Friday morning. I don't tell them that. I just schedule them for a time when I know that they're going to be the most productive. They respect me because they know how much thought I put into the scheduling and what's going on in their lives."

Judy's daughter, Jessica Barnhill, told me, "A lot of students come to my mom for advice because she's a good listener."

When students ask Judy for advice, she'll give it, but, Judy said, "I always have that hole card: 'You better call your mother.' Sometimes, their parents will come in and say, 'We really want to thank you. Our daughter told us that she was having a bad week and she talked to you and you helped her.' I'm older than most of their parents, but to the students, I'm ageless. It's like they think their parents are older than me because they are their parents. They think their parents have lost touch.

"This place becomes home base for these kids, who are in school and away from home. They are rolling in here at some time during the day, even if they're not working. They are meeting up with the other people, or exchanging a few words. It becomes a hub. Some days, some of the stuff that takes place is just hilarious. We're more of a family. I have my alumni who are spread all over the country. One of the girls who worked for me for four years is having her first baby and she e-mailed me the sonogram."

Frager's Hardware's co-owner John Weintraub raised two children in the store's Capitol Hill neighborhood in Washington, D.C. "Most of the people who work here live in the neighborhood," said co-owner Ed Copenhaver. "We used to get a lot of young people to work here because John knew them through their parents. We wanted local kids working here, because it makes our job so much easier. Most of them are smart, quick, hardworking. Hiring the young kids is a valuable asset. Not only does it enhance us in the community, but it certainly helps us in our business."

Colin Powell was a neighborhood kid in the Hunts Point section of the South Bronx in New York City, which he described in his autobiography, *My American Journey*, as "heavily Jewish, mixed with Irish, Polish, Italian, black, and Hispanic families." Through much of high school and college, Powell worked part-time at a family-owned neighborhood store on the corner of Westchester and Fox streets, called Sickser's, which sold baby furnishings and toys. Powell was close to the Sickser family and maintains the relationship to this day. "We knew the store was never our future; we were employees," Powell told me. "But we felt a part of that family. Being part of a working family—not just your own family, but a family of people you're working with, in order to support themselves—I learned some things about getting along with people; even some days when you didn't get along with them. If they do well, you do well. If you do well, they do well.

"The next thing I remember from Sickser is you do what they tell you to do. You work hard. You have a boss. The boss wants you to unload a truck; you unload a truck. He wants you to clean the merchandise; you clean the merchandise. He wants you to put together a bike; you put together a bike. Standards, working hard, giving the king his due. There is nothing dishonorable about it. Any work is honorable, as long as you're doing it well, and as long as you're making a living by doing it. I took that into the army. They gave me lots of jobs I didn't like, but they never gave me a job that I didn't do my best at. That ethic came out of New York City and came out of Sickser's."

A COMMUNITY CENTER

ALTHOUGH CHUCK AND Dee Robinson of Village Books don't have children of their own, they are certainly parental figures to the young people they've hired over the years. Chuck believes that "a business should return something to the community. It should be an integral part of the community. Our identification in the community is through the store—even though we are involved in a lot of other things. We have people who are interested in working here because we are locally owned and community based. Employees volunteer in the community. We're involved in the literacy council, women's care shelter, etc. A lot of people who are attracted to the book business come with some of those values."

Dee said that she and Chuck look for potential employees "who are friendly and interested in people, who are interested in books and who are readers, because that's the product we are dealing with. They need to understand what a service business is. We've been blessed with hiring good people who have stayed for a long time and have lots of years of experience."

To its customers, Village Books is more than a store; it's a community center. "What's thrilled us the most is creating the kind of store we wanted and have the community embrace it. Now, it has a life of its own," said Dee. Proof that the store is a community center is that when local companies are trying to lure prospective employees to relocate to Bellingham, they bring them to the store. "People tell us that one of their main determinants in moving to Bellingham is Village Books."

Carla Cohen and Barbara Meade's Politics and Prose bookstore gave their northwest Washington, D.C., community an identity as one "that respects and love books," said Cohen. "The community has built the store." When they first opened, they declared that Politics and Prose would be "a bookstore and more." If would be a gathering place "for people who are interested in reading and talking about books. We've been able to survive by playing to our strengths. Books are the same in every store. What can we offer that's different from just a book? We have a knowledgeable staff and they like books and will talk about books."

But the partners understand that they're not only in the book business, but also in the entertainment business. The store is an integral part of the Washington, D.C., literary community. From the very beginning, they brought in local authors to discuss their books. As a popular place for author appearances (particularly well-known politicians, pundits, policy wonks, and journalists), it has achieved a measure of fame as a frequent setting for those author appearances that are regularly shown on C-SPAN2's *Book TV*.

"C-SPAN has found us very easy to work with," said Meade. "Their lights are permanently installed in our ceiling. They can set up in fifteen minutes."

"I always give new bookstores this piece of advice: You always start with local authors," said Cohen. "Of course, we're very lucky because there are hundreds of people in this area who have written books. We were able to get some authors who were fairly well known and would also bring in authors who were unknown at that time, like John Feinstein [*A Season on the Brink*]. The first national person we had was J. Anthony Lukas [*Common Ground*]. I. F. Stone [the investigative journalist] was a neighbor. Herblock [Herbert Block, the Pulitzer Prize–winning editorial cartoonist and journalist] signed books for us the first year we were open. Seymour Hersh [Pulitzer Prize–winning journalist and author of *My Lai 4*], Haynes Johnson [*Sleepwalking Through History*], Jill Krementz [*How It Feels to Be Adopted*]. Authors clamor to come here. We read enough of their books to present them intelligently. They know that they're going to be treated with respect, and that there's going to be a good audience who are going to ask them good questions. We have more than ten events a week—more than any other store in Washington. We have a community of people who know each other. Eight different book groups meet in the store. We would have more if we had the room."

(Village Books also has many in-store author readings. Chuck Robinson proudly pointed out that his store once hosted a reading by first-time novelist Mackenzie Bezos, the wife of Amazon.com founder and chief executive officer, Jeff Bezos, who was a part of the audience.)

Politics and Prose also has an annual day trip to Frank Lloyd Wright's most famous residential building, Fallingwater, outside of Pittsburgh. "We get about forty-five people. It's a way for people to become friends and more solidly link with the store."

Both women feel that having a connection with customers is crucial to their longevity. They cement that relationship by working the sales floor as much as possible, particularly during Christmas.

"People love to be recognized. That's a big thing in Washington," said Carla, to which Barbara added, "You have to be visible, to be out of the floor. A customer recently said to me, 'I haven't seen you in a while. Where have you been?' I've been back here in the office. But, it's a reminder that you have to be visible."

MOM & POP POLITICS

MEADE WAS OF the opinion that "a mom & pop store would be a good school for future politicians. There are a lot of skills that they could learn in local retailing, which they can take to a political level."

She's correct. Take Margaret Thatcher, the former prime minister of Great Britain, whose father was a grocer from Grantham. According to her biographer, Hugo Young, Thatcher "often testified to the inextinguishable merit of having served in a shop . . . and having watched the meticulous reckoning of income and expenditure."

The father of Mario Cuomo, the two-term governor of the state of New York, also owned a tiny grocery store. Andrea Cuomo was a Neapolitan immigrant whose store was in South Jamaica, Queens—a poor Italian, black, German, Irish, Polish neighborhood. Cuomo has written that by watching his dad tend the shop he learned about "the dignity of work and man's instinct to survive by his own hand wherever possible. No monk bearing the inscription 'to labor is to pray' could have taught us more."

Abraham Lincoln was a better president than he was a shopkeeper. In 1833, he and his partner, William F. Berry, opened a mercantile business in the village of New Salem, Illinois, but it eventually failed. Honest Abe did have the reputation of being fair. As the story goes, after discovering that he had shortchanged a customer by six cents, he followed her home to pay her back.

Gary Locke, who is the secretary of commerce in the Obama administration, is the first Chinese American in U.S. history to be elected governor of a state—Washington state. As a young boy, he saw firsthand how his father's small grocery store, Florentia Street Market, in a middle-class Seattle neighborhood, "was a community focal point, a gathering place," Locke told me in the office of his law firm in downtown Seattle. In the late 1920s at the age of twelve, his father, Jimmy, who was born in China, came to the United States. After growing up in Seattle, he was drafted during World War II, and as a member of the Fifth Armor Division, he was part of the Normandy invasion. He landed on Utah Beach a few days after D-Day. After the war, he returned home to own and operate Sadie's restaurant in Pike Place Market before opening his store, where Gary and his two sisters worked all through high school.

"School kids would hang out in front of the store," recalled Gary, who's a graduate of Yale Law School. "People would get off work and stop off at the store on their way home. They would sit on boxes of canned goods, chatting away among themselves or with my dad, having a soda pop, or smoking a cigarette. My dad had a portable oven to heat up hot dogs or ham-and-cheese sandwiches. A lot of times, they would eat the sandwich right there, sitting with my dad, and just chatting. There was a barber shop next door. People would leave the barber shop and then come into the store to check in with my dad, to get the news of the community."

Jimmy Locke taught Gary "that personal touch: trusting customers and people, taking an interest in their lives, beyond just the sale of the merchandise. 'How are you doing? What are you up to?' He always took an interest in the kids who would come into the store for candy, and was patient with them as they tried to decide which candy they wanted. So, when I meet with little kids, I'll bend down to their level and see what they're up to. When I was governor, I always tried to have town hall meetings and meet with small groups of people and find out what issues they were concerned with. I'd go into a town and meet with the local Democratic leaders over lunch or coffee and get their ideas and observations. We'd declare a particular town the Capital for a Day. The cabinet, the top staff of all the state agencies, and the key people from my office would go to different communities throughout the state of Washington. They would meet with the local officials responsible for their respective policies—law enforcement, trade and economic development.

"At the end of the day, we'd have a big barbecue of hot dogs and hamburgers. I'd go around and mingle and chat with people as they ate. All the cabinet people would fan out and eat at different tables. We'd hear their concerns, criticisms, and questions, and refer them to the right person or agency or department. I learned that kind of community retail politics from my dad, who is a better schmoozer than I am. He would have done great in politics in a different era."

Gary Locke's is a great American story. His grandfather arrived in the United States at the turn of the twentieth century and worked as a houseboy for a family in Olympia, Washington, where he washed dishes, swept floors, and helped in the kitchen, in exchange for English lessons. Two generations later, in 1997, his grandson was elected governor, where he sat in the state capital—Olympia, Washington.

THE SOUL OF A COMMUNITY OF SOUL

WILLIE EARL BATES isn't running for political office. But it sure looked that way as I sat at his Four Way Restaurant in Memphis, and enjoyed my lunch of fried catfish, fresh turnip greens, and candied yams. I watched the man "work" the room full of happy, chatty, laughing, lunchtime customers seated at tables covered in green checked tablecloths. Dressed in a black baseball cap, blue work shirt and jeans, and a black apron, Willie Earl glided across the Four Way with a coffee pot in hand, happily refilling cups and, in his words, "spreading the good vibes."

The restoration and operation of the Four Way has been a family affair, Willie Earl told me. His wife and co-owner, JoEllen, a retired teacher of business education, serves as bookkeeper and accountant. Their son, Roman, a graduate of Ohio State University, "did much of the legwork in setting up the business," said Willie Earl. "He also worked as cashier, server, cook, maintenance person, errand person, and in whatever capacity was needed." Daughter Patrice Bates Thompson, a graduate of Xavier University in New Orleans, helped to prepare and schedule employees, as well as lend a hand where needed. Son-in-law Jerry Thompson and grandchildren Rashaan and JoElle do the same. Willie's sister, Barbara Payne, who spent most of her working as an elementary school teacher before retiring, can be found at the cash register, with a friendly smile to greet each customer.

Ever since its founding in 1946, the Four Way has been a gathering place for this part of Memphis, a spot where you can eat good food, meet good friends, and participate in community fellowship. Preachers, politicians, judges, teachers, students, and just plain folks from the community have always eaten at the Four Way. Men and women have met their future spouses at the Four Way. When LeMoyne College, which is located down the street, won the 1976 National Association of Intercollegiate Athletics basketball championship, they had their celebratory meal at the Four Way.

"When visitors from out of town would come into Memphis, they would stop by the Four Way. People left messages for each other here," said Bates. "This is where Dr. King ate one of his last meals before the great Mountain Top speech down at Mason Temple. Just like a great artist needs a canvas to draw a great picture, people need a great institution like the Four Way to meet and dine. Dr. King would come to the Four Way in the midst of his struggle, when he needed a place to steal away, a place to think, a place to regroup, a place to assure him, and give him the energy and determination for a new day."

When asked to define soul food and to explain the power of soul food to his community, Willie Earl smiled knowingly and said, "The mother or the grandmother goes in the kitchen, and takes whatever she has, puts her best effort into it, puts the flavor into it, and makes a delightful meal that is motivated by love and a desire to give to her family something that's enjoyable, that comes from the soul, and from the spirit. She's cooking because she wants to make her husband—who had worked all day—happy. She's cooking because she wants to give her children—who have been in school all day—something to look forward to.

"You put your best effort into it. That's what we do at the Four Way. We attempt to give people a replenishing: a change of pace that allows them to quench their thirst, satisfy their appetite, and to get the full measure of joy in food, conversation, and nourishment. I attempt to make the best selection I can for the nourishment of the body, because I believe that the Lord maketh man and the Lord

provides good food. If you put that food in your body, you'll operate in the spirit of the Lord. I believe that your body heals itself and
maintains itself by putting the right things in your body. That's my
motivation: to help to restore and carry on the tradition of providing good food at the Four Way."

Late in life, Willie Earl took on this big job; restoring the Four
Way has not been easy. As I listened to this proud man talk about
his mission in life, it was clear that he has put everything—
everything—into making it work.

"I didn't need to come to the Four Way after thirty-seven years
in the insurance business. I wanted somebody else to come along
and keep this great institution alive. You're talking about something far beyond a normal venture—beyond money. I would like
to do other things in my life, but I want to see the Four Way continue . . . and be here for generations." He sees the potential for a
promising future. "There is a lot of land here that can be redevel-
oped. We're networking with the Stax Records Museum. We're
part of the Memphis neighborhood that is being marketed as
Soulsville USA." As he spoke, Willie Earl gently moved from the
philosophical side to the practical side of his "best effort." He
talked about his determination "to make this restaurant work. This
is one of the greatest challenges I have ever entered into in my life.
It's not about gobbling down food real fast. It's a matter of taking
in all the nourishment of this place—the food, the environment,
the spirit of an institution like this. I'm determined to do whatever
I can. This is my commitment: I will do everything, including taking my last breath, to make sure this institution is a success."

When I asked him what he's learned from his efforts, Willie Earl
said, "Nothing worthwhile is free. There's a price that you pay for
success. Whatever business you see that is prosperous, it didn't come
easy. Somebody spent time in the trenches. Somebody sweated.
Somebody sacrificed. Somebody gave their last measure of effort to
make it possible." Then he paused for a moment. "I would have
never thought that it would take so much energy, so much sacrifice,
so much time, so much determination, so much sweat, so many
tears, so many sleepless nights, so many early risings, to get to even
this spot."

As I sat across the table from Willie Earl, and noticed a couple of tear drops fall to his cheek, I reached out and put my hand on his forearm. He put his hand on my forearm. There we were: two sixty-something men, one white and one black, holding onto each other over a piece of sweet potato pie.

But then as he looked around at the many lunchtime patrons, Willie Earl smiled and made a sweeping motion with his arm. "Even as we talk, you see in here a diverse group of individuals. I see that despite of all we've been through, the sacrifice is paying off."

Adjacent to the front door of the Four Way is a Landis No. 12 shoe-stitching machine that dates back to the 1930s. It's about five feet high. On either side are large control wheels that look like miniature automobile steering wheels. Although it's caked with rust, it stands on the property with a venerable industrial dignity. When Willie Earl was growing up in the 1940s, his mother would leave the house on Saturday mornings on her way to a full day of cooking in her employer's home, and sometimes she would drop off a bag full of her children's shoes to be fixed by the local shoemaker on that Landis No. 12.

"When we bought the Four Way and began the renovation, that machine was still in the shoe shop, but no longer in operation. The needle still had thread hanging from it. The machine reminded me of when I was growing up and how well the community was stitched together in love, and how people helped one another. I wanted to take that machine and symbolize an appreciation for those individuals who helped us along the way. It's a reminder for persons to never forget the community that you grew up in. Give back to the community."

YOU GOTTA GIVE TO OTHERS

THAT SAME SENTIMENT is shared by the Brummer brothers, who own Hobby's Delicatessen in Newark. Marc, Michael, and their father, Sam, have always believed in giving back to the community.

"Our father and mother taught us that if someone comes in off the street and says, 'I'm hungry; I haven't eaten today,' they always walk out with a sandwich," said Michael. "No one walks away hungry from Hobby's. No questions asked. I don't ask you for money. My father has always told us, 'People are hungry every day.' When my daughter was four or five years old, she would see us give food to people and she asked me why we did that. I said, 'Because people are hungry.' That's where it starts with us in the community. You gotta give to others."

The walls of Hobby's are filled with plaques and citations from local Newark groups—of every race, creed, religion, and national origin—to which the shop has donated food.

"You gotta run the business. You gotta make a living," said Marc Brummer. "It's a tough business to run. You have to run it like a businessman, which gives you pleasure when it's going well. But real pleasure—and the happiest feeling—is when you're giving back, when you're doing something for somebody. For example, we have a program with Volunteer Lawyers for Justice, a group that does pro bono work for people who can't afford a lawyer. We sell 'sponsorships' to sandwiches. For example, instead of ordering the Number Five on our menu—corned beef, pastrami, Russian, and coleslaw (our most popular sandwich)—the customer would order the sandwich by the name of the law firm that paid to sponsor it. For one day, we donate ten percent of our proceeds to the organization."

Starting in 2004, to support U.S. troops stationed in Iraq, the Brummers began Operation Salami Drop. For a ten-dollar donation, customers at Hobby's can send salamis to people in the military. "We wanted to do something for the troops in Iraq," said Michael. "When my father served in World War II, he got a salami from home. We don't twist people's arms for money. People just come up every day and give us money to send salamis. Corporations will read about it and we will get a check from them. Companies do fund-raisers. It's apolitical. Some of our biggest contributions have been from people against the war. It's a chance to show the troops that you care about them." After four years, the Brummers have sent more than twenty-four thousand salamis (over twenty-four tons) to members of the U.S. Armed Forces.

IN GOOD TIMES AND BAD

THE BEST MOM & POP stores provide an emotional connection to the community, through times of happiness and sadness.

"My drivers tell me what a great job they have because of the happiness that they distribute," said Bill Furst of Furst Florist in Dayton. You go to someone's home and you see a smile, rather than someone who's aggravated. It's been rewarding for us to see the families—the parents and grandparents—who have been our customers over the years. At holidays, I love to see people standing in line at the cash registers to get my product. Every floral arrangement that goes out of here has an impact on the community. Birthdays, wedding anniversaries, and funerals. We deliver the flowers to patients in hospitals. We deliver sympathy arrangements to help people through trying times, to let them know that they they're being thought of at a time of sorrow. The days after the funeral and the visitations can be a very lonely time. So, I like to send a little floral arrangement to the family with a card that says, 'Thinking of you.'"

Almost all the mom & pop stores would agree with Georgine Uyesugi, who told me that her family at AA Jewel Box in Tustin, California, "doesn't necessarily look at our customers as customers. They are family."

That sentiment has not been lost on her son, Steven Uyesugi, the third generation of his family to work at the Jewel Box, who noted that when his grandfather, Mas, ran the store, "people obviously came in because they needed jewelry or to have their watch repaired. But part of what they came for was companionship and someone to listen to what they had to say. My grandpa was a good listener. He felt a part of the community, but it was more as a friend to the person on the other side of the counter. He wouldn't just talk to them about jewelry. He'd talk about what was going on in their life. It was a different kind of mind-set. It was more of a get-together with friends than a retail jewelry store. That's what a lot of people remember. They came here to see friends, and do some shopping in the meantime as well. To meet with customers wasn't to sell them jewelry, it was to spend time with them. That was his way of doing a retail business. So, when they came in, they weren't coming into the Jewel Box; they were coming in to see Mas, which is a big distinction. Customers still refer to our first names instead of the name of the store. They get a cell phone call and the person calling asks where they are. They'll say, 'I'm at Allan's; I'm at Mas's.' They don't say, 'I'm at the Jewel Box.' "

Steve has a favorite story about the part the Jewel Box plays in his community.

"Early on in my career, my family and I went to the Cheesecake Factory for dinner on a weekend. From across the room, I recognized a guy who had bought an engagement ring from me a few weeks before. We watched him, from across the room, propose to his girlfriend. (She accepted.) He came in a couple of weeks later, and I said, 'How was the Cheesecake Factory?' He was surprised at the question because he hadn't noticed us in the restaurant. That scene hit home for me about what I'm doing and why I'm doing it. It reminded me that I do love what I do, and those kinds of experiences make it all worthwhile."

Georgine described Mas as "a great role model. He never hurried a customer along. If the customer wished to talk about the family first, that was fine with him. We're interested in how our customers' lives are going. If there's a problem, is there anything we can do to help you? That's what we like to do."

While we spoke, Georgine paused for a moment, turned to look at her husband, Allan, leaned forward in her chair, and said in a soft voice, "We have a longtime customer whose wife was gravely ill. Because of her illness, she retained a lot of fluid, and her wedding ring got very tight on her. It was very important to her to wear her wedding ring. Allan went to the hospital with his tools and cut her ring off for her. He took it to our bench man in L.A. to fix it for us. He worked late hours to do it. Allan brought it back from L.A., took it to the hospital, and put her ring back on her finger. She eventually passed. It meant a lot to our customer, who was our friend. We've grown up with these people. To us, that's what you do. There's no question. You just do that."

That same sentiment is shared by Joe "Swing" Flamini and his wife, Rose, who have lived and worked all their lives in Mahanoy City, Pennsylvania, where they each own and operate separate mom & pop businesses. Swing has a barber shop and Rose runs a beauty salon in their coal-mining town in the northeast corner of the Keystone State. They have both been in business for more than forty years, thanks, in great measure to their individualized, personalized service.

"You learn a lot in this business," noted the personable Swing, who used to play clarinet in a swing orchestra. "The first thirty years, I was a talker; the last ten years, I'm a listener. I've heard a few confessions in my time. Psychologically, when you cut someone's head continuously, it's a very easing type thing. After three or four years, they become very comfortable with you. Sometimes they say things that they never even knew that they said. I never repeat anything, and neither does Rose. We don't even tell each other."

Swing and Rose, whose fathers came to the United States on the same boat from Italy, met and later married (in 1954) in the Italian church in Mahanoy City. Their roots are deep in this community. Swing and Rose take their commitment to their clients way beyond the chairs in their shops. When one of their clients passes away, they are asked by the bereaved family to do the client's hair for viewing in the casket.

"They were all my friends," said Rose. "It is an emotional thing to deal with someone you loved. I love to do their hair so that they look so beautiful when they leave. Everybody goes out with style. When they had been in my shop, they were happy all the time. When I look at them in the casket, I feel that they are going to their Maker, that God is always there. He takes good care of them, and I want to make sure that they look good."

11

Hard Times

There is no education like adversity.

—BENJAMIN DISRAELI (1804–1881)

ALL OF THE STORE OWNERS I met while working on this book had to deal with adversity at one point or another. Some faced economic and physical threats that almost destroyed their shop and jeopardized their future. In almost every instance, the community helped to save the store.

Jack Weiss, the owner of Modern Carpet & Rug Company (which today is called Weisshouse) in Pittsburgh, told me about one chilling incident in the 1960s.

"During the civil rights era, my wife, Andi, and I were very active in the marches and other things," said Jack. "We were pro-busing, pro-integration. We were willing to put our kids on the bus. We were going to go on the bus with them. We felt that this was a way to have integration, and that some sacrifice had to be made."

The Weiss family home was known as a magnet for all sorts of people in Pittsburgh. According to a profile of the family in a local Pittsburgh magazine, "Entire neighborhoods were nourished physically and emotionally in the Weiss family kitchen."

"Our house on Beacon Street became central for everything: Sunday brunches, meetings, etc. Everybody came for nourishment, to be fed. This was a personal thing, which had nothing to do with the business," said Jack. "I credit my wife, Andi, more than me. She taught at Hillel Academy and the Yeshiva and those kids were always there at our house. My kids' friends were always there. My wife, being as good-hearted as she is, was constantly having people over."

One day back then, when Jack was working in his store, "These two women came in, and said they wanted us to sign an anti-busing petition. I said, 'I can't sign it. I'm pro-busing.' We were among the few in our synagogue who were pro-busing. They said if we didn't sign, they would organize a boycott against our store. These are Jews telling me this! I said, 'You can do what you feel you have to do, but I will not sign.'"

The Weisses had just bought a big house on Beacon Street, "and I was a nervous wreck," he recalled. "We used to have family meetings. I asked the kids [who were then young teenagers] how they felt. I told them we could lose the house. The consensus was that we stick to our principles. If we lose the house, we lose the house.

"It was frightening. But, after ten days, there was a backlash to the boycott. People who didn't need carpet came in to buy carpet. I sent Tony, the measure man, out to a house, and he'd call and say, 'Jack, this woman wants carpet for her bedroom. It's in good shape.' I'd call the woman up and I'd say, 'I appreciate it. But I can't sell you carpet you don't need.'"

The Weiss family was willing to sacrifice what they had for what they perceived would bring about the greater good. They dealt with intolerance head-on, and came out of the experience much stronger—as a family, as a business, and as a part of their community.

"Adversity is the trial of principle," Henry Fielding once wrote. "Without it, a man hardly knows whether he is honest or not."

The Weiss family continues to be deeply involved in Pittsburgh philanthropies. They contribute to dozens of charities, schools, and causes that cut across religious, racial, ethnic, and gender lines. There's hardly a silent auction in Pittsburgh without a Weisshouse rug in it.

The same Jewish employment agency that helped Jack get his job with Modern Carpet & Rug in 1951 is still around, and Andi works there, helping to find jobs for Russian immigrants. "It's come full circle," said Jack.

TRIALS BY FIRE

BILL FURST, THE fourth-generation florist from Dayton, Ohio, knows what it's like to have his entire family business in jeopardy.

In 1970, when Bill was thirty-two, he took over Furst Florist from his father, and for the next six years, "I borrowed all the money I could to upgrade the shop," he said. Unfortunately the shop caught fire in 1976 and was completely destroyed. Even more unfortunately, it happened in February, right after Valentine's Day—the busiest time of the year, with Easter, Mother's Day, graduations, and weddings all coming up. "All of our wedding orders burnt."

But the community rallied around Furst's to help save the florist that had supplied the flowers for their births, their parties, their proms, their weddings, their anniversaries, and the funerals of their relatives. "Everybody came together, including the phone company," Bill marveled. "It was amazing how the folks in the community came out and offered help. People offered to loan me money. Fellow florists gave me containers and other supplies, which got us up and going. We set up tables along the street. We were closed for only six hours. By mid-October, we were in our new building."

Hobby's Delicatessen has dealt with the changes that the city of Newark has gone through since the wholesale migration to the suburbs in the 1950s, when the city's population decreased from 363,000 to 266,000. (My own family left Newark during that period.) In July 1967, the tensions of that long, hot summer didn't escape Newark, where a riot broke out, resulting in twenty-six people killed, fifteen hundred wounded, sixteen hundred arrested, and ten million dollars in property damage. More than a thousand businesses were torched or looted, including 167 groceries, most of which never reopened.

Sam Brummer, the owner of Hobby's, remembered that night vividly. "The windows were smashed in places all around here, but this place was never touched. There was a group of rioters marching down Branford Place, and they were told: 'This is Hobby's.

Don't touch 'em.' I was always fair to black people. To me, I don't see color."

For a long time after the riots, Newark was in ruins, but Sam Brummer was unwavering in his decision to continue operating there. "I always had hope for Newark. It's always been good to us. We've always done well here."

In 1991, Hobby's had an electrical fire that destroyed the restaurant. The Brummers knew they were going to continue in business, but they didn't know if it would be in the same place in downtown Newark. They considered a move to the suburbs. They fielded offers from big office buildings in Newark. A change was tempting, but "eventually, we realized that it would be a better fit for us to stay here," said Marc. "That was a very difficult time for us. We got enough money to reopen. The money that would have gone to our salaries went right back into this place."

They considered a lot of cosmetic changes, which would have made the store more modern. But would the restaurant just be Hobby's in name only?

"A reporter from WBGO, the local radio station, said, 'What I love about Hobby's is that you walk into 1950s Newark.' After that, we couldn't make the changes. We're a delicatessen and that's the bottom line. It has to have that feel. It will always have that smell, but it has to have that feel," said Marc.

The smell and the feel are all-important, even to the customers who don't remember the 1950s or 1960s, but who appreciate the retro ambiance for its authenticity. Hobby's does not pretend to be anything other than Hobby's. The community, the regulars, were happy that Hobby's wasn't leaving Newark. The family's decision to stay was a vote of confidence for the beleaguered city. The Brummers put up a sign that read YOU CAN'T KEEP A GOOD DELI DOWN.

"We were closed for nine months," said Michael Brummer. "We had customers call every week just to find out when we're opening. I walked around Newark with a sandwich board at lunchtime. People would stop me and ask, 'You're really opening?'"

The return of Hobby's was practically a holiday for certain segments of Newark's population. Local TV news channels covered the official reopening, which drew a big crowd, including the mayor of Newark. Instead of cutting a ribbon, they cut a salami.

As part of the opening-day promotion, all the food was on the house. Nevertheless, said Michael, "We still took in five hundred dollars that day because people insisted on paying. People said, 'I want my food! I haven't had this for nine months.' Every day, for the next three weeks, we would get here at five in the morning and wouldn't leave until seven thirty at night. There were lines out the door. You talk about celebrity customers. Owners of big businesses in Newark were standing in line for an hour just for a table. We had to turn down orders because we couldn't physically make them. We got so many plants with good-luck notes, and 'Thank God you're back.'"

Looking back on how Hobby's and the community responded to the fire, Marc said, "If there was ever a question as to what we meant to the community, it was answered then. When I think about how people reacted, I still get tears in my eyes."

SHOTS IN THE DARK

TWO SONS OF grocery store owners had their lives turned upside-down when their fathers were shot while working in the store.

When Gary Locke, the former governor of the state of Washington, was just finishing law school, his father, Jimmy, was severely injured in a robbery attempt in his shop, Florentia Street Market. "It was really touch and go," Gary recalled. "We had no health insurance. Mom had to take care of Dad. I had two younger siblings still at home. She closed the store for about a month and a half. But the neighbors took up a collection just to help my dad. The 7-Eleven, which had just come into the neighborhood, had a kitty for my dad on their counter, too. The community banded together. There was this tremendous outpouring of support and good wishes for my dad."

Barry Schwartz, the former chairman and chief executive officer of Calvin Klein, Inc., got his early business education working for his father, Harry, who in 1950 opened grocery a store in Harlem, on Lenox Avenue between 118th and 119th streets.

"In those days, they called it a supermarket," said Schwartz. "It was thirty-five-hundred square feet of selling space, with a full produce department, full butcher department, frozen foods, etc. Today, with the advent of the bigger supermarkets, you'd call it a bodega, but back then it was a supermarket. Calvin's father was a Harlem grocer as well, on 138th Street and Lenox Avenue—twenty blocks away. Most mornings, my father and Calvin's father met at the coffee shop on the corner of Bainbridge Avenue and 205th Street, had their breakfast, and took the train into Harlem. Neither of them drove a car."

As a young boy, Barry began working in the store on Saturdays, doing odd jobs, such as "pushing shopping wagons out of the way. My first salary was two hours for seventy-five cents. It wasn't thirty-seven-and-a-half cents an hour; it was two hours for seventy-five cents," he said with a laugh.

After he graduated high school at age sixteen, he became a full-time employee, training under his father, who "believed in teaching me the business from the ground up. I spent the first six months in the frozen food case, which was probably the worst job in the whole store. Then he made me a produce man. I shucked corn, and stacked collard greens, and learned how to set up a produce department, whether it was trimming lettuce or stacking apples or pears, or cutting watermelons so that the seeds don't show. I spent about a year in the produce department. I took to that and I really liked it. Then he tried to make me understand what the butcher part of the operation was all about. That was a disaster. I did not do well with that at all. I guess I had a fear of those great big band saws. I remember cutting oxtails, and beef liver. The whole front of my white gown would be red from the blood."

Schwartz, who had intended to follow in his father's footsteps, told me that "everything I learned about business in my entire life I learned from my father. He was a hardworking guy who worked fourteen-hour days, six days a week. He was very good at explaining to me how you should interact with your help. He told me, 'Never ask somebody to do something you wouldn't do yourself.'

That included sweeping the floors, stacking shelves, or moving a crate that was in somebody's way. He led by example. He was of the school that the customer is always right. Don't get into fights with them. He'd say, 'You get into a fight with a customer, they're going to walk out and forget about it, and you're going to be aggravated all day.' That was a valuable lesson. That was my education. I didn't go to college. People would ask me what school I went to, and I would answer 'Harlem U.' "

Barry was drafted into the United States Army in July 1964, and was sent to Fort Dix in New Jersey for basic training. Three months later, on October 15, 1964, Harry Schwartz was fatally stabbed in a holdup in his store.

"There were a couple of thousand people at the funeral," Barry recalled. "Half of them were neighborhood people who had shopped with him for so many years. We had a tremendous amount of our clientele on welfare. People would struggle in between welfare checks, which they got twice a month. He always gave them credit. The outpouring of support we got from people in the neighborhood was incredible. To me, it said a lot about my father's character."

Barry was discharged from the army and returned to take over the store. He was twenty-two years old.

Calvin Klein, Schwartz's friend from early childhood, was trying to break into the fashion business as a designer of women's apparel. To make extra money during this time of struggle, Klein worked the cash register in Schwartz's store on Saturdays. Klein was at a frustrating point in his career, questioning whether he should continue to design clothes. Schwartz suggested a backup plan for both of them. They could become partners in the grocery business. "We would open stores, and we would be supermarket barons," said Schwartz with a smile.

But when Klein told his friend that he couldn't give up his dream, Schwartz responded by loaning Calvin ten thousand dollars to launch his own company. (Schwartz would later give Klein an additional twenty-five thousand dollars.) While Schwartz had intended the money only as gesture of support, Klein was adamant that they were partners in the new venture, which opened officially on March 18, 1968, the day before Barry and Sheryl were married. They moved their apparel business into offices on Seventh Avenue, in the center of Manhattan's garment district, and Klein eventually produced his first small collection of ensembles—dresses or skirts, blouses, and coats. Schwartz continued running the grocery store in Harlem.

But everything changed on April 4, 1968, when Martin Luther King Jr. was assassinated in Memphis, Tennessee. There were riots in Harlem, and Schwartz's store, like many others in the neighborhood, was wrecked. After he arrived in Harlem and looked at the devastation, "I filled up four shopping bags of what we could salvage," said Schwartz, "and I threw the keys into the rubble and never went back."

Schwartz joined Klein in the apparel business, about which he knew absolutely nothing. He soon discovered that "business is business; the basic principles are the same. You want to keep costs down and quality up. I had to learn the apparel business, and I had some great help from people who were really kind to help explain it to me." The two childhood friends built Calvin Klein into one of the most famous brands in the world. In 2003, Schwartz and Klein sold Calvin Klein, Inc. to Phillips-Van Heusen Corp. for $430 million.

When asked what mom & pop store lessons he took with him to the fashion business, Schwartz told me, "We had two brands of turkeys. One of them was really expensive, the other wasn't. My father would always say, 'They'll forget the price, but they'll remember the taste. Make sure you give the customer a quality product.' Calvin used to say that one of the great things about going partners with me was that I didn't grow up in the apparel business, so I didn't know the wrong way to do everything. I didn't know the shortcuts—the ways to cut corners—and that was a big advantage. The only way I knew how to do it was the right way. I learned that from working in my father's store."

FROM ONE LITTLE PIZZA RESTAURANT

WHEN DANIEL CARNEY was seventeen years old in 1948, his forty-six-year-old father, Mike, passed away suddenly, leaving a wife, seven young children, and a neighborhood grocery store on the east side of Wichita, Kansas, appropriately named Carney's Market.

From the age of twelve, Dan had been stocking shelves and delivering groceries on his bicycle to his neighbors on the east side of town, which was predominantly Catholic. After his father died, Dan (the oldest son and the second-oldest child) ran the grocery store with his mother, Margaret, through the rest of his high school years and four years of college. While in graduate school, he and his wife and three children (they would eventually have four more) survived, in part, on food that couldn't be sold to customers, such as bruised, overripe fruits and vegetables, and dairy products and meats that were past their use-by dates.

Dan always had a desire to own his own business, a desire he inherited from his father. Before opening the shop in 1944, Mike Carney had toiled for twenty-one years at the Wichita facility of the giant Cudahy Packing Co., one of the nation's leading food suppliers. Although he eventually rose to the position of supervisor, "My dad had been very unhappy working for someone else," Dan told me, as we sat in his office in Wichita, Kansas. "He always told me: 'If you have a choice, be in business for yourself, because you get the satisfaction that you know that if you fail or you win, it's yours. You don't have somebody over you who's not giving you good opportunities to succeed.'"

In November 1957, Dan and his younger brother, Frank, received a visit from their landladies at Carney's Market. They came with an article from the *Saturday Evening Post*, which was then one of America's most popular magazines, about a hot new food concept called "pizza." The article, entitled "Crazy About Pizza," explained what this then-exotic dish was and included a series of color illustrations to show how it was made. The landladies asked Dan if he and Frank were interested in opening a pizza restaurant in one of their nearby commercial properties that was about to be vacant. They quickly said yes.

To get the business off the ground, the Carneys borrowed six hundred dollars from a fund established from Mike Carney's life insurance to pay for his children's college tuitions. With part of the money, the brothers bought secondhand cooking equipment, and cheap chairs and tables.

As the business began to take shape, the next question was what to call it. The local Coca-Cola distributor provided a complimentary small outside sign that was wide at the top and tapered down at the bottom. There was room for only five letters on the top line and three letters on the bottom line. "Pizza" obviously had to be on top. But Pizza what? Pizza Pad? Pizza Inn? Pizza Pan? Pizza Jug? Dan's wife, Beverly, mentioned that she thought the building looked like a hut. The decision was made. The name of the pizzeria would be Pizza Hut.

The night of the Pizza Hut opening, the place was packed with friends and relatives who had known the Carney family for a long time—from the community, school, college, and church—and they continued to support the new venture through its early mom & pop years. The Carneys rapidly expanded their business with the help of friends and associates, who became franchisees, and today Pizza Hut, a division of YUM Brands, has ten thousand stores all over the world.

But the lessons about how to run Pizza Hut came out of Dan Carney's experience working at Carney's Market, where "I learned how to handle money and how to work with profit and loss statements. We learned how to get by on very, very little expenditures. We had a delivery truck that continually had flat tires because we couldn't afford new ones, which wouldn't have made the economics work. And I also learned how to treat people—both your customers and the people who work for you."

BOOKS VS. BOMBS

It seems as if in any reporting of war-torn countries, the first indicator of a return to normalcy is when the shops and markets reopen, because if the merchants are feeling more confident, that's the signal for the rest of the population to get back to their routine. Iraq has been no exception.

Nabil al-Hayawi owns a family bookshop on Baghdad's famed Mutanabi Street. Named after a celebrated tenth-century poet, Mutanabi Street has long been the location of a popular Friday book market, where sellers set up displays on the street, and thousands of buyers and sellers exchange ideas, while sipping strong, steaming-hot tea in small glass beakers with china saucers. A familiar Arab saying is "Cairo writes. Beirut publishes. Baghdad reads."

Al-Hayawi lost his brother and his only son in a car bombing in 2007 that almost destroyed the family's bookshop and nearly took his life as well. He endured five operations and had difficulty standing up. With shrapnel still in his body, he took medication to deal with physical pain and depression.

The violence in Baghdad forced millions of people, including many intellectuals and professionals, to flee the country. But al-Hayawi, whose bookstore has the apt name of Renaissance, refused to be defeated because "if you live with fears, how can you live?" he asked. "Iraq is my soul. I go and come back. But I will never leave."

The al-Hayawi family sold their house in Baghdad and used the proceeds to retire their debts, replenish their stock of books, and rebuild their two shops, which employ seven people, including members of the third generation. Observing the renewed activity on Mutanabi Street during the summer of 2008, Nabil al-Hayawi told *Financial Times* how happy he was when "I discovered the people still reading."

A mom & pop store always represents hope—the hope of the proprietor and the hope of the community.

HURRICANE KATRINA

Tom Lowenburg and Judith Lafitte, owners of Octavia Books in New Orleans, have a keen understanding of the hope their store represented to the customers in their community. They learned it the hard way after Hurricane Katrina in 2005.

Before opening the twenty-five-hundred-square-foot store in 2000, Tom had worked for fifteen years for the nonprofit Alliance for Affordable Energy, which he cofounded "to challenge the local electric and gas utility companies who had made imprudent decisions that would unfairly drain billions of dollars from the local economy and to work to convince the utilities to invest in energy efficiency resources." His wife, Judith, worked as an office manager for an international construction company while she finished earning her college degree.

When asked if it was a little crazy to open an independent bookstore at a time when independent bookstores continued to struggle, Lowenburg responded with a smile. "Of course it's crazy. If people did things purely for calculated reasons, the world would be a lot less interesting place. In 2000, the American Booksellers Association said that there was just a handful of new bookstores opening in the United States. Many stores were closing, too, of course. Conventional wisdom said you couldn't do this. We had to prove that wrong. Also, we wanted to do something together. I didn't envision myself being here full-time, but that's how it turned out."

Once they decided to go forward with their plan, it took Lowenburg and Lafitte almost two years to open the store, which is located on a quiet block in the old Uptown residential neighborhood, near Magazine Street, one of the longest commercial streets in the country. It's a good location, not far from Tulane University, and about four miles from the French Quarter.

"When I grew up in this neighborhood, there were a lot of empty buildings on Magazine Street," said Lowenburg. "Now it's a hot, very vibrant area." Adding to the vibrancy is Octavia Books, which occupies a hundred-plus-year-old corner commercial building that had once been the stable for the Laurel Street streetcar line and is now a lovely, bright retail space with high ceilings, exposed New Orleans hard-tan brick walls, a coffee bar, an outdoor courtyard and waterfall, a goldfish aquarium, and tropical plants. The store won Best of New Orleans Architecture honors from *New Orleans* magazine and a Golden Hammer award from the City of New Orleans. The remainder of the two-story building includes a

228 / The Mom & Pop Store

yoga studio, bakery, judo school, and financial services company upstairs.

Like many aspiring booksellers, Judith was motivated by her love of books, particularly children's books. "Getting children's books, for me, is like Christmas every day," she said. "The fact that I get to read them before I put them on the shelf is exciting to me. I love spending time on the floor, hand-selling all the books I love."

Tom takes a pragmatic approach: "We try to be smart about running our business. There are no guarantees. When you're a small business, you have to be optimistic enough that you're going to be able to survive. We get more optimistic as we go along. If you only think of books as a commodity, then you are only competing on a dollar basis, and Borders and Barnes & Noble can beat us at that. We thought a lot of about how we could make this a special place. We specialize in local books. We provide good service. We are very personal. We try to be excellent at what we do."

Like all New Orleanians, Tom and Judith have their own stories about how they dealt with Hurricane Katrina, one of the most devastating and deadly Atlantic hurricanes in history, which hit New Orleans on August 29, 2005.

"We initially evacuated north of Mobile, Alabama, where my mother lived," said Lowenburg. "We lost power there at the end of the week. Our cell phones didn't work very well because the circuits were overloaded and the cell towers were down, although we were able to text message. We heard from some people—who had not immediately evacuated the area—that the building looked OK from the outside. Our neighborhood did not flood because we're close to the Mississippi River, on a natural levee, on high ground. Even though the city looks flat, it's really bowl shaped."

Lowenburg and Lafitte, like everyone else, wanted to get back to New Orleans as soon as possible, but they were thwarted by Hurricane Rita, another Category Five storm, which hit Louisiana about four weeks after Katrina.

"I was so mad when I couldn't get into New Orleans in that window between the hurricanes," said Lowenburg. "I was not going to be stopped again after Hurricane Rita. We were able to go online and print out a business pass from the city," which would allow them to return. But as they approached the city, they faced a road-block, with National Guard soldiers carrying automatic weapons. "They asked us why we had to come into the city. We said we had a business. They said they were only allowing essential businesses. I said, 'I have a bookstore.' They said, 'Make a U-turn, buddy.' We didn't make a U-turn; we made a left turn, and got in at the next location. If you were determined to get in, you could do it."

Tom and Judith were relieved to discover that "everything in the store was basically the way we left it," he said. "Even the goldfish in the courtyard fountain were swimming and living off of the mosquitoes that landed on the water. They were waiting for us to feed them their traditional fare. Other than a not-too-pleasant smell that came from the refrigerator, our house was in pretty good shape, relatively speaking. There was about forty inches of water in our basement, where we had our air-conditioning and heating equipment. A lot of papers were floating around in the basement. Our tile roof was badly damaged."

Six weeks after the storm, Octavia Books reopened.

"We did it because we thought that a bookstore is not just a mom & pop business," said Tom. "A bookstore is a special kind of business, where people meet and exchange ideas. It's a place where people can get inspired to do things. It's a building block for building the city back."

Judith described Octavia Books as "a place for people to feel comfortable talking about anything they like. We don't stifle any conversation in our store. We're noisier than a library. It's a nice community space. We see ourselves as a community meeting place. We have a very strong commitment to bring the city back. We didn't know if anyone was going to show up at first, but we knew it was important to get open, and to make the statement."

Tom and Judith were most heartened by the reaction from their customers when they reopened.

"We put together some makeshift signs around the neighborhood saying that we were now open, and I sent an e-mail to those on my customer list," said Tom. "People from all across the country were reading it. I got responses from people telling me their stories. The idea that a paradise for them would be here when they got back made a huge difference in their outlook. I got more response from that e-mail than from any I ever sent out. It was the warmest, most supportive, heartbreaking, thrilling response you could possibly imagine."

Octavia Books' reopening made a difference to even non–book readers. "A neighbor said she came into the store because there was no television reception and she couldn't rent a video. Her faith in the power of books was stronger than she ever imagined it would be."

After Hurricane Katrina, "the independent stores really brought the city back," said Lowenburg. "Barnes & Noble waited for six months before they reopened. I could have come up with plenty of reasons not to open, too. What do you do when you have people in other places without a commitment [to this area], making corporate decisions, waiting to see what was going to happen? We didn't have time to wait and see. People understand the local economy now better than before, because of what we've gone through. They are loyal to local companies."

FOOD, FLOOD, AND FRIENDS

IN NEW ORLEANS, I visited two very different eateries to discuss how each dealt with Hurricane Katrina and its aftermath.

The first restaurant was RioMar, on the corner of Julia and South Peters streets in the historic Warehouse District, two blocks from the Morial Convention Center. RioMar, the brainchild of business partners Nicolas Bazan from Argentina and Chef Adolfo Garcia from Panama, is a seafood restaurant inspired by the owners' heritages and the fresh local seafood of the Gulf of Mexico, and beyond. RioMar is well known for its variety of ceviche dishes (featuring Louisiana fish fillet) and Spanish tapas, as well as Chef Garcia's unique take on fish and shellfish.

Nick Bazan, who is originally from Bahia Blanca, south of Buenos Aires, came to New Orleans in 1981 and soon found himself in the restaurant business, eventually moving up to management. Through his sister, he met Adolfo Garcia, who is considered one of the best chefs in the city. They opened RioMar in August

2000, and soon developed a popular following among the local savvy foodies in the Warehouse District, where many old warehouses have been converted to upscale condominiums that are occupied by mostly single young professionals.

"It started out only Adolfo and I," said Bazan. "I was waiting tables and he was cooking. But we knew that if we wanted to go to the next step, we couldn't do it alone. We had to delegate and we had to believe in people and give them a chance. We did it with the right people."

A few miles away from RioMar is Vincent's Italian Cuisine, a classic neighborhood restaurant, which since 1998 has been in business on St. Charles Avenue in the Uptown section of New Orleans. This is the second Vincent's restaurant launched by native New Orleanian Vincent Catalanotto, who opened his first eponymous eatery in 1989 in suburban Metairie. Both Vincent's are famous for the corn and crab bisque served in a toasted bread bowl, veal and spinach stuffed cannelloni (the house specialty), and the gigantic seafood stuffed pork chop. Diners listen to the crooning of Frank Sinatra, Dean Martin, and Jerry Vale, while enjoying the food in a casual, cozy, candle-lit atmosphere.

I met co-owner Tony Imbraguglio for lunch at the St. Charles location, where diners enter by passing almost-life-size replica statues of Venus de Milo and Michelangelo's *David*, which stand outside on the brick steps. Located on the route of the historic St. Charles streetcar line, the place has been a popular destination for tourists and locals for more than a hundred years. From 1929 to 1998, it was called Compagno's Restaurant and for the last four-plus decades of that run the place was run by the husband-and-wife team of Sal and Maria Compagno. "Miss Maria," as everyone called her, "was in the kitchen cooking for forty-two years," said Imbraguglio, who added another tidbit of local trivia: "The city of New Orleans had a contract with the Compagnos so that the train conductor could use their restroom."

Like all the people I met along the way, Imbraguglio has brought his passion to his job and everything it entails.

"This is a job that I love—to see our regulars come in, and look at their faces, and make 'em happy and smile. We treat them like friends. You touch people. They feel like they're coming home. It's like they're sitting in their La-Z-Boy in their home, relaxing with a glass of wine and some food. I got customers who are here three or four nights a week. They want you to have a bottle of wine with them, to share something with you. They want to give you something. It's like a family. There's so much wealth in the stories that people share with you. They share everything with you. Restaurant people say you hear all the stories when you're behind the bar. That's a bunch of bull. When you're out on the floor and you're sitting down with these people and you talk with them, you get a perspective of who they are. You can live vicariously through the people that come through the door. They'll tell you about trips and things they've done, and war stories, and working on the pipeline and going underwater spearfishing.

"They're all waiting for you to come to their table. You gotta be careful whose table you go to first and whose table you go to last. The funny thing about it is that the ones you go to last are your most special. You know that when you go to that table you're not just going to say hello and good-bye. You're going to sit there and talk to them. If you don't sit down with them, they're not happy. They expect it. They'll say, 'What's the matter, Tony, are you too busy to talk to me?' So, it can be a mixed blessing."

Both RioMar and Vincent's survived Hurricane Katrina.

"The devastation in this area was not bad. We did not get flooded," said Nicolas Bazan of RioMar, who temporarily relocated to Baton Rouge, Louisiana, about one hundred miles away. "But there was looting throughout the area, which is about two blocks from the Convention Center."

A short time after Bazan returned to check on RioMar, a member of the Louisiana National Guard came by and said that he had been "holed up here with a family, which he fed with my food. There were some canned goods that we left behind. There were some babies here who were fed with our condensed milk. Whatever they could find. He told me that he was here with a couple of compadres with machine guns, and protected our restaurant from be-ing destroyed."

Although looting was rampant, Bazan was forgiving. "There's a human element. Who knows what you or I would have done if they left us here for seven days with no food or water? I don't blame them for doing what they had to do. They had to survive. People thought they were going to die. A lot of people did die."

Commuting two to three hours every day each way, between Ba-ton Rouge and New Orleans, Bazan and Garcia and their staff set about getting the restaurant back in business. Three months after the storm, RioMar reopened, initially only for lunch because they could secure only a limited amount of ingredients.

As trying as the aftermath of Katrina was for him and his partner, Bazan looked back on it as "an amazing experience. I wouldn't trade it for anything—to see the city come back, to see the locals come back and tell me their stories, to see the optimism that they had. Purveyors came back as soon as they could. We couldn't have done it without them. We are a seafood restaurant. We thought the fish estuaries or oysters or crabs were going to be destroyed. But, no, there were actually more oysters, more shrimp, more fish than before. There were a lot of boats that were destroyed, so the [com-petition among] fishermen was less. The oysters were actually bet-ter. Huge shrimp. The crab has been amazing. The seafood came back stronger.

"The thing about New Orleanians is that we don't give up. I found that out after Katrina. New Orleanians are full of life and par-ties, drinking and good food. We like to have a good time as much as possible. But after Katrina, people really picked up the pieces and got to work."

The importance of mom & pop stores to the community was never more true than in New Orleans, in the aftermath of Hurri-cane Katrina. When the RioMar restaurant reopened its doors, "people were so happy that they were almost in tears," Bazan told me. "They wanted to give us hugs and kisses. They finally had a place where they could come back together with their neighbors and friends. People went out of their way to go out to eat and support us. Not because they had to, but because they wanted to.

"A restaurant is an anchor for the people in the neighborhood, where they can get together. They recognize faces from the neighborhood and know their names. What I enjoy the most is taking care of the regulars. Being a regular is about asking the kitchen to do something slightly different from what's on the menu. People need that. I need that. That's why I go to restaurants myself. People recognize me and know me. New Orleans is a small town, especially after Hurricane Katrina. My regular customers come here once a week. One couple who live a block away have been coming here every Thursday for the last seven years. If they're going out of town, they come on Wednesday. They need to come here to get their fix, which is for food and recognition. We need that for our soul. We give the tourists the respect and the service, but the locals are what get us through, not just financially but emotionally.

"The restaurants like ours are leading the way. This is what the culture is: music and food, and the festivals we put together with music and food. We are bringing our culture back. If you look at the numbers, we have more restaurants now than before Katrina. We opened a second restaurant, a steakhouse, La Boca. That was another opportunity, thanks to Katrina. The flavor of New Orleans is strong. We're getting it back."

Tony Imbraguglio and his staff at Vincent's were able to get back about four weeks after the hurricane.

"No flooding. No looting. We were absolutely blessed. I had boarded everything up. The windows were nailed. The front door was boarded. After the hurricane, we had two holes in our roof—one in the kitchen, one in the back. Luckily, it didn't rain for about thirty-something days after. We just put tarps over the holes. I assembled a small crew. We came in and cleaned the coolers. It was the worst, most disgusting thing. There was nothing you could put on your face to mask the stench. It was pathetic."

Vincent's lost its chef, who had to leave town after his house was flooded. Imbraguglio needed help with figuring out how to prepare some of the restaurant's signature dishes. The first person he thought of was the venerable Johnny Mancuso, whom he described as "a classic Italian waiter, and the most entertaining person you've ever met. He used to sing for us in the restaurant. I went to Johnny's house, he opened the door, and he said to me, 'Tony, I *knew* you were coming for me today.' It was really weird, because I hadn't seen him in a year and a half. I said, 'Well, ain't this something.' I asked him how we made the meatballs and he showed me. He made the red sauce, which is the same red sauce we use to this day. He was a jack-of-all-trades. He orchestrated all the things in the kitchen that needed to be done."

Once the restaurant crew got Vincent's in reasonable shape, they put up a two-by-floor plywood sign that proclaimed: VINCENT'S IS OPEN.

"We didn't know what to expect," said Imbraguglio, a good-humored man with red hair and a quintessential New Orleans accent. "People were coming down the street, honking their horns, giving us the thumbs up, and saying thank you. It was every single car. It was like a parade."

The restaurant opened its doors for dinner at five o'clock. They had to use paper plates and plastic knives, forks, and spoons because they couldn't wash dishes with contaminated water. Every morning, they had to fill up buckets of water or buy containers of water. All the pasta was boiled in that water, which was a two-hour chore.

"The first few nights we had candles on the wall," said Tony. "People just love that memory, and still talk about it to this day. Somebody said we should do it again, with paper plates and plastic forks. The simplicity of it just made people feel good."

The impact of reopening the restaurant "didn't dawn on me until a couple of weeks later when people would come in and be very emotional. They would cry. They would say, 'Thank you. This is our sanity. This is our sanctuary. This is something that shows us that there's hope in the city of New Orleans.'

"Katrina taught me how to work again, how to get in there and make a mess of the kitchen, work all day, and just get back to the nuts and bolts. That was probably one of the most common things that was mentioned among all the business owners that I had met in every field, not just the restaurant field." Back in the prosperous years before Katrina, "some of them just kind of took the easy life and hired managers to do most of the work. After Katrina, they had to come back to work. They had to roll up their sleeves like the old times, and learn how to do it, all over again."

12

If Your Neighbor Has It to Sell . . .

> When we were younger, we always wanted to
> change the world, or thought we could. Now, I think
> we're smart enough to know that we're just here to
> help the neighborhood.
>
> —RICK DANKO (1942–1999),
>
> BASS PLAYER AND SINGER, THE BAND

M Y TWO YEARS ON and off the road, talking with shop owners far away from home, changed the way I viewed the
mom & pop shops I visit almost every day in my own neighborhood.

For three decades, more than half my life, I've lived in Seattle—
more specifically the community of West Seattle. If you've ever been
to Pike Place Market and looked out onto Elliott Bay, you'll see an
isthmus. That's West Seattle. We're connected to land (not Seattle,
but the area south of the city), but we think, and view ourselves, as
if we live on an island. We have an island mentality. We believe that
everything—well, almost everything—we need is right here.

We're a tight-knit group. My wife, Marybeth, is third-generation
West Seattle. We live less than ten blocks from her parents and sister, ten blocks from another sister, and fifteen blocks from her
cousin. West Seattle is still the kind of place that embraces, reveres,
and perpetuates its traditions and values. We have our own pa-
rades, organizations, and ways of doing things. Colorful murals on
some of the buildings give people a glimpse into the neighborhood's
history, such as the old streetcar line and press day at the *West
Seattle Herald*, the weekly paper.

For most of the twentieth century, West Seattle was connected to the city by two low-level drawbridges for eastward and westward traffic. Before that, travel was by ferry, railway trestle, and winding wagon road. Today, we're separated from Seattle by a soaring 160-foot, six-lane bridge (built in 1984) that spans the Duwamish Waterway, an industrialized estuary that's part of the Green River. At the apex of the bridge, a driver can see the Cascade Mountains (including Mount Rainier on the days that it's "out"), Safeco Field (home of the Mariners baseball team), Qwest Field (home of the Seahawks football team), the industrial waterfront, downtown Seattle, the Space Needle, and the headquarters of Starbucks Coffee Company and Amazon.com.

Back in the days of the old drawbridges, Seattle people considered West Seattle as "out there" somewhere. Even though downtown Seattle is less than fifteen minutes by car from my home, there are many people who still think of my community as "out there." As someone who grew up in Perth Amboy, New Jersey, I understand the slight and I find it amusing.

Although they are twenty-five hundred miles apart in distance and two hundred years apart in age, West Seattle and Perth Amboy have much in common. West Seattle is on Elliott Bay; Perth Amboy is on Raritan Bay. When you look west from West Seattle, you see Bainbridge Island and (on a clear day) the Olympic Mountains. When you look east in Perth Amboy you see Staten Island. (Sorry, no mountains.) Like Perth Amboy, West Seattle is working-class. When the community was settled in the early part of the twentieth century, it attracted blue-collar workers who toiled in the nearby steel mill, shipyards, lumberyards, cement plants, and Boeing airplane facilities. The egalitarian, working-class, no-frills attitude is unchanged.

Both Perth Amboy and West Seattle had great early expectations and aspirations. While Perth Amboy was dubbed *portus maximus* by its boosters, the twenty-two men, women, and children (many of whom were from New York) who in 1852 arrived at Alki Point, Seattle's birthplace, dubbed the location Alki New York, meaning New York By and By. It didn't take long for the first mom & pop to be opened by brothers Charles and Lee Terry, who launched a general store called the New York Store. Soon after, Lee Terry returned to New York, leaving Charles to run the store. As other entrepreneurs set up shop, Alki became a business hub, albeit a short-lived one. The area was eventually logged and cleared, and later developed for residences, a process that continues to this day. Not long after arriving at Alki Point, some of the pioneering families headed over to the eastern portion of Elliott Bay, where they began the development of what would become Seattle at the most level portion of the southern part of Elliott Bay. Alki boasts its own miniature version of the Statue of Liberty, and it was the place where we gathered on September 11, 2001.

ALASKA JUNCTION

WEST SEATTLE'S ANSWER to Perth Amboy's Smith Street is California Avenue SW—the spine of our community—a six-mile stretch of road, which is said to be the longest and straightest street in the whole city. In 1907, a boggy woodland was drained and cleared, and two streetcar lines were connected at a junction on California Avenue SW and SW Alaska Street. Real estate agents soon enjoyed a brisk business selling lots in the area that would come to be known as the Alaska Junction—the commercial, civic, and social heart of the community.

While California Avenue has had, at one time or another, JCPenney, Woolworth's, and Kress's five-and-dime stores, the street is home base for mom & pop stores, which draw a loyal neighborhood following.

I believe in the principle that was expressed in the 1930 Newark, New Jersey, directory: "If your neighbor has it to sell, give him your business. Like consideration from your neighbor adds prosperity to both." If a small, independent mom & pop store has what I need, I will give it my business, even if it's slightly more expensive. It's worth it to me to keep that store in business.

Our stores are the kind you'd find in a small town—pet supplies, beauty supplies, opticians, jewelers, framers, pharmacies. You can buy a cupcake, an electric train, a laptop computer, new and used music on compact discs or vinyl records, and patriotic teddy bears. We have a wood furniture store that has a suit of armor standing guard at the outside entrance. Working behind the counter at Ron's Cobbler Shop is Yefim Spektor, who emigrated from the same part of Ukraine that my family comes from and has been repairing shoes at the Alaska Junction for many years. Although we are not related, when I stop in with a pair of shoes, I like to greet him as my cousin.

To compete with the malls, West Seattle merchants chip in to provide free parking for shoppers on the street as well as in several parking lots. To make the streets even more pedestrian friendly, at the corner of Alaska and California we have a "scramble" light that, when green, allows pedestrians to cross all streets, straight as well as diagonally. If we had angle parking instead of parallel parking, the Alaska Junction would look like Mayberry, the fictional town that was the setting of the old Andy Griffith television show.

YOU WANT YOUR USUAL?

In Mayberry, everybody knew everybody. It's not quite that way in our neighborhood, but the shopkeepers certainly know their regular patrons, who represent the lifeblood of their business. Is there any one of us who doesn't enjoy being recognized and acknowledged when we walk into our friendly neighborhood restaurant or hardware store or butcher shop or barber shop? Tag along with me, on a typical day in my neighborhood, while I visit the places where I'm a regular. But this visit will be different because we're going to stop and talk to the owners, to find out what life is like from the other side of their counters.

Wherever I've lived, my connection to the community starts with breakfast in the morning. It began for me, as a thirteen-year-old, with my father and uncle as we sat on the counter stools at Perth Amboy's Texas Lunch, where the owner, Evie Mariolis, would look me in the eye and ask, "You want your usual?" I like having a "usual"—a customary, normal, typical, standard order. We identify with our usual. It helps define who we are—to the outside world as well as ourselves. We like the fact that our barista, our bartender, our sandwich maker knows us, and knows our tastes. And if we decide to change our usual, the person on the other side of the counter will smile and make a joke about it, which only the two of us can truly appreciate with a smile and a wink.

I work out of my home, so every morning I need to get out into the world and find out what's happening in my community. I need someone in addition to my darling wife to say, "Good morning, Robert." As I drive along California Avenue, I see lots of people stopping off at bakeries, coffeehouses, blue-collar restaurants—and many are probably ordering their usuals. My destination is Hotwire Online Coffeehouse, a tiny 350-square-foot space with exposed brick, that buzzes every morning with activity and good cheer. Owner Lora Lewis is usually behind the counter, teamed up with one of her young employees or, on some occasions, Lora's teenage daughter, Jessie. In Hotwire's intimate space, the espresso machine is placed to the side so that customers can watch their drinks being made, and the baristas can converse with the customers. It's a lot nicer than looking at the barista's back, or having the barista hidden behind the espresso machine.

Because it's adjacent to our large, busy main U.S. post office on California Avenue, there is a steady stream of postal workers who line up for their morning jolt of java. With a couple of parochial high schools in the neighborhood, the morning rush includes platoons of bleary-eyed teenagers ordering sweet coffee drinks topped with whipped cream—nothing like caffeine and sugar to start the day. Lora has a word to say to virtually each person who comes in: "Hello, my darling. Your usual triple grande soy vanilla? Perhaps a pastry to go with that?"

Although the place is tiny, I never feel rushed. In fact, for a coffee shop, the atmosphere is relaxed. The four computer terminals equipped with DSL Internet service are all occupied while customers quietly check e-mail, stock quotes, and online newspapers. The purchase of a coffee drink enables a customer to have free use of a computer for the first fifteen minutes, with a charge of ten cents for each additional minute. Lewis does make money from the computers.

"All emotions aside, I still am an entrepreneur, so I'm going to make sure that whatever services I offer are going to give me a positive cash flow," Lora told me one summer morning as we sat at a table outside Hotwire in the tiny courtyard that accommodates three additional tables.

"Most coffee bars have very much of a fast-food mentality. Their thinking is: 'How many people can I put through the cash register in sixty minutes?' I wanted to integrate a concept that would slow people down, take a breath for just a minute, and allow them to enjoy a beverage. Even if it's to do some mindless Web surfing on our computer terminals to see what events are coming up this weekend, or checking a quick e-mail or two."

Lora, a forty-something mother of two, once was an executive with a large U.S. insurance company. By the year 2000 "I discovered that I have a strong entrepreneurial spirit that was always a part of me. I really wanted to try a small business. It took me a couple of years to figure out who I was as an entrepreneur, and to build a business plan. I made a conscious decision to remove myself from the corporate environment," said Lora, who sports a big smile, curly blonde ringlets, a pierced nose ring, and a constellation of stars tattooed on her left forearm. "I sold my house and all my stocks. To get my espresso machine out of hock, I had to sell my BMW. *That* was a commitment."

Hotwire occupies West Seattle's oldest commercial building, built in 1905 for the local lighting and gas company. (In Seattle, anything over a century old is considered ancient.) Up until 1940, the lighting and gas company building served as a carriage house for horse-drawn vehicles. Then it was vacant for the next sixty-two years until Hotwire's opening in 2002.

"It was in a horrid state of disrepair. We started with a shell. The roof was rotted. One of the doors was somehow still connected to the building by one rusty hinge. There were rats. The night before we opened we were up until three in the morning. The last thing I did was write out our drinks and prices on the chalk board, which I had left outside. Of course, it rained and everything I had written had been washed away. When I came back, four hours later, I was outside rewriting the chalk board. People were coming in for coffee drinks. My barista was asking me how much a drink cost, and I said, 'Uh, two-fifty? Sounds good?'"

I asked Lora why anyone would open a coffee shop in Seattle, the home of Starbucks, as well as any number of smaller chains and a multitude of independents just within a couple of blocks of her shop. Her answer: "Like a lot of entrepreneurs, I did my due diligence. I looked at the economic core here in West Seattle. I felt that this community could support another coffee shop. It goes back to the entrepreneurial spirit that you believe you have the best of everything. No matter what's out there, yours is going to be better than everyone else. That flame of desire is one of the things that drives an entrepreneur.

"The shop relates back to my core beliefs of life. I grew up in England, in a close-knit community in a small beach town. I was surrounded by family. My community had a very defined core, a soul, so to speak. I've been in this country since I was twelve, and traveled and lived back and forth between these two countries for the last twenty years. I found that in the U.S., because of its size and social structure, I was having a hard time finding a soul—a place where I could go and really connect with others in my community. So, my driving force to open a coffee shop was my finding that social center, again."

Lora is one of the forces of energy in our little part of the world. "Every decision I make goes back to my basic philosophy of bringing people together. I create events that bring people together." As vice president of the West Seattle Junction Association, a group of local merchants, Lora runs the annual summer series of outdoor movies, which are shown on a large blank wall behind Hotwire. The entertainment includes films such as *Who Framed Roger Rabbit*, *Best in Show*, *Monty Python and the Holy Grail*, and *Edward Scissorhands*, which are targeted to both grown-ups and kids.

On a warm summer night, several hundred people spread out on lounge chairs and blankets, and chat with neighbors. While bringing the community together, the movies also help to raise awareness for local nonprofits and charities, such as Friends of the Animals Foundation, West Seattle Food Bank, West Seattle Helpline, and Westside Baby, which is a nonprofit organization that collects previously owned items for children and babies and distributes them free of charge to South King County families in need. Lewis also chairs the monthly West Seattle Art Walk, in which all kinds of local businesses—restaurants, retailers, realtors, even other coffee shops—exhibit locally created works of art, "which brings more people into this area and creates a community of art lovers."

She believes that part of her job description is to mentor the young people who work for her. "It's important for me to have young people who are working here, to provide them solid, collaborative leadership. These people are starting off in their work lives. A lot of them are in college. They can be influenced by a poor employer, who does not appreciate what they bring. On the other hand, they can also be influenced by someone who gives them a voice in the operations of the coffee shop. My collaborative leadership skills, I hope, have helped those people—whether they're with me now or they've gone on and graduated college and moved out of the area—in whatever they do, just like my own children."

"YOU GET WHAT YOU GIVE"

AFTER I GET my latte at Hotwire, I walk down to the end of the block to the Forsythe Studio where the owner, Jessica Forsythe, has cut my hair and trimmed my beard since the late 1990s. I'm at the Forsythe Studio about three times a month to get my beard trimmed. Jessica finds places to fit me in for the trim, in between applying color or doing a permanent for other clients. We enjoy bantering and she gives as good as she gets.

The shop has four other hairdressers working there, so there's a lot of activity with customers getting ready to get married, have babies, get their hair done for the prom. Of course, there's the exchanging of community news—getting the word on new restaurants, or what stores are opening or closing. There is no gossip at the Forsythe Studio. Jessica says you can talk about Brittany Spears or the latest reality-based TV shows, but nothing about local people or politics. This is a small town; watch what you say because somebody's cousin may overhear what you're saying about her.

Jessica, an attractive blonde who grew up in the neighborhood, opened her first shop down the street in 1998 because "I wanted to create a customer-service-focused, professional environment that spoke to people, and that reflected me. I had confidence that I could do it. I've always had the cup-half-full, I-can-do-it, no-one's-going to-stop me, Taurus, only-child kind of thing. I was raised by a single mom. You can't tell me no. I got a five-thousand-dollar line of credit, and opened my own 250-square-foot shop, at age thirty." Eighteen months later, she opened her 1,100-square-foot shop.

Jessica is a bighearted, giving woman, and that attitude permeates her salon. She decorates for every holiday, and when I say she decorates, that's an understatement. At Halloween, it seems like every inch of the place is covered with ghosts and ghouls and cobwebs and weird animals making strange sounds. Thanksgiving, Christmas, and Valentine's Day get the same kind of treatment. It's one celebration after another.

Like most other operators of small shops, Jessica is a source of information. "I have the menus of the latest restaurants. I want to support them. If I like a restaurant or a place, I'll go on and on about them. People trust me. I'm not going to recommend something I don't believe in. I'll tell clients about pediatricians, dentists, where to get their shoes shined.

"We give back to the community. I donate to everybody's schools. We do volunteer work for MOPS (Mothers of Preschoolers) who have a spa day that is put on by Westside Presbyterian Church. We do benefits for people's causes. When some of my clients who worked for Boeing were on strike, I charged them less during the strike. After the strike, we went back to full price. We're a community. We're all in this together. The bottom line is that I would not be here without the clients, the community. You get what you give, and I'm going to give as long as I can, and enjoy life."

EASY STREET

WHEN I'M IN the mood to shop for music, I don't go online to iTunes. I keep walking down California Avenue and turn in to Easy

Street Records, a funky iconoclastic space that has become the un-likely shopping anchor at the corner of Alaska Street and California.

Easy Street is the brainchild of Matt Vaughan, who as a teenager in the early 1980s worked for a little record shop on California Av-enue called Penny Lane as well as another shop in Bellevue, which is the city across Lake Washington from Seattle. In the late 1980s, both stores were going out of business. That was a tough time for music retail, with the introduction of music on compact discs, which required reconfiguring the stores to fit the new format that would eventually replace vinyl albums. Vaughan brought together the owners of the two music stores to combine inventory at Penny Lane. The plan was for Penny Lane to go out of business and for the eighteen-year-old Vaughan to take over ownership of a new entity. "The owner of Penny Lane told me, 'You can handle this. If you can pay me eight grand within the next two years, great. If you can't, so be it.' That was it. I paid him the eight grand.

"I was the only employee for two years," said Vaughan, who dropped out of Seattle University on registration day of his sopho-more year. "I had a couple of friends working for me under the table, and I worked seven days a week and had a bed in the back room. I expanded very organically. I'd only add a new employee if I could afford to do it." To pay the bills and increase sales, Vaughan bought and sold used CDs, which was a business that few record stores were involved with at that time. Because the used CDs were cheaper, traffic in the store increased.

In the late 1980s and early 1990s, the Alaska Junction was rid-dled with vacant storefronts and was a neighborhood ready for transition. Every day Vaughan would pass by the empty storefront at the corner of California and Alaska that had been the home of a longtime drugstore that had closed amid scandal (too many pre-scriptions for too many painkillers), and he began to think bigger thoughts. "This corner location was just sitting there. I was intrigued by it, even though there was flooding and damage." As business im-proved, Vaughan made the move to the new space. "I was nineteen at the time. I negotiated the lease for twelve hundred dollars a month. That was a very cheap price, although it didn't seem so at the time. I did all the work to fix the place up. I fell in love with the space. I knew every nook and cranny of it and behind every wall."

The challenges Vaughan faced were a motivation for him to innovate. Like every successful entrepreneur, he got creative. "There comes a point where you go beyond being a record store owner or a deli guy or a bar owner. You have to become an entrepreneur. That's not what I envisioned. I was all about being a record store owner. But changes forced me to dig deep. That's stimulating. You are either a businessman or you're not."

In the late 1990s, faced with increased competition from music-downloading sites such as iTunes, Vaughan expanded his space and added a café, because "I needed to find something that would immunize me from the competition and make something unique that would expand on the social aspect of the business. We looked around and realized that there wasn't a great place to get great coffee, diner food, a beer, and an occasional live show, all in one place."

The café is a wide open space of exposed concrete walls and linoleum floor with posters of the latest CDs. There are plastic chairs and tables, a couple of upholstered booths, and a telephone pole with a street lamp that stretches almost as tall as the space's eighteen-foot-high ceilings. (There's another telephone pole with a street lamp on the music side of the space.) Looking around at the lunch crowd, it's typically West Seattle. A young waitress, heavily tattooed and pierced, jokes with a table of white-haired Boeing retirees and fills up their coffee cups, while the band Eagles of Death Metal's "Coca-Cola" blares out over the speakers.

The café, where food is served all day, offers a menu full of colorful names such as the Billy Burrito and the Betty Burrito. The Billy (two scrambled eggs with black bean salsa and cheddar, wrapped in a Spinach tortilla) was named after a friend of Vaughan's who had helped him with some odd jobs and was the first person to try the burrito. The Betty (two scrambled eggs with hash browns and cheddar wrapped in a spinach tortilla) got its name from a cherished eighty-year-old customer who enjoyed listening to old country and swing music. Other dishes include James Browns (hash browns topped with diced ham, sausage, veggie links); the Salad of John and

Yoko (mixed greens with veggie bacon, avocado, red onions, olives, and tomatoes); and the Soundgarden Burger. Named after the Seattle band, it is a (nonvegan) garden burger served with lettuce, tomatoes, onions, and Easy Street's own sauce on a burger bun, with fresh-cut fries.

West Seattle was one the foundations of Seattle's storied music scene in the late 1980s and early 1990s. "A lot of the bands, who went on to become world famous," said Vaughan, "were living in West Seattle. Rent was cheap. You could get a decent postwar home at a reasonable price. There were a lot of garages out here, where bands could practice. Neighbors wouldn't complain about the loud music like they would in other Seattle neighborhoods. A lot of the best rehearsal spaces were underneath the West Seattle bridge and no one would bother you.

"Eddie Vedder [the lead singer for Pearl Jam] moved here from San Diego to join Mother Love Bone, a band that became the basis of Pearl Jam. He bought his music here—and still does. He became friends with the store and he even worked a shift back in 1995, when we needed a shift covered. Soundgarden and Mudhoney lived out here. This is where a lot of bands got their start. This is where they saw their records sold, where they bought their records. There was a pride being in West Seattle and being in a band. The wild, wild West."

In 2005, Pearl Jam performed a long set at Easy Street in support of the Coalition of Independent Music Stores. The album, *Live at Easy Street*, was released exclusively to independent record stores. A reviewer in *Rolling Stone* wrote, "Here's a good reason why cool bricks-and-mortar record shops still matter: seven songs cut live and hot in front of fans and customers at Easy Street Records in Pearl Jam's hometown of Seattle, then released through indie stores and priced to move."

Easy Street's reputation is well known among musicians from across the country, who often venture to West Seattle to stack up. Vaughan recalled Patti Smith visiting the store to buy a box set of the music of Seattle native Jimi Hendrix. Lou Reed, after he played an in-store set, bought some David Bowie music. Tim Robbins, Bo

Derek, Ben Harper, Avril Lavigne, and the Beastie Boys have all been spotted in the store.

"There's something poetic about having a corner record store that's become an anchor for the community. There's something to be said for having a place where people like to hang out. It creates more activity. There's something good-natured about it. It becomes the place where your older brother used to go, and now you go there. There's a connection to your own family and community and how you were brought up."

In 2002, Vaughan opened a second store in the Seattle neighborhood of Queen Anne, not far from the Space Needle. He took over a space that had been occupied for years by Tower Books, a division of the then-giant Tower Records chain, which had a store a few blocks away.

"That was a huge undertaking for me," Vaughan told *Seattle Weekly*. "The World Trade Center tragedy, 9/11, occurred soon after I signed my lease, and my business loan never transpired. So, I had to refinance my house and do what I could to get the store open. I felt that Seattle deserved a good-sized, centrally located independent that carried more than just specialized music; that was a true reflection of Seattle, its heritage, and its future. I also wanted to host in-stores [concerts] in a way that hadn't been done before. Treat the artists as if they were playing a real venue, have a real P.A. system, have a real sound guy and enough room so that you could see and hear the performance while showcasing their talent and latest release in a respectful manner."

Easy Street is a testament that an innovative brick-and-mortar store can survive.

"The digital providers are having a tough time," Vaughan told me. "They thought they would take over music retail. It just hasn't happened. They have twenty percent. The forecasters predicted that people like me would be gone. Buying music is impulsive. It triggers your brain waves different than if you were sitting in a chair at your computer. It's hard to get a smile when you're downloading that ninety-nine-cent song. You're not cracking a smile. It's more like a duty. You're crossing something off your to-do list.

"When you're walking in the Junction, you don't necessarily know where you're headed. You just know you're being in your community. You're seeing smiles. You're recognizing faces—your favorite barista or your favorite record seller. You're enjoying where you live. Seattleites want to shop in an independent store. People are spending their money for family, schools, and a better place to live. They are doing more than just buying their record at Easy Street. They are buying that record in support of their community."

WEST SEATTLE'S LOCAL WATER COOLER

AFTER MY LUNCH at Easy Street, I remember I have to make some copies of a document and overnight the package to New York. I drop by my house, get the document, and then I drive five blocks to Alki Mail & Dispatch, where owner Don Wahl or one of his capable staff will take care of everything for me, including providing me with the airbill and envelope.

Alki Mail & Dispatch (think the UPS Store with soul) is a friendly little neighborhood place where you can pick up your mail from your post office box, send packages, print, copy, notarize documents, and pick out a card for Mother's Day. Don has merchandised the place with lots of impulse items: postcards, greeting cards, newspapers, mugs, sweatshirts, T-shirts, and plastic pig key chains that light up and oink.

While I'm at Alki Mail—which bills itself as West Seattle's Local Water Cooler—I order another latte (hey, this is Seattle), and take it upstairs, three steps up on a raised platform where there are a couple of tables, easy chairs, and three computer terminals for people to check e-mail or surf the Web. Local artwork covers the walls. As I address my airbill, I watch the parade of people coming in and out.

Behind the counter, either at the coffee area in the front of the store or the mailing counter in the back, you'll usually find Don Wahl, a tall, lanky man, who as a college student in the 1980s ventured west from his hometown of Lincoln, Kansas, to study jazz and West African dance and "to enjoy the outdoors and the progressive community of Seattle." Eventually, he and his boyfriend, also named Don, came up with the idea for an independent mail-shipping business. They opened Alki Mail & Dispatch in a six-hundred-square-foot space (two hundred of it for storage) on Alki Avenue, not far from where the Denny Party landed on Alki Point.

Both men immediately took to the new venture, particularly in how it connected them to the neighborhood.

"I grew up in a fifteen-hundred-person town, so I was accustomed to knowing everybody in town. That's a sense that West Seattle had—a small community, where people knew each other. The people who came in were your clients/friends, people you'd see in the neighborhood. That sense of community has grown on me over the last twenty years. I've really come to appreciate what it means to be part of a community. Respect and appreciate and honor that. There's a certain responsibility that you have to be a small business in the community."

Don keenly felt that appreciation for the neighborhood in 1994 when his partner died of AIDS. "I had lost the love of my life," he said. "It was healing to talk about it. I know people who never talked about it. I felt complete about my grieving process. That was a gift for me. It was hard, but as a result of that support from the community, it made dealing with the greatest loss of my life possible.

"It's the people who create the community atmosphere—being able to learn about people's lives, and for them to learn about my life. If all I did was send faxes, steam milk, and wrap boxes all day long, I'd go crazy. The community is why I'm still doing this. After twenty years, I've lived through births of children, marriage, death. Life happens. We get a hundred fifty people every day. You can participate in a hundred fifty people's lives. Someone got married; someone had a baby; someone died; someone's having a great day; someone's having a crisis. I need to manage that input into my psyche, so it doesn't overwhelm me."

Since early 2005, Alki Mail & Dispatch has occupied a new, bigger, and better location in a 1937 building on Admiral Way, a major artery heading either toward Alki Beach or toward Seattle. Talk about locations, location, location. There's a bus stop right outside, so the shop's espresso bar is in the front, with a serving window so that commuters waiting for the bus can get their morning coffee without having to go into the store.

"We didn't dress up the folksy, inviting aspect of the business because we're the only business in the neighborhood, which is zoned residential. Our business has been grandfathered in. I love the fact that people come here in their bedroom slippers and pajamas for their coffee."

PUTTING THE SERVICE IN SERVICE STATION

DRIVING NORTH ON Admiral Way, toward downtown Seattle, I notice my gas tank is empty, so I better stop off at Barnecut's to fill it up. (The official name is Barnecut Admiral Way Super Service, but all of us just call it Barnecut's.) Because I'm driving north, it would be more convenient for me to stop for gas at the Safeway Supermarket Gas Station on that side of the street. Uh-uh. I'm going to make a left turn into Barnecut's, which is not just a place to get cheap gas; it's a service station with the emphasis on service. It's a family-owned business that has been here since 1932.

I pull in to the full-service side so that Rudy can see if my tires are inflated correctly and check under the hood. There used to be service stations like this everywhere, but they are on the endangered species list. We're lucky to still have a Barnecut's, where Andy Barnecut (the third-generation owner) or longtime workers Rudy or Tim will help you replace your wiper blades, or get that nail out of your tire, or pick you up at home if your car won't start.

"When we go out and help people they can't believe it. They say it's like the good old days," said Dick Barnecut, whose father, George, opened the station in 1932. "We try to treat you like you'd like to be treated. If they call us to fix a flat or start their car, what they are really saying is, 'Do you want my business?' If you respond in a satisfactory way, a lot of people—not all—will remember that." Dick started work at his father's service station while in high school in 1940 and continued until he joined the military during World War II. After the service and marriage in 1947, he returned. "I've been here ever since. I took over January 1, 1953, when I bought it from my dad. I have two brothers and a stepsister. They all worked in it; I'm the only one who stayed."

Dick has four children, but just one, forty-four-year-old Andy, his youngest, stayed and now runs the business.

A few years ago, the Safeway supermarket chain built that big self-service discount gas station across the street from Barnecut's. For Safeway, gas is a loss leader. If a Safeway supermarket customer buys fifty dollars' worth of groceries, she gets a break on the gas or oil, which is all the station sells.

"Safeway did hurt us," Dick told me. "But, we're adjusting to it. We still have a nice core of loyal customers that are appreciative."

SHUT UP AND EAT

WELL, BY NOW it's dinner time and I feel like sushi, so Marybeth and I head over to Mashiko Japanese Restaurant, across the street and a few doors down from Easy Street Records, where Hajime Sato, the iconoclastic goateed owner and chef, stands behind the sushi bar, watching all the proceedings while doing his artistry. You might even spot Eddie Vedder or Soundgarden's Chris Cornell. I like to sit at the sushi bar and ask Hajime or one of the other chefs to choose what they think I'd like. It's called *omakase*, or let the chef decide. That's the fun of a sushi bar. "I want you to try new things and ask questions. I want people to laugh and enjoy food and life," said Hajime. So, you might get a plate of hamachi cheek, the most flavorful section of the yellowfin tuna, or tobiko, which is flying fish roe. I always order Kurosawa sake, which is easy for me to remember, because it's the same name as the famed Japanese film director.

Hajime is from the town of Utsunomiya in the prefecture of Tochigi, about one hundred miles north from Tokyo. "When I was growing up, it was a rural area. I learned how to fish with my hands." He arrived in the United States in 1989 as an exchange student in Coeur d'Alene, Idaho, and later moved to Seattle, where he attended a community college and got a job working at a sushi restaurant on the waterfront, where he was an apprentice, then sous-chef. The owners of that restaurant wanted to open another one in Coeur d'Alene, and asked all the people on the staff if anyone wanted to go there. No one did. "So I volunteered," Hajime said.

By 1994, Hajime was ready to go off on his own. "Believing that food is one of the most powerful languages in not only defining cultures but also in integrating them, I wanted to open a Japanese restaurant that would transcend the traditional way of presenting and thinking of food from my country. I wanted to create new and interesting ways to interpret Japanese food and sushi. I feel as if I'm representing Japan. Maybe someone doesn't know other Japanese people. I want to give them the information I have on the food."

In the late 1980s and early 1990s, the shopping and dining at the Alaska Junction was bleak. Many storefronts were closed and even loyal West Seattleites preferred shopping downtown or at the malls. Hajime had actually wanted to open his restaurant in another part of town but it was too expensive. He said his landlords "thought I was going to fail. People didn't think a sushi restaurant in West Seattle was going to work out. But I really believe in myself. I have confidence that if I do a good job people will come—not just from West Seattle but all over Seattle. I wanted to have a really good neighborhood restaurant that's affordable. I can provide a high quality of food, but for a lesser price. That was my goal.

"You'll never hear traditional Japanese music in Mashiko, because it reminds me of two things: grammar school and death. Believe me, if you've ever been to an elementary school in Japan . . . death isn't too bad. So we play new and interesting music that we hope will compliment the food."

When I told Hajime about my own experience working in my father's shop, and how much I hated it, he smiled broadly and I knew that I had struck a chord.

"My father was a golf greenskeeper in Japan. He started his own business building golf courses. I had to work there. My first job in summer: you get up a three in the morning to water before the sun comes up. The fairway needs to be patched. You have to carry the sod. You have to carry the dirt up the steps. Oh, my God, my father was mad that I didn't take over his business. It was only just recently that he accepted my path. I'm doing the same thing as him: doing my own thing, making people happy."

"IT'S LIKE A PARTY ALL DAY LONG"

Now that I've had my sushi, I've left a little room for some ice cream, and fortunately, the shop next door to Mashiko is Husky Deli, which is ground zero for ice cream in West Seattle. Husky Deli has been at the Alaska Junction since 1932, and is a three-thousand-square-foot neighborhood institution. In the center is a spacious rectangle-shaped space where a half dozen or so employees and/or members of the owner's family are making sandwiches, slicing cold cuts (there are four slicing machines), selling bread, soft drinks, mustards, candy, etc. In the center of the rectangle are two massive wooden chandeliers in the shape of octagons. On each side of the octagon is the carved name of a famed food region, such as Roquefort and Gruyere.

As you enter the store, on the lefthand side is the ice cream counter, which, in the thirty years I've been coming here, is usually overseen by gangly teenage boys whose voices are changing. Husky offers forty-five flavors of homemade ice cream, using Dutch cocoa and real bananas, strawberries, and other fruit, much of it from the weekly West Seattle Farmers' Market. Husky churns out as much as a thousand gallons a week.

There are plenty of places to sit in the front of the store while people come in to enjoy their ice cream. When my daughter, Fae, was in elementary school, this is where we would bring her to meet her friends after a school play. On summer nights, people sit outside on the benches in front of Husky, licking their ice cream cones and watching the pedestrians parade by on California Avenue.

You might also see one of the employees from Mashiko carrying some supplies back to the restaurant, because the owner of Husky provides supplementary refrigerator and freezer storage for Mashiko, his tenant and neighbor.

Husky was started by Herman Miller. After breeding cattle in Indiana, he arrived in Seattle in the mid-1920s to sell Kelvinator commercial refrigerators. In 1932, he bought the Edgewood Farms Grocery store in West Seattle, and soon after he purchased a machine to make ice cream in the store's front window, which attracted passersby. Herman served a giant scoop of ice cream that was dipped in chocolate, rolled in peanuts, and put in cones. It was comparable to the more established Nutty Buddy. He called his creation Husky and in 1937, he changed the name of the store to Husky and trademarked the ice cream. During the Depression, he sold his Huskies to public school lunch programs, which kept his business going.

"We still have the racks that we made them on," said Herman's grandson, Jack Miller, a round, smiling man in his fifties, with a closely cut salt-and-pepper beard, who runs the store today.

Herman Miller repaid the customers for their business during the Depression by letting some run a tab if they could not afford to pay for their groceries. Husky has been embraced by the community ever since.

A couple of years ago, a Ben & Jerry's ice cream store opened at the busiest intersection of the Junction—across from Easy Street Records and down the block from Husky. There was no boycott. In fact, no one said much of anything. They just didn't show up at Ben & Jerry's, which closed less than a year after it opened. Locals didn't even bother to use the franchise's coupons that had been handed out on the street for one complimentary ice cream cone.

After serving in World War II, Herman's sons, John and Bob, came back to the store and converted it to a deli. Husky eventually became a place where customers could get imported grocery goods. "We had a lot of Europeans living in the community. As time went on, we became a deli that catered to the customers' requests. We carried things you couldn't find anywhere else," said Jack Miller. Husky has a great selection of domestic and imported mustards, salad dressings, marinade sauces, crackers, wine, and chocolates, but fancy it is not. Overhanging roof shingles line the three display walls of the store and add to the cozy feeling. Hanging high on the rear wall of the store are photographs of previous generations of Millers.

Jack Miller began working in the store as a boy in 1966. "My dad would wake up my brother and me in the middle of the night," he said, "and ask us if we'd help him make ice cream. We couldn't say no. On a Saturday morning, we'd start to make ice cream at two in the morning, and we wouldn't finish until two in the afternoon. Then he'd work here until he closed at ten o'clock at night. That was standard for him."

My conversation with Jack was occasionally interrupted when Jack greeted a customer, and exchanged some pleasantries or stories.

Jack, who is the kind of West Seattle personality that lights the community Christmas tree, is one of nine children, but he is the sole member of his generation still working in the store. His brother Joe retired and went into commercial real estate. Husky is set for the next generation after Jack. Between Jack and his siblings, there are twenty-four children—eight of them are already working in the store, the oldest of whom is in his midthirties.

People come to Husky for more than just shopping, although that's certainly a part of it. "You run into people you know. That's what makes West Seattle fun. When September Eleventh hit, we were packed. People wanted to come to a place where they would know other people. It's kind of a comfort thing to go out and shop with people who know who your dog is and what you're all about. You'll pay a little more if you have to, but lots of times, you don't."

One need only see the smile on Jack's face to believe him when he said, "I love to do this. In my whole life, I've never not wanted to go to work. It's like a party for me all day long. I have a relationship with almost everybody who comes in here.

"There are some people who come in because they don't have a lot else going on in their life. Going into Husky every day is a huge part of their life. They get recognized. Someone talks to them. Even if it's the same conversation every day. People ask me questions like 'What should I do with my money?' 'I need some dental work done, who should I call?'

"When people who used to live here come back to town, they come to Husky to see if it's still here and still doing the same thing. Husky provides the sense of history in West Seattle."

THE FARMERS' MARKET

EVERY SUNDAY, ALL year-round, West Seattle has its own farmers' market, which is set up in a parking lot that is emptied out at the Alaska Junction, around the corner from Easy Street Records. During the peak spring and summer seasons, some forty or so farmers bring their wares to the market, as do artisans who make cheese, ciders, jams, salad dressings, and baked goods. You can get your knives sharpened, sign up for a political cause, meet and talk with friends, and listen to folksingers warble "Turn, Turn, Turn."

All over the country, farmers' markets, which are as old as commerce itself, are enjoying a renaissance as consumers rediscover the benefits of buying locally grown food (preferably organic), which is fresher, tastier, and supports the local economy. Farmers' markets provide us with a pleasurable social atmosphere, where we can get information on the food from the people who have grown it, the people who still have the soil under their fingernails, who have planted, nurtured, grown, harvested, and displayed the fruits and vegetables of their labors.

Seattle's Neighborhood Farmers Market Alliance, a community-based organization, supports the state's small farms and farming families by providing places where they can sell their food firsthand—the clearest, most direct, immediate, and honest type of exchange. The Germans have a term for it: *auge-in-auge handel*, "eye-to-eye trading."

At the West Seattle market, Marybeth and I first stop at the display of Whistling Train Farm, which is run by Mike and Shelley Verdi, who have been farming together for ten years in Kent, Washington, less than a thirty-minute drive to Seattle, in the fertile Green River Valley. Whistling Train Farm lies between the tracks of the Burlington Northern and Union Pacific railroads, hence the name. Although Kent was once completely populated with farms, much of the real estate has been filled and built over. While warehouses and industrial parks dominate the landscape, there are still some farms around, but you have to go off the freeway to find them. Mike Verdi's parents came from Italy and settled in an area south of Seattle, which is today occupied by the large Southcenter Mall. His father was one of the founding farmers of the Pike Place Market, and his mother, Pasqualina, was literally the face of Pike Place Market. Her wise, smiling visage was used in many advertisements. My wife, Marybeth, like so many of Pasqualina's old customers at Pike Place Market, remembers her taking out a head of romaine lettuce, and saying in her thick Italian accent: "You want this lettuce wet [washed] or dry [unwashed]?" Pasqualina would wash the lettuce, only when she was ready to display it. "Dry is better," she would add. "It comes straight from the fields. Last longer." She'd hand you a piece of bitter arugula and say, "Try it. You never taste anything like this. I eat it if you don't."

Shelley, who had always wished she had grown up on a farm, works with Mike on their fifteen acres, which encompass several microclimates and soil types that make it perfect for growing a wide variety of crops and making harvest possible for ten months of the year. They grow vegetables and herbs and raise chickens (for eggs and meat) and Berkshire pigs. They also keep cows and ducks, and are assisted by their two young children, Della and Cosmo.

"We grow a lot of things that you can't find in the grocery store," said Shelley. "We enjoy exploring new varieties, as well as improving on the standards. We want you to enjoy new foods—like pea shoots, Japanese turnips, or Romano beans—or at the very least, to break out of the grocery store box." Depending on the time of year, they might be selling Gold Nugget or Sugarloaf squash, heirloom Italian shelling beans, Italian torpedo onions, cinnamon basil, Deer Tongue lettuce, radicchio, broccoli, or carrots—all assembled in a colorful, inviting display.

In the late 1990s, Marybeth and I began purchasing a subscription to Whistling Train Farm. For two hundred fifty dollars a season, we get a bag full of groceries every week for sixteen weeks. There's something different every week. We eat with the seasons. The vegetables we buy from Shelley and the other producers at the market were in the ground a day or two earlier. *That's* fresh.

Is it any wonder that farmers' markets have returned to popularity? They provide another connection to the community of people who are providing us with our food. More and more, people are starting to realize the value of trading with men and women who know their product and can tell you the best way to consume it.

BUTCHER SHOPS

IN THIS AGE of mass processing of meat, where supermarkets save costs by stocking precut meat, there is still room for the butcher who knows what he's doing—people like the Wassler brothers in Cincinnati and Garry Moen in London. All over the United States, we are seeing the return of independent butcher shops where meat is cut, trimmed, and ground to order. Meat that comes from massive slaughterhouses (which cut and ship the meat "wet aged" in shrink wrap) does not have the rich flavor that comes from dry aging. Many independent butchers age the beef themselves and cut and trim it according to the customer's preference. Yes, the prices may be slightly higher, but the return is more flavorful and healthful meat—and as an added bonus, you know where it came from and whether all that hamburger meat came from the same animal.

We don't have a local butcher, but we do have Skagit River Ranch, which is run by George and Eiko Vojkovich, who raise, slaughter, and butcher their animals on their organic (no antibiotics, steroids, growth hormones, or animal by-products) farm in the fertile Skagit Valley about ninety minutes' drive north of Seattle. George and Eiko, who are assisted by their daughter, Nicole, sell their wares at a couple of farmers' markets in the Seattle area, where they are well known for their 100 percent grass-fed beef and pork, as well as their pastured chicken and fresh eggs.

"We sell what we feed our family," said Eiko.

BUY LOCAL

JACK MILLER, OWNER of Husky Deli, mentioned to me that he had just bought a washing machine from Wiseman's Appliance and TV, a second-generation mom & pop, and a West Seattle institution since

1963, which is located a couple of miles north of Husky on California Avenue. In this era of big-box appliance and television chains, Wiseman survives by selling not just merchandise, but also support and customer service. "I could have saved ten bucks," Jack said, "by buying it from a big store, but Wiseman will bring the new washing machine down to your house and take your old one away. Keep the spending in your town, otherwise you won't have choices. Some people, in order to save a dime, lose sight of that."

Gary Foust, who owns the Barber Pole in Savannah, Georgia, said that instead of having lunch at a chain restaurant, "I'd rather go around the corner to the State Street Café, where John, the owner, knows me. I can call ahead and place my order. Sometimes, when I'm busy, he'll slide out the back door of the restaurant and bring me my lunch. I want to support him because he and his two boys are my customers. 'Buy local' makes a lot of sense for so many of us who are in small businesses. I trade with people who trade with me."

Carla Cohen, the co-owner of the Politics and Prose bookstore in Washington, D.C., said, "Right now, young people's definition of cool is to go online and buy something. They think, 'Why should I bother going to a store when I can get it online?' We have to find a way to make it cool to buy local from community-owned enterprises. The thing that we have to do is make idiosyncratic mom & pop shopping as popular for the young people. They want pure water, organic food; they will support that in restaurants, grocery stores. They've got to know that the future depends just as much on local individual retailers."

Tapping into that sentiment are activist groups that are spreading the gospel of buying local. The Business Alliance for Local Living Economies (BALLE) is a San Francisco–based network of dozens of local business groups, which was formed in 2001 to provide, in the words of the organization's charter, "a vision for a more democratic, community-based alternative to corporate globalization," and has organized tens of thousands of aspiring entrepreneurs in the United States and Canada. In Bellingham, Washington, Bellingham Sustainable Connections, the local BALLE network, claims more than five hundred members, who want to keep the small community's reputation as a haven for unique businesses.

The American Independent Business Alliance (AMIBA), based in Bozeman, Montana, is a national coalition, network, and resource hub for community-driven groups supporting local independent businesses. AMIBA's main goals are to preserve distinctive community character, ensure opportunities for entrepreneurs, build and strengthen local economies, and help local businesses fight the chains. AMIBA members focus on educating citizens, local government, and media about the importance of supporting community-based businesses, and the issues that those businesses face.

In many parts of the country, independent stores are joining together to help protect themselves from big chains. For example, the Vermont Alliance of Independent Country Stores, a nonprofit organization, was formed to offer promotion and support—moral and marketing—for the owners, and to play on their unique heritage and contributions to their communities. Membership is limited to stores built before 1927. The Alliance's more than fifty member stores hold tastings of products such as cheese, honey, syrup, ice cream, and milk. The group has also launched Vermont Village Foods, which is a line of homegrown goods, such as sodas, soaps, bread mixes, and condiments that are available exclusively through members' stores. The Web site features online tour maps and offers the publication *Country Stores of Vermont: A History and Guide*.

These organizations are having an impact on how communities view large retailers. Over the past several years, big retail expansion efforts have been meeting with increasingly stiff, stubborn opposition from a broad cross section of groups, including local and national grassroots organizations, small-business associations, guerrilla street-theater activists, consumer groups, populist politicians, and legal advocates, ranging from libertarian to progressive.

"I'M FROM THE GOVERNMENT AND I'M HERE TO HELP YOU"

SMALL BUSINESSES ACCOUNT for about 50 percent of the private gross domestic product of the United States and create, on average, about two thirds of net new jobs annually. They are the greatest source of new employment in inner cities, comprising more than 99 percent of establishments and 80 percent of total employment. American small business is the world's second-largest economy, trailing only the United States as a whole. Small businesses employ more than half of private-sector employees, and they represent 99.7 percent of all employers.

And yet, many municipalities all over the United States are constantly finding ways to stick a finger in the eye of small businesses. Elected officials offer tax incentives to big-box stores and help them through the often-complicated permitting process, because all they see are the raw number of new jobs that the big store will provide. Politicians enjoy appearing at ribbon-cutting ceremonies for these new businesses. They like to cite the number of new jobs they've added to the community. That's a lot sexier than helping small businesses add a couple of new employees here and there, and achieve the same number of new jobs over time.

When Tom Lowenburg and his wife, Judith Lafitte, initially tried to open their store, Octavia Books, they ran into obstacles from the city of New Orleans. Although the space for the store had been a commercial building for a hundred years, "I had to get the entire city council to approve putting in the bookstore," said Lowenburg. "It took a long time and a lot of patience. It would scare away most people who didn't have the time or resources. We couldn't grease the wheels."

At the same time I was in New Orleans to visit with Tom and Judy, there was a big announcement by city officials that Borders was going to open up a new twenty-four-thousand-square-foot store between Octavia Books and the Garden District Book Shop, another well-established independent. The Borders location, at the corner of Louisiana Avenue on the St. Charles Avenue streetcar line, was formerly the Bultman Funeral Home, which had been at that location since 1943. Only the façade of the building was preserved as a part of a nine-million-dollar project that used low-cost Gulf Opportunity Zone bonds (intended for Hurricane Katrina recovery) to finance the first chain bookstore on St. Charles Avenue.

"People think there's something magical about giving to a big business," said Lowenburg. "We're not asking for [money from the state] and we're not expecting it. But I do have a problem with the unlevel playing field. An outside big business organization sucks money out of the local economy. We should be doing the kind of economic development that helps local businesses keep money in the economy. Stop pinning your hopes on bringing someone in from the outside. We're not going to sit on our hands and do nothing. You have to be an active optimist. You have to make the best decisions for your business."

Lowenburg and Lafitte have joined together with other owners of independent neighborhood bookstores in New Orleans to educate the public on the benefits—socially and economically—of buying local and keeping their dollars and loyalties within the community.

If there's one thing officials of local and state governments enjoy more than giving incentives to big companies, it's hassling small businesses with lots of rules and regulations. Clearly, these elected officials and bureaucrats have never run a business. Too often, city, county, state, and federal taxing entities spend their time trying to squeeze money out of the most vulnerable contributing taxpayers: mom & pop stores. And if they're not after the money, they are trying to find ways to control commerce in the form of licenses. According to an editorial in the *Wall Street Journal*, more than 20 percent of the U.S. workforce is required to get a permit to do their jobs—as compared to a mere 4.5 percent in the 1950s.

In New York City, in 2007, the administration of Mayor Michael Bloomberg made the notorious move of raising revenue by issuing tickets and fines to small businesses—including many immigrant entrepreneurs across the five boroughs. One of the biggest money-makers for the city was citations for "dirty sidewalk" violations issued by the Department of Sanitation, for "failing to clean eighteen inches into the street."

"Every morning at eight thirty, we have to clean up our area, or else, in ten minutes, there will be somebody coming by to give us a two-hundred-fifty-dollar ticket. They don't care. Other than that, we've been pretty lucky," said Abby Fazio, owner of New London Pharmacy in Manhattan. Fazio, who is in competition with large drugstore chains, has to deal with regular government audits of the prescriptions she dispenses. "I can't afford the manpower to look at every single prescription. The little guy can't do everything that the big guy does."

Norm Dinkel, the third-generation owner of Dinkel's Bakery in Chicago, told me that he once wrote to Mayor Richard M. Daley "about how it's important that we don't overregulate and that we don't try to make it so cumbersome that we force small businesses out of business. State, local, and federal governments put in these edicts and you just can't comply. It's a joke. It's a challenge. I see it all over. We have way too much government regulation. Cities need to work with their small businesses. I once got a letter from the city of Chicago that my sign, which has been around since 1946, was illegal. It's a landmark. It's been featured in movies [*Straight Talk* with Dolly Parton]. It helped my mail-order business. I had to sort things out with the mayor's office."

In Milwaukee, Sandy and Angie D'Amato, who have two businesses in a historic building in Milwaukee's Third Ward—the Coquette restaurant and the Harlequin Bakery—ran afoul of the local Architectural Review Board.

"We rented some space that was along the window in the front of the building so that we could get some exposure to the street," said Angie. There are three window panels that face the street. "The Harlequin logo was in the middle panel, and on the side panels we put on decal lettering of the items for sale: baked goods, coffee and tea, etc. We were told that our signage hadn't been approved by the Architectural Review Board of the Third Ward, so we had a hearing with them. They said that the righthand panel was over its quota of lettering by two percent and that the lefthand panel was under by two percent. We needed to change the decals so that we would be in line. It didn't matter that one panel was over and one was under. It was just silly. We had a decal on the window that said 'handmade artisan chocolates.' I scraped off 'handmade' and I was immediately in compliance."

In Seattle, the tax people came up with a bizarre, convoluted new tax on square footage—which is derived from a combination of floor space and revenue generated outside Seattle city limits. I won't bore you with the details, but a certified public accountant was quoted as saying, "I don't think anyone's written a more complex, less intuitive taxing statute that is harder to comply with."

Sometimes politicians do learn the errors of their ways, but often it's too late. In 1988, seven years after he had left the U.S. Senate, George McGovern, the three-term senator from South Dakota and the Democratic Party nominee for president in 1972, fulfilled a lifelong fascination with hotels, inns, and restaurants, and bought Connecticut's Stratford Inn—a combination hotel, restaurant, and public conference facility. It was a failure.

After having spent more than two decades creating rules and regulations as a legislator, the senator learned what it was like to be on the receiving end of federal, state, and local rules and regulations written by people who have never had to meet a payroll. "Too often, however, public policy does not consider whether we are choking off those opportunities," McGovern wrote in a 1992 article in *Nation's Restaurant News*. He added that even well-meaning legislators often ignore this basic question: "Can we make consumers pay the higher prices for the increased operating costs that accompany public regulation and government reporting requirements with reams of red tape." Senator McGovern expressed a wish that "during the years I was in public office I had had this first-hand experience about the difficulties business people face every day. That knowledge would have made me a better U.S. senator and a more understanding presidential contender."

Compare this attitude to the country of Honduras, which until recently had not been famous for accommodating capitalism and entrepreneurship. The mayor of the capital city Tegucigalpa cut the number of steps to acquire an operating license from 108 to 25. Some aspiring entrepreneurs could get their business off the ground by filling out just three forms. The time it took to get a municipal operating license was cut from a month-plus to a day. As a result, the city sharply increased the number of newly registered restaurants, workshops, grocers, and other businesses. The mayor's offices feature posters that proclaim the slogan of the city council:

ATIENDE, ENTIENDE, RESUELVE." ("We pay attention, listen, and sort things out.") How many local government offices in the United States could say those words with a straight face?

YOUR NEIGHBOR HAS IT TO SELL

INDEPENDENT RETAILERS NEED and deserve support from their local government administrations. That's where most of the new jobs will be coming from—not from the General Motors or Citibanks or Starbucks of the world. They are going to come from people like Nicolas Bazan and Adolfo Garcia in New Orleans, and Chuck and Dee Robinson in Bellingham, Washington, and Valeria Safran and Marcie Turney in Philadelphia. Let's help them survive and thrive as we head into a golden age of mom & pop stores. In a time of economic turmoil, we turn to our neighbors and our neighbors turn to us. Our neighbor has something we need and we have something that our neighbor needs. It's that simple. I learned those lessons many years ago from my own mother and father, who taught me how to contribute to the well-being of my community.

Mom & pop stores represent the past, the present, and the future. They touch every aspect of our lives, just as they did for our parents and grandparents, and just as they will for our children and grandchildren. Although the stores will change, and the neighbors will change, and the neighborhoods will change, what will not change is our yearning for connection. The imperative of mom & pop stores will remain because they are essential to who and what we are—our neighborhood, our community, our collective soul.

As I write these words, on a chilly fall morning, I'm sitting at a table in the corner of Hotwire Online Coffeehouse, observing the steady parade of regulars coming in for their usual—their coffee, their conversation, their connection to their community. It's all so beautiful and it's all so mundane, and it makes me feel good to be a part of it. I'm ready for a refill.

ACKNOWLEDGMENTS

FIRST AND FOREMOST, my profound thanks and deep appreciation go to my agent, Elizabeth Wales, for her steadfast support and encouragement for this project. Elizabeth was with me every step of the way as we worked, reworked, and reworked every aspect of this book, from idea to proposal to finished product. At one point during this lengthy process, I remarked to my wife, Marybeth, "I think Elizabeth knows this book better than I do."

Thank you to my Marybeth. I could not have done this without you. Thank you for being there through the agony, the ennui, and the ecstasy, and for reading, rereading, rereading this manuscript. I promise you, you'll never have to read it again, unless, of course, you want to.

Jacqueline Johnson has been the kind of editor that an author hopes for: wise, kind, gentle, encouraging, decisive, and firm. Thanks, Jackie.

George Gibson, publisher extraordinaire. Thank you for being a friend—and for being so wise and prescient to offer me a contract.

My appreciation to the 2008 Seattle Mariners, who lost 101 games. Because my hometown baseball team was unwatchable, I had plenty of extra time to write this book.

Along the way, I was aided by Peter Armato, Stan Baranowski, Ann Berger, Daniel Carney, Alan Cheuse, Kenneth Duberstein, Etta Fielek, David Fujita, David Fuller, Jennifer Giannobile, Jack Greenstein, Michelle Greenstein, Ernest Horvath, Samuel Kagan, Bill Kodilla, Dana Kubick, Stan Laegreid, Barry Lafer, Jane Lees, Gary Locke, Lisa Lockwood, Michelle Long, Evelyn Mariolis, Michelle Mooney, Tom Moriarty, Dr. Raymond Philips, Colin Powell, Susan

Roane, Barry Schwartz, Sharon Penn Sigmund, Bob Spitz, Neal Swain, Paul Steinke, Buddy Toig, Irving Warhaftig, and Marjorie Young.

My appreciation to John Eckberg of the *Cincinnati Enquirer*, Linda Forgosh of the United Jewish Communities of MetroWest New Jersey, Patricia Gandy of the Perth Amboy Public Library, the late Charles F. Cummings of the New Jersey Information Center of the Newark Public Library, Murray Meld for translating Yiddish, and Professor Frank Trentmann of the School of History, Classics and Archaeology, Birkbeck College, London, for recommending several useful books on the history of retailing,

A special thanks to my cousins Seymour Handler, Harvey Spector, and Jules Spector for their memories of our grandparents and their time working at Spector's Meat Market.

During the long period of research, I lost two dear cousins, Claire Handler Warhaftig and Beatrice Okner Ferber, who both died in their eighties after living rich, full lives. Claire was invaluable in her observations about our grandparents, Isadore and Mindel Spector. Bea filled in blanks about my mother, who was her aunt (but more like a big sister), and other members of the Okner family. They were remarkable women and I miss them both.

Finally, thanks to my own mom & pop, Florence and Fred Spector, for the example they gave to my sisters and me. This is their book.

Robert Spector
Seattle, Washington

NOTES

1: WORKING-CLASS HERO

20 "came in the middle of every night": Fernand Braudel, *Civilization and Capitalism 15th–18th Century*, vol. 1, trans. Sian Reynolds (New York: Harper & Row, 1979), 33.

26 Gay Talese, whose parents: Ron Kovach, "Gay Talese on the Art of Creative Nonfiction," *Writer*, February 2005, 21.

2: PERTH AMBOY

32 "I have never seen such before in my life": William A. Whitehead, *Early History of Perth Amboy* (New York: D. Appleton & Company, 1856), 211.

32 "a convenient town . . . air, soil, and situation": Federal Writers' Project of the Works Progress Administration of the State of New Jersey, *New Jersey: A Guide to Its Past and Present* (New York: Viking Press, 1939), 362.

34 "gardeners, ploughmen . . . cooks and bakers": Myra Jehlen and Michael Warner, *The English Literatures of America, 1500–1800* (New York: Routledge, 1997), 97.

34 "A society cannot . . . leave off consuming": Karl Marx, *Das Kapital*, vol. 1, sec. 7, ch. 23, cited in Fernand Braudel, *Civilization and Capitalism 15th–18th Century*, vol. 2, trans. Sian Reynolds (New York: Harper & Row, 1979), 25.

34 "on any spot . . . the weary traveller": Morris Birkbeck, *Notes On A Journey In America, From The Coast Of Virginia To The Territory Of Illinois* (Whitefish, Montana: Kessinger, 2008), 99.

35 "what people seldom . . . when they retire to Perth Amboy": Fletcher Knebel, *New York Times*, January 11, 1976, New Jersey section, 2.

36 "I now have . . . fresh coat of mosquito bites": Russell Baker, *New York Times*, August 6, 1986.

36 "were not thinking . . . doesn't suffice on Broadway": Brendan Gill, *New Yorker*, December 2, 1985, 144.

36 "I had been trying all afternoon . . . Perth Amboy": James Thurber, *My Life and Hard Times* (New York: Bantam Books, 1933 and 1961), 63–64.

3: ZEYDE (GRANDFATHER)

50 "Sleep, my baby sleep . . . soon you will join him": Words by Sholem Aleichem. Smithsonian Center for Folklife and Cultural Heritage, accessed at http://www.smithsonianglobalsound.org/trackdetail.aspx ?itemid=7996.

50 "a matrix . . . dull gabardines": Henry Roth, *Call It Sleep* (New York: Noonday Press, 1991), 9.

50 "If they could afford it . . . borrowing and pawning": Irving Howe, *World of Our Fathers: The Journey of the East European Jews to America and the Life They Found and Made* (New York: Monticello Editions, 1989), 60.

51 "If one does speak 'broadly,' . . . without industrial experience": Howe, *World of Our Fathers*, 59.

52 "They put us into lines . . . running away from": Ellis Island Immigration Museum exhibit, New York.

52 "Dinner: beef stew . . . milk for women and children": Ellis Island exhibit.

53 "Mecca of visitors . . . came in hundreds": John T. Cunningham, *Newark* (Newark: New Jersey Historical Society, 2002), 195.

53 "undergoing a powerful and dynamic transformation": Mervyn Rothstein, "To Newark with Love. Philip Roth," *New York Times*, March 29, 1991, B1.

53 "In my childhood imagination . . . 'No, it wasn't' ": Ibid.

54 "Our store was opened . . . for their needs": Advertisement, *Druggist*, March 1922.

57 "eternal desire . . . of the Russian immigrant": Anzia Yezierska, *How I Found America: Collected Stories of Anzia Yezierska* (New York: A Karen & Michael Braziller Book, Persea Books, 1991), 6.

60 "if thy wife be fair . . . at the door": Quoted in Dorothy Davis, *Fairs, Shops, and Supermarkets: A History of English Shopping* (Toronto: University of Toronto Press, 1966), 110.

60 "You are full . . . of rings?": William Shakespeare, *As You Like It*, act 3, scene 2, in *The Complete Works of William Shakespeare*, (London: Abbey Library, n.d.), 233.

61 "Arabella Brown . . . with Punctuality and Dispatch": Julie Anne Lambert, *A Nation of Shopkeepers: Trade Ephemera from 1654 to the 1860s in the John Johnson Collection* (Oxford, UK: Bodleian Library, 2001), 72.

61 "David Jacobs . . . Breeches Makers": Ibid., 75.

61 "Chandler's Shop": Ibid., 74.

4: THE RISE OF THE MERCHANT

67 "If you are unskilled . . . will teach you": Quoted in Fernand Braudel, *Civilization and Capitalism 15th–18th Century*, vol. 2, trans. Sian Reynolds (New York: Harper & Row, 1979), 30.

68 "it is not from . . . their own interest": Adam Smith, *An Inquiry into the Nature and Causes of the Wealth of Nations* (Chicago: University of Chicago Press, 1976), 18.

68 "The old-fashioned grocer . . . in exchange for a coin": Molly Harrison, *People and Shopping: A Social Background* (London: Ernest Benn Limited, 1975), 117.

69 "One of the accepted . . . just such a response": Penrose Scull with Prescott C. Fuller, *From Peddlers to Merchant Princes: A History of Selling in America* (Chicago and New York: Follett Publishing Company, 1967), 247.

70 "Every retailer . . . by a soul-less corporation": Quoted in Richard Tedlow, *New and Improved: The Story of Mass Marketing in America* (New York: Basic Books, 1990), 272, from Frank Farrington, *Meeting Chain Store Competition* (Chicago: Byxbee Publishing Co., 1922).

70 "opens vistas . . . trees or underbrush": Ellen M. Snyder-Grenier, *Turnpike Treasures: The Souvenirs and Stuff That Celebrate an American Phenomenon* (Newark: New Jersey Historical Society, 2001), 16.

71 "locusts . . . producer and the consumer": William Cobbett, *Rural Rides in the Counties of Kent, Sussex, Hampshire, et al.* (London: William Cobbett, 1830), 649.

71 "Merchant and pirate . . . piratical morality": Friedrich Wilhelm Nietzsche, accessed at http://thinkexist.com/quotes/with/keyword/mercantile/.

71 "of greedily gotten gains . . . monstrous stone": Edward C. Bursk, Donald T. Clark, and Ralph W. Hidy, eds., *The World of Business: A Selected Library of the Literature of Business from the Accounting Code of Hammurabi to the 20th-Century "Administrator's Prayer,"* vol. 1, Harvard Business School (New York: Simon & Schuster, 1962), 165.

72 "When I see a merchant . . . an axe to grind": Charles Miner, "Who'll Turn Grindstones," in *Essays from the Desk of Poor Robert the Scribe* (New York: W. E. Rudge, 1930), first published in the *Wilkesbarre Gleaner* (1811).

72 "tricks enough to delude . . . fleece behind them": N. H., *The Compleat Tradesman* (1684), cited in Dorothy Davis, *Fairs, Shops, and*

Supermarkets: A History of English Shopping (Toronto: University of Toronto Press, 1966), 102.

73 "I think about my farm . . . bye-bye 'Buy!' ": Aristophanes, *The Complete Plays of Aristophanes*, trans. B. B. Rogers (New York: Bantam Classics, 1984), 44.

73 "propensity to truck . . . with another dog": Smith, *Wealth of Nations*, 17.

74 "It was some time in the year . . . not even to the nobility": James Lackington, *Memoirs of the First Forty-five Years of the Life of James Lackington* (London: n.p, 1792), 336.

76 "a salmon as thick . . . between the fists": Harrison, *People and Shopping*, 24.

76 "A good butcher . . . thought to be cruel": W. Stanley Jevons, *Political Economy* (New York: D. Appleton and Co., 1880), 58.

78 "You break your back . . . if delayed": Cited in Braudel, *Civilization and Capitalism*, vol. 2, 74.

78 "We write you . . . I write you": A. D. Isere cited in Braudel, *Civilization and Capitalism*, vol. 2, 74–75.

79 "insists on being paid . . . quite harmless": Beatrix Potter, *The Tale of Ginger & Pickles* (London: Frederick Warne & Co., Ltd., 1909), 75.

81 "if outlaws hatch . . . put to death": C. H. W. Johns, trans., *The Oldest Code of Laws in the World; The code of laws promulgated by Hammurabi, King of Babylon B.C.* (Edinburgh: T & T Clark, 1903), p. 19.

82 "if the threads . . . ought to be burnt": Harrison, *People and Shopping*, 17.

82 "It is dangerous to buy . . . like leopard skin": A.-P. Faugere, ed., *Journal du voyage de deux jeunes Hollandais (MM. de Villers), à Paris en 1656–1658* (Paris: L. Marillier, 1899), 87, cited in Braudel, *Civilization and Capitalism*, vol. 2, 36.

84 "Within the city . . . hopes and ambitions": L. B. Alberti, *On the Art of Building in Ten Books*, trans. J. Rykwer, N. Leach, and R. Tavernor (Cambridge, Massachusetts: MIT Press, 1988), 152, cited in Evelyn Welch, *Shopping in the Renaissance: Consumer Cultures in Italy 1400–1600* (New Haven and London: Yale University Press, 2005), 125.

85 "because of their worries . . . to the sack": Welch, *Shopping in the Renaissance*, 146.

86 "A series of craftsmen . . . customers and traders alike": Braudel, *Civilization and Capitalism*, vol. 1, 509.

87 "There is no city . . . as we go along": Davis, *Fairs, Shops, and Supermarkets*, 102.

87 "The Retail Tradesman . . . scarce bids for anything": Daniel Defoe,

The *Compleat English Tradesman* (Cambridge, UK: Charles Riving-
ton, 1727), cited in Davis, *Fairs, Shops, and Supermarkets*, 181.

87 "to speak fluently . . . or a handsome face": Harrison, *People and
Shopping*, 87.

87 "Let every order . . . may bring forth": Ibid., 85–86.

6: INDEPENDENCE

117 "the specialty food business . . . and knowledgeable service": Rob
Kaufelt, "Who Moved My Arugula?" *New York Times*, January 18,
2003, op-ed page.

119 "I think I have a romantic vision, period": Cynthia Zarin, "Big
Cheese," *New Yorker*, August 23, 2004, 42.

121 "No, Sir . . . a good tavern or inn": John Boswell, *The Life of Samuel
Johnson* (New York: Alfred A. Knopf, 1992, first published by Every-
man's Library, 1906), 613.

121 "In Southwark . . . For Canterbury": M. H. Abrams, general ed., *The
Norton Anthology of English Literature*, Major Authors Edition
(New York: W. W. Norton & Company, Inc., 1962), 14.

123 "wine of Apollo . . . dream and dialectic": Kenneth Davids, *Coffee:
A Guide to Buying, Brewing, and Enjoying*, 5th ed. (New York: St.
Martin's Press, 2001), 219.

123 "For persons much concerned . . . indisposed for business": William
Ukers, *All about Coffee* (New York: Tea and Coffee Trade Journal
Co., 1922), 71.

123 "These houses . . . transaction of business": R. J. Mitchell and M. D. R.
Leys, *A History of London Life* (London: Longmans, Green and Co.,
1958), 206, quoting from *Misson de Valberg's Memoirs of Travels
over England*, trans. Mr. Ozell (London: D. Browne, A. Bell, et al.,
1719, originally published in 1698).

130 "Carla is . . . whoever has the most persuasive argument": *Politics
and Prose 15th Anniversary Newsletter*, Washington, D.C., 1999.

8: REINVENTION

151 "In business . . . will swallow you": William Knudsen, accessed at
http://quotationsbook.com/quote/5165/.

157 "Good luck is another name . . . purpose": Ralph Waldo Emerson, accessed at www.gaia.com/quotes/topics/tenacity.

9: THERE GOES THE NEIGHBORHOOD

173 "The majority of the stores . . . whole other world": Timothy Williams, "In Changing Harlem, Soul Food Struggles," *New York Times*, August 5, 2008.

173 "The old order changeth, yielding place to new": Alfred Tennyson, "The Coming of Arthur and The Passing of Arthur," from *Idylls of the King* (London and New York: Macmillan, 1891), 21.

10: CONNECTION

197 "left Arkansas for good . . . cigar-box guitars": Maya Angelou, *I Know Why the Caged Bird Sings* (New York: Bantam Books, 1970), 2.

199 "Other methods of . . . commercial institution": Gerald Carson, *The Old Country Store* (New York: Oxford University Press, 1954), 215–20.

199 "I am a storekeeper . . . would be acceptable": Ibid., 311.

206 "often testified . . . income and expenditure": Hugo Young, *One of Us: A Biography of Margaret Thatcher* (London: Pan Books, 1993), 4.

206 The father of Mario Cuomo: Mario Cuomo, *Diaries of Mario M. Cuomo: The Campaign for Governor* (New York: Random House, Inc., 1984), 8.

11: HARD TIMES

217 "Adversity is the trial . . . honest or not": Henry Fielding, accessed at http://www.quotationspage.com/quote/29136.html.

226 "if you live with fears . . . people still reading": Sudarsan Raghavan, "Bookshop Holds Hope of Iraqi Renaissance," *Financial Times*, July 12, 2008.

SELECTED BIBLIOGRAPHY

Alexander, Nicholas, and Gary Akehurst, eds. *The Emergence of Modern Retailing, 1750–1950*. London: Frank Cass and Company Limited, 1999.

Angelou, Maya. *I Know Why the Caged Bird Sings*. New York: Bantam Books, 1970.

Aristophanes. *The Complete Plays of Aristophanes*. Translated by B. B. Rogers. New York: Bantam Classics, 1984.

Baron, Salo W. *The Russian Jew under Tzars and Soviets*. New York: Macmillan, 1976.

Benson, John, and Laura Ugolini. *Cultures of Selling: Perspectives on Consumption and Society Since 1700 (The History of Retailing and Consumption)*. Hants, UK: Ashgate Publishing, 2006.

Braudel, Fernand. *Civilization and Capitalism 15th–18th Century*. 3 vols. Translated by Sian Reynolds. New York: Harper & Row, 1979.

Bursk, Edward C., Donald T. Clark, and Ralph W. Hidy, eds. *The World of Business: A Selected Library of the Literature of Business from the Accounting Code of Hammurabi to the 20th-Century "Administrator's Prayer,"* vol. 1. Harvard Business School. New York: Simon & Schuster, 1962.

Cannadine, David, ed. *Making a Living in the Middle Ages: The People of Britain 850–1520*. The New Economic History of Britain Series. New Haven: Yale University Press, 2002.

Carson, Gerald. *The Old Country Store*. New York: Oxford University Press, 1954.

Chuihua, Judy Cheng, Jeffrey Inaba, Rem Koolhaas, and Sze Tsung Leong, eds. *Project on the City: The Harvard Design School Guide to Shopping*. Koln, Germany: Taschen GmbH, 2001.

Cipolla, Carlo M. *Before the Industrial Revolution: European Society and Economy, 1000–1700*. 3rd ed. New York: W. W. Norton & Co., 1994.

Cobbett, William. *Rural Rides in the Counties of Kent, Sussex, Hampshire, et al.* London: William Cobbett, 1830.

Cunningham, John T. *Newark*. Newark: New Jersey Historical Society, 2002.

Cuomo, Mario. *Diaries of Mario M. Cuomo: The Campaign for Governor*. New York: Random House, 1984.

Davidson, James N. *Courtesans & Fishcakes: The Consuming Passions of Classical Athens*. New York: Harper Perennial, 1997.

Davis, Dorothy. *Fairs, Shops, and Supermarkets: A History of English Shopping*. Toronto: University of Toronto Press, 1966.

———. *Shopping*. London: Routledge & Kegan Paul, 1967.

Federal Writers' Project of the Works Progress Administration of the State of New Jersey. *New Jersey: A Guide to Its Past and Present*. New York: Viking Press, 1939.

Gillespie, Angus Kress, and Michael Aaron Rockland. *Looking for America on the New Jersey Turnpike*. New Brunswick, New Jersey: Rutgers University Press, 1992.

Harrison, Molly. *People and Shopping: A Social Background*. London: Ernest Benn Limited, 1975.

Hendrickson, Robert. *The Grand Emporiums: The Illustrated History of America's Great Department Stores*. New York: Stein and Day, 1979.

Howe, Irving. *World of Our Fathers: The Journey of the East European Jews to America and the Life They Found and Made*. New York: Monticello Editions, 1989.

Jacobs, Jane. *The Death and Life of Great American Cities*. New York: Modern Library, 1993.

Kotkin, Joel. *The City: A Global History*. New York: Modern Library, 2005.

Lambert, Julie Anne. *A Nation of Shopkeepers: Trade Ephemera from 1654 to the 1860s in the John Johnson Collection*. An exhibition in the Bodleian Library. Oxford, UK: Bodleian Library, 2001.

Lebhar, Godfrey M. *Chain Stores in America: 1859–1959*. New York: Chain Store Publishing Corporation, 1959.

León, Vicki. *Working IX to V: Orgy Planners, Funeral Clowns, and Other Prized Professions of the Ancient World*. New York: Walker & Company, 2007.

Miers, Earl Schenck. *Where the Raritan Flows*. New Brunswick, New Jersey: Rutgers University Press.

Morris, A. E. J. *History of Urban Form: Prehistory to the Renaissance*. London: Halsted Press, a division of John Wiley & Sons, 1974. First published in 1972 in Great Britain by George Godwin Limited, London.

Newhouse, Alana, ed. *A Living Lens: Photographs of Jewish Life from the Pages of the Forward*. New York: Forward Books, W.W. Norton & Company, 2007.

Oldenburg, Ray. *The Great Good Place: Cafés, Coffee Shops, Bookstores, Bars, Hair Salons and Other Hangouts at the Heart of a Community*. New York: Marlowe & Company, Avalon Publishing Group, 1999.

Origo, Iris. *The Merchant of Prato: Francesco di Marco Datini, 1335–1410*. Jaffrey, New Hampshire: David R. Godine, Nonpareil Books, 1986.

Powell, Colin, with Joseph Persico. *My American Journey*. New York: Random House, 1995.

Reeves, Pamela. *Ellis Island: Gateway to the American Dream*. New York: Barnes & Noble Books, 1998.

Roth, Henry. *Call It Sleep*. New York: Noonday Press, 1991.

Satterthwaite, Ann. *Going Shopping: Consumer Choices and Community Consequences*. New Haven: Yale University Press, 2001.

Scull, Penrose, with Prescott C. Fuller. *From Peddlers to Merchant Princes: A History of Selling in America*. Chicago and New York: Follett Publishing Company, 1967.

Seguine-LeVine, Joan. *Images of America: Perth Amboy*. Dover, New Hampshire: Arcadia Publishing, Chalford Publishing Corporation, 1966.

Smith, Adam. *An Inquiry into the Nature and Causes of the Wealth of Nations*. Edited with notes and marginal summary by Edwin Cannan. Chicago: University of Chicago Press, 1976.

Snyder-Grenier, Ellen M. *Turnpike Treasures: The Souvenirs and Stuff That Celebrate an American Phenomenon*. Newark: New Jersey Historical Society, 2001.

Terkel, Studs. *Working: People Talk about What They Do All Day and How They Feel about What They Do*. New York: Pantheon Books, a division of Random House, 1972.

Welch, Evelyn. *Shopping in the Renaissance: Consumer Cultures in Italy 1400–1600*. New Haven and London : Yale University Press, 2005.

Whitehead, William A. *Early History of Perth Amboy*. New York: D. Appleton & Company, 1856.

Yezierska, Anzia. *How I Found America: Collected Stories of Anzia Yezierska*. New York: A Karen & Michael Braziller Book, Persea Books, 1991.

Young, Hugo. *One of Us: A Biography of Margaret Thatcher*. London: Pan Books, 1993.

INDEX

AA Jewel Box, 97–102, 213–215
Acme supermarket, 59–60
adaptation. *See* reinvention
adversity
   Daniel Carney and, 224–225
   community connection and,
     219–220
   Furst Florist and, 218
   Nabil al-Hayawi and, 226
   Modern Carpet & Rug Company
     and, 216–217
   Octavia Books and, 226–230
   RioMar and, 230–234
   Barry Schwartz and, 220–223
   Vincent's Italian Cuisine and, 232,
     234–236
Alberti, Leon Battista, 84–85
Aleichem, Sholem, 50
Alito, Samuel J., 92
Alki Mail & Dispatch, 250–252
Allyn's Shoes, 37
Amazon.com, 74
American Booksellers Association,
   227
American Independent Business Al-
   liance (AMIBA), 262
Amy's Bread Bakery Café, 120
An American in Paris (film), 36
Angelou, Maya, 1, 197–198
A. N. Weissman & Sons, 45
A&P, 59–60, 118
Argyros, Eleni, 189
Aristophanes, *Archarnians*, 72–73
Arluck, Norman, 165–167
Astor, John Jacob, 1–2
Atlantic magazine, 7

Bacon, Francis, 33–34
Baker, Russell, 36
Balducci's, 117
Baranowski, Stan, 20
Barber Pole, 143–145, 198, 261
Barnecut, Andy, 252–253
Barnecut, Dick, 252–253
Barnecut, George, 252
Barnecut Admiral Way Super Service,
   252–253
Barnes & Noble, 228, 230
Barnhill, Jessica, 124–127, 202
Bassett, Eric, 109
Bassett, Lewis Dubois (L. D.), 107
Bassett, Lewis Lafayette (L. L.), 107,
   146–147
Bassett, Roger, 107–109, 146–147
Bassett's Ice Cream Company,
   107–109, 146–147
Bates, JoEllen, 208
Bates, Magnolia Gossett, 135,
   136, 137
Bates, Roman, 208
Bates, Willie Earl, 7, 10, 134–137,
   138, 208–211
Batista, Fulgencio, 149
Bazan, Nicolas, 230, 232–233, 267
Bellingham Sustainable Connections,
   261
Ben-Gurion, David, 166
Benjamin, André, 155
Ben & Jerry's, 147, 256
Benning, James, 154
Berry, William F., 206
Berry Bros. & Rudd, 153
Beychok, Katherine, 52

A NOTE ON THE AUTHOR

Robert Spector is the author of *The Nordstrom Way*, *The Nordstrom Way to Customer Service Excellence*, *Lessons from the Nordstrom Way*, *Amazon.com: Get Big Fast, Anytime, Anywhere*, and *Category Killers*. He has appeared on the *National Business Report*, CNN, CNBC, Fox News, Bloomberg Business, CNET News.com, CEO Exchange, NPR's *Marketplace Report*, and numerous radio shows. He has written on business for the *Wall Street Journal*, *USA Today*, *UPI International*, *NASDAQ* magazine, *Customer Service Management*, and *Corporate University Review*; on fashion for *Women's Wear Daily* and *Details*; and on civil liberties for *Parade*. He gives dozens of talks every year to business organizations and groups all over the world. Spector lives in Seattle, Washington. Visit his Web site www.robertspector.com.